MW00415737

THE POST-TRIB,
PRE-WRATH RAPTURE

THE POST-TRIB, PRE-WRATH RAPTURE

DR. ROLAND RASMUSSEN

RARE CHRISTIAN BOOKS
19275 Highway 28
Dixon, MO 65459
Ph./Fax: (573) 336-7316

The Post-Trib Research Center
7644 Farralone Avenue • Canoga Park, California 91304

THE POST-TRIB, PRE-WRATH RAPTURE

Copyright © 1996 by Dr. Roland Rasmussen. Published by The Post-Trib Research Center, 7644 Farralone Avenue, Canoga Park, California 91304.

All rights reserved. No part of this publication may be reproduced, stored in a retrieval system or transmitted in any form by any means, electronic, mechanical, photocopying, recording, or otherwise, without the prior written permission of the publisher, except as provided by USA copyright law.

Most of the italicized emphases in this book are the author's.

Scripture quotations are from the King James Version of The Holy Bible unless otherwise indicated.

Cover design: Louis Ujueta

Printed in the United States of America

Library of Congress Catalog Card Number 96-092137

ISBN 0-9651789-0-0

CONTENTS

ACKNOWLEDGMENTS

First, I wish to thank my Lord and Saviour Jesus Christ, Who saved me in 1949 and Who opened my eyes to the truths contained in this book. Without His wonderful and gracious help, it would have been impossible for me to write this book.

I also wish to express my warm thanks to my wife Linda for her love and patience during the time it has taken to write this book; to Beth Wood, my secretary, who has typed and retyped the manuscript in its many revisions; to Clay Pierson, my son in the faith, who has tested my views, given insightful input in regard to the fifth seal vision, and prepared the manuscript for camera-readiness to be sent to the printer; to Steve Labins and Stephania Rasmussen for their invaluable help in proofreading the manuscript; to my son, Roland Rasmussen, Jr., for his contributions to the preface and help in the proofreading process; to Louis Ujueta for his creative art and graphic contributions for the cover and charts and assistance in readying the manuscript for the printer; to Pat Brooks, author of several books, for her practical suggestions and helpful hints; to Allison Castner for her computer consultation; and to Dave MacPherson, author of *The Rapture Plot*, for his initial proofing of the manuscript.

PREFACE

The pilot of our flight from Singapore to Taipei had just been notified about an anonymous caller who said that a bomb had been planted on board our plane.

We were cruising at 35,000 feet, only halfway to Taipei, and below was nothing but the deep, blue ocean, dotted with whitecaps. The flight attendants informed the passengers that the aircraft was being diverted to Hong Kong.

Sitting beside me was a former Air Force pilot who was extremely concerned about the reason for the diversion. He demanded of our stewardess the reason for re-routing our flight to Hong Kong, which was nearer to our immediate position, yet out of the way. With fear evident in her eyes and voice, the flight attendant answered, "The captain will make an announcement at the appropriate time." The former pilot asked, this time more sternly, "Why are we being re-routed?" The stewardess said again, "The captain will make an announcement at the appropriate time." The flight attendants would say nothing more.

Recognizing the near panic in the eyes and on the faces of the flight attendants, and the fear in the voice of the former pilot sitting next to me, I realized that we were in a life-threatening situation.

While others might have thought about their families, and the possibility of their lives coming to a sudden end, I had one dominating thought. That thought was about the need for this book. Previously, I had only considered writing a book to set forth the views the Lord had shown me through my study of the Bible. I was overpowered by the thought of the need for this book. I promised the Lord that I would write this book setting forth those things which He had shown me, if He would get me safely back home.

Our plane landed at Hong Kong, and as the tires smoked upon touching the runway, the pilot finally made the announcement informing us of the bomb threat. The plane came to a stop far from any buildings and other aircraft. Fire engines waited in the distance, and all of the plane's exits were used for an emergency evacuation.

We were detained for four hours. The aircraft, all luggage, and the passengers were carefully searched. No bomb was found. The flight to the U.S.A. was resumed, and a promise had been made. <u>The Post-Trib, Pre-Wrath Rapture</u> is the result of that promise.

If you have been led to believe that Christians will be delivered from the Antichrist and the Great Tribulation by a supposed pretribulational rapture of the church, reading this book may be one of the most important things you will have ever done. Read on, and see the evidence that proves pretribulationism is a hoax.

INTRODUCTION

Did you know that the King James Version of the Bible teaches that Christ will not come to rapture the church until *after* the Antichrist has been revealed as the son of perdition? This fact means that Christ's coming to rapture the church is neither imminent nor pretribulational. Furthermore, out of the more than 5,300 extant manuscripts, all but three of them have the same reading as the King James Version in the crucial passage which is the source of the above facts. Not only that, the three manuscripts upon which most pretribulationists rely to evade the doctrines taught in the King James Version are so corrupt that in Luke 2:33 they teach Joseph was the father of Jesus Christ.

Did you know that the Day of the Lord will not begin until *after* the Great Tribulation? This Bible truth means that the unparalleled wrath of the Lamb, which will be poured out in the Day of the Lord, will not be poured out in the Seventieth Week of Daniel, the last half of which is the Great Tribulation. This truth is devastating to pretribulationists, who desire desperately to smuggle the unparalleled wrath of the Lamb into the Seventieth Week. Why? In order to make necessary a pretribulational rapture to deliver the church from wrath.

Did you know that "the tribulation" will *not* be characterized by the pouring out of the unparalleled wrath of the Lamb? Rather, the Great Tribulation will be the time during which the Antichrist will make war with the saints and overcome them.

Did you know that John Walvoord wrote, "One of the problems that face both pretribulationism and post-tribulationism is the fact that their point of view is an induction based upon scriptural facts rather than an explicit statement of the Bible"? It is true that *pretribulationism is an induction*, but it is a false induction. On the other hand, posttribulationism is not an induction, but rather an explicit statement of the Bible. *The Post-Trib, Pre-Wrath Rapture* demonstrates this fact. Walvoord further admits, "While both pretribulationists and posttribulationists have strained to find some specific reference in support of their views, most adherents of either view usually concede that there is no explicit reference . . . ." Once again, it is true that there is no explicit reference that supports pretribulationism. On the contrary, the Bible explicitly teaches and supports a posttribulational rapture of the church. This book explains clearly these specific references.

The Post-Trib, Pre-Wrath Rapture proves from Scripture that the unparalleled wrath of the Lamb will be poured out in the Day of the Lord *after* the Great Tribulation. This truth, which is devastating to pretribulationism, is plainly taught in the Scriptures, and it is demonstrated in this book.

Dwight Pentecost has twenty-eight arguments to support the pretribulational rapture. Hal Lindsey has two favorite arguments to support the pretribulational rapture. All of these arguments are refuted in the chapter entitled "Pretribulationism's Preposterous Pillars."

Posttribulationism is not only the historical position of the church, but it is also the majority position of the church. John Walvoord writes, "Posttribulationism has long been a common doctrine held by the majority of the church."

Dwight Pentecost writes, "The literal method of interpretation, consistently employed, can lead to no other conclusion than that the church will be raptured *before* the seventieth week." In this book, you will see that pretribulationists, including Scofield and Pentecost, are not always literal in their interpretation of Scripture. You will see that at crucial times they use a symbolical interpretation to support a pretribulational rapture. This author is more literal than Scofield and Pentecost combined, and he believes that the literal method of interpretation, consistently employed, can lead to no other conclusion than that the church will be raptured *after* the Great Tribulation.

Because of Dave MacPherson's new book entitled *The Rapture Plot*, many pretribulationists are becoming edgy. MacPherson, in his new book, documents plainly that pretribulationism had its origin in 1830. Margaret MacDonald, a fifteen-year-old Scottish girl, had a vision in which she saw part of the church raptured prior to the emergence of Antichrist. In her vision she saw the remainder of the church go into the fiery trial of the Great Tribulation. Margaret's vision taught both a pretribulation rapture and partial rapturism.

A cultic group called the Irvingites, in their September 1830 edition of *The Morning Watch*, were the first to publish pure pretribulationism. Pretribulationism's origin is thoroughly documented in *The Rapture Plot*. Now pretribulationists are desperately trying to find writers who were pretribulational prior to 1830. They have come up with four men whom they claim were pretribulationists before 1830. This writer calls these men "mythical" pretribulationists. *The Post-Trib, Pre-Wrath Rapture* shows that these men who are being called pretribulationists were not pretribulationists at all. Three of the four writers simply held a two-stage coming of Christ, as does this writer. One can see for himself how far pretribulationists have gone in their all-out attempt to show that pretribulationism existed prior to 1830.

The author of five books who proofread *The Post-Trib, Pre-Wrath Rapture* manuscript wrote the following in a recent newsletter:

> The new pretrib-demolishing prophecy book by our friend Roland Rasmussen (pastor of the huge Faith Baptist Church of Canoga Park, CA who was featured in Dollar's 1973 *History of Fundamentalism*) will be out soon. Having been allowed to see the manuscript, I'm sure that pretribs will <u>not</u> welcome it! And Tommy Ice of the *Pre-Trib* Research Center will freak out when he learns that this new book is being published by the Post-Trib Research Center!

ONE

TWO DAYS OF INFAMY

"But if the watchman see the sword come, and blow not the trumpet, and the people be not warned; if the sword come, and take any person from among them, he is taken away in his iniquity; but his blood will I require at the watchman's hand."

— *Ezekiel 33:6*

The first day of infamy occurred on December 7, 1941. That dreadful day is described by Walter Lord, who writes:

In they hurtled--Lieutenant Commander Takahashi's 27 dive bombers plunging toward Ford Island and Hickam . . . Lieutenant Commander Murata's 40 torpedo planes swinging into position for their run at the big ships. Commander Fuchida marked time off Barbers Point with the horizontal bombers, watching his men go in . . . the ships were sitting ducks.

A few minutes earlier, at 7:49 A.M., Fuchida had radioed the signal to attack: 'To . . . to . . . to . . . .' Now he was so sure of victory that at 7:53--even before the first bomb fell--he signaled the carriers that the surprise attack was successful: 'Tora . . . tora . . . tora . . . .'

Back on the Akagi, Admiral Kusaka turned to Admiral Nagumo. Not a word passed between them. Just a long, firm handshake.

On the Nevada at the northern end of Battleship Row, Leader Oden McMillan waited with his band to play morning colors at eight o'clock . . . . As they moved into formation, some of the musicians noticed planes diving at the other end of Ford Island. McMillan saw a lot of dirt and sand go up, but thought it was another drill. Now it was 7:58--two minutes to go--and planes started coming in low from southeast Loch. Heavy, muffled explosions began booming down the line . . . enough to worry anyone. And then it was eight o'clock.

The band crashed into 'The Star-Spangled Banner.' A Japanese plane skimmed across the harbor . . . dropped a torpedo at the Arizona . . . and peeled off right over the Nevada's fantail. The rear gunner sprayed the men standing at attention . . . . The executive officer of the supply ship Castor shouted, 'The Japs are bombing us! The Japs are bombing us!'

. . . A seaman on the destroyer Monaghan told Boatswain's Mate Thomas Donahue, ' . . . I didn't even know they were sore at us.' . . . Commander Vincent Murphy was still phoning Admiral Kimmel about the Ward's sampan report when a yeoman burst into the room: 'There's a message from the signal tower saying the Japanese are attacking Pearl Harbor, and this is no drill.'

. . . the Arizona blew up . . . the bomb landed alongside the second turret, crashed through the forecastle, and set off the forward magazines . . . a huge ball of fire and smoke mush-roomed 500 feet into the air . . . . On the Arizona, hundreds of men were cut down in a single, searing flash. Inside the port antiaircraft director, one fire control man simply vanished--the only place he could have gone was through the narrow range-finder slot. On the bridge Rear Admiral Isaac C. Kidd and Captain Franklin Van Valkenburgh were instantly killed. On the second deck the entire ship's band was wiped out. Over 1000 men were gone. [1]

---

[1] Walter Lord, *The Day of Infamy* (New York: Holt, Rinehart & Winston, 1963), pp. 63, 64, 67, 68, 70, 71, 73, 94, 95.

December 7, 1941, was indeed a day of infamy, but did so many Americans need to die at Pearl Harbor? The sad truth is that most of the men who died could have escaped if only the ships had been dispersed at sea before the sneak attack. However, the Americans were caught completely by surprise. The Japanese leaders had spent many months planning their surprise attack to insure its success.

Presently, unknown to most, preparations are being made for another terrible surprise--a far worse day of infamy. This day of infamy will occur when you will be required to take the *mark* in order to buy or sell. The Bible says:

> He causeth all, both small and great, rich and poor, free and bond, to receive *a mark* in their right hand, or in their foreheads; and that *no man might buy or sell, save he that had the mark*, or the name of the beast, or the number of his name. Here is wisdom. Let him that hath understanding count the number of the beast: for it is the number of a man; and his number is *six* hundred threescore and six.[2]

In spite of denials by many leaders, the Bible clearly reveals that there will be a one-world government headed by the Antichrist at the end of the age. Regarding the coming Antichrist, the Bible says:

> . . . all the world wondered after *the beast*. And they worshipped the dragon [Satan] which gave power unto the beast; and they worshipped the beast, saying, Who is like unto the beast? *Who is able to make war with him?* And there was given unto him a mouth speaking great things and blasphemies; and *power was given unto him to continue forty and two months*. And he

---

[2] Revelation 13:16-18.

opened his mouth in blasphemy against God . . . *and it was
given unto him to make war with the saints, and to overcome
them: and power was given him over all kindreds, and tongues,
and nations.* And all that dwell upon the earth shall worship
him, whose names are not written in the book of life of the
Lamb . . . .[3]

The beast will not come to power through the regular
political process; the Bible says:

And the ten horns which thou sawest are ten kings, which have
received no kingdom as yet; but receive power as kings one hour
with the beast. *These have one mind, and shall give their power
and strength unto the beast.* These shall make war with the
Lamb, and the Lamb shall overcome them: for he is Lord of
lords, and King of kings . . . .[4]

While the Bible speaks plainly of the coming world
government, other informed persons such as Commander
William Guy Carr of the Royal Canadian Navy also warn
of a conspiracy to bring about a world government. Carr
writes:

Propaganda put out by those who direct the Luciferian conspiracy has caused the general public to believe all who oppose
Christianity are Atheists. This is a deliberate lie circulated to
hide the secret plans of the High Priests of The Luciferian
Creed . . . The High Priests of the Luciferian Creed work from
the darkness. They remain behind the scenes. They keep their
identity and true purpose secret, even from the vast majority of
those they deceive into doing their will and furthering their
secret plans and ambitions. *They know that the final success of
their conspiracy to usurp the powers of the world government
depends upon their ability to keep their identity and true*

---

[3] Revelation 13:3-8.
[4] Revelation 17:12-14.

purpose secret until no cunning or power can prevent them crowning their leader King-despot of the entire world.[5]

Even as the Japanese leaders carefully prepared for the sneak attack on Pearl Harbor, evil men working to bring in the New World Order are even now preparing for the next surprise attack.

America is being disarmed. While most Americans remember President Clinton's closing of U.S. military bases, few understand the significance of the closings. In "Top-Down Treason," John McManus writes:

When they first hear about the disarmament program our nation has been implementing for over 30 years, many Americans are incredulous that officials in the highest offices of our government would commit such a blatant act of treason. Yet, such a plan exists and is unfolding at an alarming pace. *It calls for the United States to disarm itself and simultaneously build the military capability of the United Nations.*

It all began in September 1961, when President Kennedy formally presented the official U.S. disarmament program described in State Department Publication 7277. Entitled Freedom From War: The United States Program for General and Complete Disarmament in a Peaceful World, the program calls for the nations of the world--including the U.S.--to disarm, turn over their military might to the UN, and make the world body an unchallengeable military power.[6]

---

[5] Commander William Guy Carr, *Pawns in the Game* (USA: printed privately, n.d.), p. XVII.

[6] John F. McManus, "Top-Down Treason," *The New American Magazine*, Volume 11, 3 April 1995, p. 11.

Freedom From War says,

> In Stage III progressive controlled disarmament and continuously developing principles and procedures of international law would proceed to a point where *no state would have the military power to challenge the progressively strengthened U.N. Peace Force . . . .*[7]

The writer has seen video footage showing the mass destruction of B-52 bombers in the Arizona desert. He has seen a newspaper headline that says, "Giant Guillotine chops B-52's for Peace." He has seen video footage of American armor being driven over the side of a ship into the ocean.

Bob Fletcher, a former Florida U.S. congressional candidate, told of U.S. National Guard units being sent to Russia while Russian troops have been sent to National Guard locations in this country.

He then told of Russian tanks and trucks being shipped into this country through Florida and Mississippi, and he showed video footage of the following:

1. 750 Russian trucks equipped for chemical and biological warfare, parked in a depot in Mississippi;

2. 1,500 Russian trucks equipped for chemical and biological warfare, parked in a depot in Louisiana;

---

[7] Ibid.

3.   A Russian T-72 heavy battle tank on a flatbed truck, photographed in front of an Exxon gas station in Texas;

4.   Railroad flat cars in Montana carrying Russian tanks;

5.   Railroad flat cars in the Midwest carrying Russian military vehicles;

6.   A Russian missile launcher with a 50-mile range, capable of delivering chemical, biological, or nuclear warheads, photographed in the U.S.A.

Fletcher further said that thousands of Russian tanks are just across the border in Mexico.

Detention centers for civilians have been set up across America. There are forty-three primary detention centers and hundreds of smaller ones. On my desk is a photograph of a huge facility in Oklahoma City. The caption beneath the photograph says:

> This is the new federal maximum security prisoner sorting and transfer center adjacent to Will Rogers Airport in Oklahoma City. This is believed to be part of the secret FEMA prison complex. The center is capable of handling up to 2,500 prisoners at any one time.[8]

Before me is another picture of a sprawling FEMA complex in Birmingham, Alabama. Regarding the prisons that have been built and those that are being built to incarcerate U.S. citizens, *The Spotlight* says:

---

[8] Mike Blair, "FEMA Connections Exposed," *The Spotlight*, 26 September 1994, p. 12.

In addition, according to findings of *The Spotlight*, the Pentagon is still not leveling with the American people about the urban warfare operations, which many view as training to ultimately disarm the American people by force and thus eliminate their Constitutional right to keep and bear arms, as guaranteed by the Second Amendment.

As an example, The Pentagon indicated that the exercises have no connection with the Federal Emergency Management Agency (FEMA), which in 1979, by an Executive Order signed by then President Jimmy Carter, was established to take over running the country during a presidential-declared national emergency. Such an emergency could be invoked by the stroke of a presidential pen on any number of pretexts, ranging from a natural disaster to a crime and drug crisis.

According to what Perrett told [reporter] McClendon, FEMA is 'wholly separate [from the urban warfare operations].'

Not true.

The Spotlight has obtained a copy of a U.S. Army field manual (FM 41-10), titled Civil Affairs Operations, which is purposely disguised to sound like some type of cooperative public affairs effort with the civilian population.

On the contrary, however, the effort is fully coordinated with FEMA and is detailed in the field manual, which bears the warning on its cover page:

'DESTRUCTION NOTICE: Destroy by any method that will prevent disclosure of contents or reconstruction of the document . . . .'

In the large manual, about three-quarters of an inch thick, the part played by FEMA in the Civil Affairs Operations are [sic] detailed, as are the methods of rounding up civilians and placing them in detention centers.

Included in the manual, dated January 1993, *are diagrams of detention centers, as well as illustrations of the FEMA chain of command and the regional boundaries of its field installations.*[9]

Americans looking to Newt Gingrich and Robert Dole for deliverance are in for a major disappointment. In 1990, Gingrich put together HR 4079. This bill calls for the providing of a five-year, national emergency call for the creation of prison camps at military bases. These camps were to be created for the holding of civilian laborers. Gingrich also called for tents in the middle of the desert to be used for the holding of civilian prisoners. The bill sponsored by Gingrich was stopped, but *the same provisions are in the new crime bill.*

Texe Marrs writes:

House Speaker Gingrich (member of the World Future Society) and Senate Majority Leader Robert Dole (a 33rd-degree Mason) have lied to us. In their highly vaunted 'Contract With America' the legislators promised to repeal Clinton's unconstitutional Crime Act of 1993. Instead, these Republican overlords are now unconscionably cramming even tighter Big Brother measures-- such as HR 666--straight down our gullets.[10]

United Nations troops are already here in the United States of America. Bob Fletcher said that 44,000 UN troops were trained in Georgia; Canadian troops were trained in California under the UN umbrella; they were using white or cream-colored United Nations military vehicles; German troops were in Arkansas, and Gerkas

---

[9] Blair, "FEMA Connections Exposed," p. 12.
[10] Texe Marrs, "Beast-like '666' Laws Forced on American Citizens," *Flashpoint*, March 1995, pp. 1, 2.

from Nepal were in the State of Washington. UN troops are being trained to enter civilian homes for the purpose of search and seizure.

Marines stationed at the base in Twentynine Palms, California were given a questionnaire asking if they would be willing to shoot American citizens. One fourth of those questioned said they would shoot American citizens. Pilot sweeps of neighborhoods have already taken place in America and American possessions. A sweep was conducted in New Orleans. One was conducted in Chicago. Another was conducted in Puerto Rico, an American possession. On Saturday morning, April 1, 1995, at 4:00 A.M., 800 officers from the Los Angeles Police Department, the FBI, and other agencies arrested 53 people in about 150 raids across the Los Angeles area. The sweep reached as far away as Long Beach, Palmdale, and San Bernardino.

An inside police source said that the Los Angeles sweep was a practice run. The source further said that persons arrested would be taken to boot camps where gang members are being trained. It has been reported that boot camps exist in Georgia and Texas, where gang members are being trained to work as "civilian police" in the search-and-seizure program. Moreover, it has been reported that hoodlums are being trained to break into houses to search and seize whatever they wish. A former intelligence officer explained that two armed men will come to the door in the middle of the night. Three armed men will stand in the street to cover the two men at the door, and two armed men will take positions behind the house. The seven men will wear black ski masks and black clothing.

Recently, a Christian mother who lives near our church was awakened at 4:00 A.M. by three policemen who knocked on her door. These three were covered by another policeman with an assault rifle. The pretense for frightening this Christian lady at 4:00 A.M. was that burglars were reported to have been in the area. This Christian lady had been distributing literature warning of the New World Order.

On my desk before me is a copy of HR 666. HR 666 passed the House of Representatives February 8, 1995. Regarding HR 666, Texe Marrs writes:

> More recently, the same network of anti-American legislators slam-dunked through the House of Representatives HR 666. It is advertised by its sponsor, Representative Bill McCollum (Dem.-FL), as a bill 'to control crime.' But what it really does is control people! If passed by the Senate and signed into law by President Clinton, the Orwellian HR 666 will suspend the constitutional rights of Americans. This monstrous, new law allows federal and local law enforcement agencies--including the Gestapo-like DEA, FBI, Fincen, etc.--to search and ransack people's homes and property without a search warrant.[11]

While detention centers for civilians are being readied, guillotines are being stored in warehouses in the U.S. The writer has obtained this information from seven separate sources. Three of the sources are eyewitnesses who have actually seen the guillotines. Fritz Springmeier writes:

> One couple who subscribed to this newsletter grew skeptical of the newsletter and asked to be dropped from receiving it. Later, a man with connections to American Intelligence was visiting them. They happened to mention that Fritz Springmeier had

---

[11] Marrs, "Beast-like '666' Laws Forced on American Citizens," p. 1.

reported guillotines being imported into the U.S. by the thousands. The man's eyes got big, and he said that the guillotines were top secret and that his friend who works for the CIA had been part of the operation to import the guillotines. His amazement that my newsletter gave away top secrets revived their interest to receive it again.[12]

Again Springmeier writes:

One of the big lessons from history is that mankind doesn't learn from history. The history of the Krupp family which is in the Illuminati would provide the world with a loud and clear warning for today.

The first lesson that could be learned is how a military buildup and military intentions can be totally concealed for decades. Today, the New World Order has brought in hundreds of thousands of foreign troops into the United States, they have brought in thousands, if not hundreds of thousands of guillotines for executions, they have built a network of unused concentration camps across the U.S., they have built crematoriums next to these concentration camps, and yet most Americans appear to believe the lies . . . like they believed the lies of Krupp, and the German Chancellors *before* Hitler, and the German military leaders who were all well aware of the secret German buildup that began immediately after W.W.I ended!

We are about to go into a New World Order that will be worse than Hitler's New World Order, but the power behind the scenes is the same--the Illuminati getting their power from their centuries-old generational satanic practices.[13]

---

[12] Fritz Springmeier, *A Newsletter from a Follower of Christ*, June-July-August, 1995, p. 5.

[13] Ibid., p. 80.

The shocking fact that guillotines are presently being stockpiled in the U.S.A. is very interesting in the light of Revelation 20:4, which says,

> . . . and I saw the souls of them that were *beheaded* for the witness of Jesus, and for the word of God, and which had not worshipped the beast, neither his image, neither had received his mark upon their foreheads, or in their hands; and they lived and reigned with Christ a thousand years.

This Scripture teaches that the beast will put his victims to death by beheading them. Think about that for five minutes.

The media is turning the public against Christians. *Time* says:

> The grisly mix of fertilizer and hatred that detonated in Oklahoma City last week appears to provide stark evidence of something many Americans have denied; the existence of paranoid, violent thinking within our borders. Just what are the tenets of this thinking? And did they figure in last year's election returns?

> Like other political movements before it, the radical right in America today has its extremist component, which plainly was a force in the 1994 elections. For instance, George Nethercutt, the giant-slayer Congressman who knocked off former House Speaker Tom Foley in Washington State, drew strength from radio shows where callers talked about sightings of black helicopters and U.N. plans to set up a secret compound in the state . . . .

> These politicians and others drew on widespread mistrust and even hatred of government power in Western and rural areas. *Their coalition included* well-known elements of far-right thought: tax protesters; *Christian home-schoolers*; conspiracy theorists influenced by the John Birch Society's fear of one-

world government; Second Amendment activists (mostly men) for whom guns are an important part of an independent way of life . . . .[14]

Waiting in the wings at this very moment is a man who claims that he is the Christ, the world teacher. The writer first had his attention called to Lord Maitreya by a full-page advertisement that appeared in the *Los Angeles Times* on April 25, 1982. It read as follows:

The world has had enough . . . of hunger, injustice, war. In answer to our call for help, as world teacher for all humanity, the Christ is now here.

How will we recognize Him? Look for a modern man concerned with modern problems--political, economic, and social. Since July, 1977, the Christ has been emerging as a spokesman for a group or community in a well-known modern country. He is not a religious leader, but an educator in the broadest sense of the word--pointing the way out of our present crisis. We will recognize Him by His extraordinary spiritual potency, the universality of His viewpoint, and His love for all humanity. He comes not to judge, but to aid and inspire.

Who is the Christ? Throughout history, humanity's evolution has been guided by a group of enlightened men, the Masters of Wisdom. They have remained largely in the remote desert and mountain places of earth, working mainly through their disciples who live openly in the world. This message of the Christ's reappearance has been given primarily by such a disciple trained for his task for over 20 years. At the center of this 'Spiritual Hierarchy' stands the World Teacher, Lord Maitreya, known by Christians as the Christ. And as Christians await the Second Coming, so the Jews await the Messiah, the Buddhists the fifth Buddha, the Moslems the Imam Mahdi, and the Hindus await

---

[14] Philip Weiss, "Outcasts Digging in for the Apocalypse," *Time*, 1 May 1995, p. 48.

Krishna. These are all names for one individual. His presence in the world guarantees there will be no third World War.

What is He saying? My task will be to show you how to live together peacefully as brothers. This is simpler than you imagine, My friends, for it requires only the acceptance of sharing. How can you be content with the modes within which you now live: when millions starve and die in squalor; when the rich parade their wealth before the poor; when each man is his neighbor's enemy; when no man trusts his brother? Allow me to show you the way forward into a simpler life where no man lacks; where no two days are alike; where the Joy of Brotherhood manifests through all men. Take your brother's need as the measure for your action and solve the problems of the world.

When will we see Him? He has not yet declared His true status, and His location is known to only a very few disciples. One of these has announced that soon the Christ will acknowledge His identity and . . . will speak to humanity through a worldwide television and radio broadcast. His message will be heard inwardly, telepathically, by all people in their own language. From that time, with His help, we will build a new world.

Without sharing there can be no justice; without justice there can be no peace; without peace there can be no future. [This is veiled communism.]

This full-page advertisement appeared in major newspapers around the world on the same day--April 25, 1982.
Maitreya expects to fulfill His mission through the United Nations. The New American, February 20, 1995, printed an article entitled, "The 'Master' on Earth: New Age Messiah Makes an Appearance." The article says:

According to Monte Leach, the United States editor of *Share International* journal, the 'Master of all the Masters and Teacher alike of angels and men' is alive and among men today. Leach is a disciple of Benjamin Creme, the British Theosophist who speaks on behalf of 'Lord Maitreya,' an enigmatic ersatz messiah who resides in the Indian quarter of London . . . . According to Leach, Maitreya is the most exalted member of an occult brotherhood--variously referred to as the 'Great Teachers,' the 'Ascended Masters,' or the 'Spiritual Hierarchy.'

. . . The 'Masters' intervene in human affairs by 'overshadowing' individuals, according to Leach, and such 'overshadowings' have been common in mankind's past: 'Anybody you can name in history who has been a leader--Socrates, Buddha, Jesus--is a disciple of the Great Masters, whether they knew it or not.' . . . Creme and his followers believe that the same process is the means whereby Jesus of Nazareth became Christ, and that the very same 'Master' who supposedly accomplished these transformations has been reincarnated in the person of 'Maitreya.'

. . . The Theosophical Society, to which Benjamin Creme belongs, was founded by 19th-century Russian occultist Helena Petrovna Blavatsky, whose successors included Fabian socialist Anne Besant and Luciferian Alice Bailey. Blavatsky professed to have been initiated into the 'secret wisdom' of the ages by two 'Masters' named Koot Hoomi and Morya. Leach states that 'Blavatsky was the first in recent times to talk about the Masters, and that was the first phase of the modern teaching. The second phase came with Alice Bailey, who expanded the teaching. The third phase began just a little over a decade ago' when Creme began promulgating Maitreya's doctrines.

Leach was at the IDC [International Development Conference] on behalf of Creme's organization, *'Share International,'* a UN-recognized nongovernmental organization (NGO). *Share International, the organization's monthly journal, is published in association with the Department of Public Information at the United Nations.* Predictably, the magazine retails the UN's party line on issues like 'sustainable development.' It also details recent 'appearances' of Maitreya and evangelizes on behalf of his gospel of global wealth redistribution.

Furthermore, the 'Masters' are reportedly prepared to create the 'new world religion and the Universal Church.'

. . . Many Christians would interpret these statements as tidings of the impending arrival of the Antichrist . . . . *the United Nations . . . is intended to be the instrument through which the 'Christ' will consummate his vision.* That event is nigh upon arrival, according to Creme and his 'Master.'

Since December 1988, Maitreya has forecast a major event that he now says will occur in the near future. That event, according to Maitreya, will be an international stock market crash beginning in Japan. It has been announced that he will appear on television within weeks or at the most months after the crash. According to Creme, arrangements have been made for Maitreya to appear on major television networks with only a few days' notice.

Every issue of *Share International* includes a message from "The Master," who is identified as "a senior member of the Hierarchy of the Masters of Wisdom." Supposedly communicating via telepathy with Creme, "The Master" issues edicts to the world regarding spiritual affairs.

The New American, April 3, 1995, printed an article entitled, "One World Worship." The article said:

The December 1994 issue of *Share International* reports that Maitreya and his associates are rapidly constructing 'the One Church and the New World Religion [which] will gradually emerge as a mutual tie to unite men with closer bonds.' The same issue contains a warning issued by 'The Master' via Creme: *'Very soon now, a most unusual event will allow the world to know that the Masters do, indeed exist . . . when men see Maitreya, they will know that the time has come to choose; to go forward with Him into a future dazzling in its promise-- or to cease to be.'* If 'empowerment' of the UN continues apace,

Creme's threat may become a hideous reality for those who refuse to bend the knee . . . .

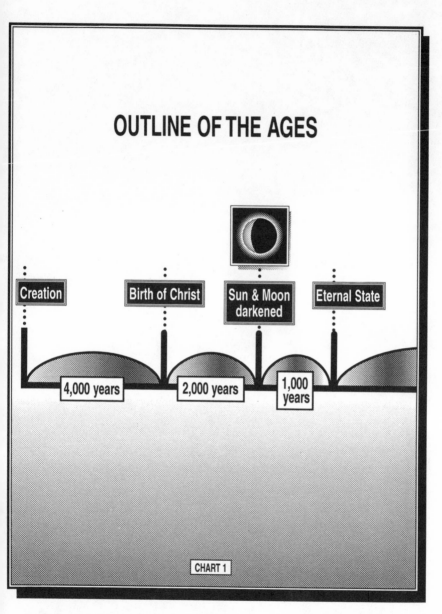

This time line portrays a general overview of the ages from Creation to the Eternal State.

TWO

THE DAY OF CHRIST

"Now we beseech you, brethren, by the coming of our Lord Jesus Christ, and by our gathering together unto him, That ye be not soon shaken in mind, or be troubled, neither by spirit, nor by word, nor by letter as from us, as that the day of Christ is at hand. Let no man deceive you by any means: for that day shall not come, except there come a falling away first, and that man of sin be revealed, the son of perdition . . . ."

— *II Thessalonians 2:1-3*

Christians everywhere are looking for the coming of Jesus Christ. The coming of Christ to catch up His church is often referred to as the *rapture*. The *word* "rapture" is not found in the Bible, but it is used to describe the catching up of believers to meet Christ in the air when He comes for His church. As we approach the end of the age, the time of the rapture has become a hotly debated issue. Can the coming of Christ to rapture the church occur at any moment as pretribulationism claims, or must certain events occur first? Is the rapture pretribulational, midtribulational, or posttribulational? Are there explicit scriptures that decisively answer these questions?

Believers have sought answers to these questions ever since the first public presentation of pretribulationism in the September, 1830 issue of *The Morning Watch* (cf. Appendix D - Mythical Pre-tribs). In Toronto, during a large conference in December of 1879, George Müller addressed this issue. Roger Steer wrote:

> On the final afternoon Müller publicly replied to nine written questions one of which was as hotly debated then as it is in some quarters today. The question was: 'Are we to expect our Lord's return at any moment, or that certain events must be fulfilled before He comes again?' Hundreds of pulses beat a little faster as Müller rose to his feet to deliver his reply.

> 'I know that on this subject there is a great diversity of judgment, and I do not wish to force on other persons the light I have myself. The subject, however, is not new to me; for having been a careful student of the Bible for nearly fifty years [Müller read the Bible through over 100 times], my mind has long been settled on this point, and I have not the shadow of doubt about it. *The Scriptures declare plainly, that the Lord Jesus will not come until the apostasy shall have taken place, and the man of sin, "the son of perdition"* (or personal Antichrist) *shall have been revealed, as seen in second Thessalonians chapter 2* [verses 2, 3]. Many other portions of the Word of God distinctly teach, that certain events are to be fulfilled before the return of our Lord Jesus Christ. This does not, however, alter the fact, that *the coming of Christ*, and not death, *is the great hope of the church*, and, if in a right state of heart, we (as the Thessalonian believers did) shall "serve the living and true God," and--wait for His Son from Heaven.'[1]

The question asked of Müller was "Are we to expect our Lord's return at any moment, or that certain events must be fulfilled before He comes again?" George Müller believed that a decisive biblical answer to this question is

---

[1] Roger Steer, *George Müller Delighted in God!* (Wheaton, Ill.: Harold Shaw Publishers, 1981), p. 255.

found in II Thessalonians 2:2, 3. To the troubled Thessalonians, Paul wrote:

> Now we beseech you, brethren . . . That ye *be not soon shaken in mind, or be troubled*, neither by spirit, nor by word, nor by letter as from us, *as that the day of Christ is at hand*. Let no man deceive you by any means: for *that day shall not come, except there come a falling away first, and that man of sin be revealed, the son of perdition* . . . . [2]

George Müller's definition of the Day of Christ is the key to his answer. Müller equated the Day of Christ with "the coming of Christ . . . the great Hope of the Church." According to a rule of grammar, "that day" in II Thessalonians 2:3 must refer to "the day of Christ" in the preceding verse. Müller said,

> The Scriptures declare plainly, that the Lord Jesus will not come until the apostasy shall have taken place, and the man of sin, 'the son of perdition' (or personal Antichrist) shall have been revealed . . . . [3]

Accordingly, Müller did not believe in imminency, that is, an any-moment coming of Christ.

WHAT DOES THE BIBLE SAY ABOUT THE DAY OF CHRIST?

Having the correct definition of the Day of Christ is critical in ascertaining the time of the rapture. To arrive at the correct definition, we must carefully consider the six passages that refer to the Day of Christ besides II Thessalonians 2:2, 3.

---

[2] II Thessalonians 2:1-3.
[3] Steer, p. 255.

First, Paul said, "So that ye come behind in no gift; waiting for the coming of our Lord Jesus Christ: *who shall* also *confirm you unto the end, that ye may be blameless in the day of our Lord Jesus Christ.*"[4] According to Webster, confirm means, "to make firm or firmer: *strengthen.*" Accordingly, this Scripture teaches that *in* the Day of our Lord Jesus Christ, believers will be blameless. They will be blameless because *the confirming* (sanctifying) work of Christ, which is presently being performed in believers, will be completed *when* the Day of Christ comes.

The time when believers will be wholly sanctified is taught clearly by John, who writes, "Beloved, now are we the sons of God, and it doth not yet appear what we shall be: but we know that, *when he shall appear, we shall be like him*; for we shall see him as he is."[5] Therefore, the Bible teaches plainly that believers will be wholly sanctified at the rapture.

Moreover, not only is Christ currently confirming believers, but He will also continue to confirm them *unto the end.* A crucial conclusion must be drawn from this Scripture. *Since Christ will confirm believers unto the end, the rapture, at which time believers will be wholly sanctified, cannot occur until the end.* Then, *believers will be blameless in the Day of Christ.* Being blameless is a blessing for which believers long.

Second, the Bible says, "To deliver such an one unto Satan for the destruction of the flesh, *that the spirit may be saved in the day of the Lord Jesus.*"[6] This verse

---

[4] I Corinthians 1:7, 8.
[5] I John 3:2.
[6] I Corinthians 5:5.

teaches that in "the day of the Lord Jesus" the spirit of the believer will be saved--a blessing for the believer.

Third, Paul said, ". . . *we are your rejoicing, even as ye also are ours in the day of the Lord Jesus.*"[7] This verse teaches that in the Day of Christ there will be rejoicing by believers--a blessing for believers.

Fourth, in Philippians 1:6 Paul said, "Being confident of this very thing, that *he which hath begun a good work in you will perform it until the day of Jesus Christ.*" This Scripture teaches plainly that the good work (namely, sanctification) which the Lord has begun in believers is presently being performed in them and will continue to be performed in them *until the Day of Jesus Christ.* Why only until the Day of Jesus Christ? The good work will no longer need to be performed after the Day of Christ comes, for it will have been completed when that Day comes. According to Webster, perform means, ". . . to do; to execute, to accomplish . . . ." Accordingly, the work of *progressive sanctification* is presently being per-formed in believers, and it will continue to be performed in them until the Day of Jesus Christ. It is crucial to lay hold of the truth that believers will be wholly sanctified when the Day of Christ comes, that is, at the rapture. This glorious truth is established by John, who wrote, ". . . *when* he shall appear, we shall be like him . . . ."[8]

This truth was confirmed by Henry C. Thiessen, who wrote:

> *Conformation to the image of Christ is the positive aspect of sanctification . . . Scriptures that deal with this phase of sancti-fication are the following*: Rom. 8:29: 'For whom he did fore-

---

[7] II Corinthians 1:14.

[8] I John 3:2.

know, he also did predestinate to be conformed to the image of his Son, that he might be the firstborn among many brethren.' . . . *Phil. 1:6: 'Being confident of this very thing, that he which hath begun a good work in you will perform it until the day of Jesus Christ'* . . . I John 3:2: 'Beloved, now are we the sons of God, and it doth not yet appear what we shall be: but we know that, *when he shall appear, we shall be like him*; for we shall see him as he is.' *Clearly this is a process extending throughout life and coming to full fruition only when we shall see the Lord.*[9]

Moreover, Peter Ruckman writes:

. . . 'he which hath begun a good work in you *will perform it until the day of Jesus Christ'* . . . 'the day of Christ' (as in II Thessalonians 2) is NOT 'the day of the Lord' . . . . A small boy at a prayer altar was heard praying: 'Lord, make a good job of me! Make a good job of me!' Well, the passage says that He will do it! . . . God will 'perform it until the day of Jesus Christ.' . . . The One who works *in* the Christian . . . placed Himself within the Christian . . . and He will not 'knock off for lunch,' cut down to a '20 hour week,' take a paid vacation, quit before the whistle blows, or 'retire at 50.' He will work on and on until His workmanship is faultless before the presence of his glory' (I Thessalonians 5:23, Jude 24!) . . . .[10]

A crucial conclusion must be drawn from this scripture. *Since Christ will perform the good work* (namely, sanctification) *which He has begun in believers until the Day of Christ, then the rapture, at which time believers will be*

[9] Henry C. Thiessen, *Introductory Lessons in Systematic Theology* (Grand Rapids, Mich.: Wm. B. Eerdmans Publishing Co., 1951), p. 379.

[10] Peter Ruckman, *The Books of Galatians, Ephesians, Philippians, Colossians* (Pensacola, Fla.: Bible Believers Press, 1973), pp. 363, 364.

wholly sanctified, cannot occur until the Day of Christ.
Think about that for five minutes. The completion of the
work that the Lord has begun in believers, when the Day
of Christ comes, will be a *blessing* for believers.

Fifth, in Philippians 1:10 Paul says, "That ye may
approve things that are excellent; that ye may *be sincere
and without offence till the day of Christ . . . ."* This
verse implies that when the Day of Christ comes, the believer's battles, trials, and testings will be over. The end
of battles, trials, and testings will be a *blessing* for believers.

Sixth, in Philippians 2:16 Paul says, "Holding forth the
word of life; that I may *rejoice* in the day of Christ, that I
have not run in vain, neither laboured in vain." This
Scripture teaches that in the Day of Christ there will be
reward and rejoicing for believers--*a blessing for believers.*

From the above six references, we are able to ascertain that the Day of Christ begins with the rapture, at
which time believers will be wholly sanctified. Furthermore, we learn that the Day of Christ relates to the
rewarding, rejoicing, and blessing of saints at His coming.

WHAT DO LEADING
PRETRIBULATIONISTS SAY
ABOUT THE DAY OF CHRIST?

The Scofield Reference Bible notes read, "The 'day of
Christ' relates wholly to the reward and blessing of saints
at His coming, as 'day of the Lord' is connected with
judgment."[11]

------

[11] The Scofield Reference Bible, p. 1212.

Lewis Sperry Chafer writes, "The Day of Christ is the termination of the Church's pilgrim journey on the earth . . . [by the rapture] and includes . . . the judgment seat of Christ . . . and the marriage of the Lamb . . . ."[12]

Gerald Stanton writes, "The day of Christ is distinguished by the fact that it is universally spoken of as a time of blessing."[13]

Dwight Pentecost writes:

> It thus appears that two separate programs are in view when these two expressions [the Day of the Lord and the Day of Christ] are used, although not two separate time areas. *They cannot be made to refer to the same event.* In each case in which Day of Christ is used, it is used specifically in reference to the expectation of the Church, her translation, *glorification*, and examination for reward.[14]

George Ladd, a posttribulationist, agrees when he writes, "The day of Christ is indeed a day of blessing and reward, and the day to which the believer eagerly looks forward." [15]

Peter Ruckman was also correct when he wrote in 1973, "'the day of Christ' (as in II Thessalonians 2) is NOT 'the day of the Lord' . . . ."[16]

---

[12] Lewis S. Chafer, *Systematic Theology, Volume VII* (Dallas, Tex.: Dallas Seminary Press, 1948), p. 110.

[13] Gerald Stanton, *Kept from the Hour* (Grand Rapids, Mich.: Zondervan Publishing House, 1956), p. 71.

[14] J. Dwight Pentecost, *Things To Come* (Findlay, Ohio: Dunham Publishing Co., 1962), p. 232.

[15] George Ladd, *The Blessed Hope* (Grand Rapids, Mich.: Wm. B. Eerdmans Publishing Co., 1956), p. 92.

[16] Ruckman, pp. 363, 364.

In summary, as the New Scofield Reference Bible notes read:

> 'The day of Christ' in all six references in the N.T. is described as relating to the reward and blessing of the Church at the rapture and in contrast with the expression 'the day of the Lord' . . . which is related to judgment upon unbelieving Jews and Gentiles, and blessing on millennial saints . . . . [17]

MUST CERTAIN EVENTS OCCUR BEFORE THE DAY OF CHRIST?

Now that we have established the definition of the Day of Christ from the Scriptures, let us consider carefully Paul's revelation to the Thessalonians. Paul writes:

> Now we beseech you, brethren . . . that ye *be not soon shaken in mind, or be troubled*, neither by spirit, nor by word, nor by letter as from us, *as that the day of Christ is at hand.* Let no man deceive you by any means: *for that day shall not come, except there come a falling away first, and that man of sin be revealed, the son of perdition* . . . . [18]

In verse two, Paul teaches plainly against the doctrine that Christ could come immediately. A.T. Robertson confirms this when he writes:

> . . . evidently some one claimed to have a private epistle from Paul which supported the view that Jesus was coming at once . . . . The use of <u>hos</u> <u>hoti</u> ['as that'] . . . means 'to wit that' [to know that] . . . . Certainly it flatly denies that by conversation or by letter he had stated that the second coming was immediately at hand . . . . It is enough to give one pause to note Paul's

---

[17] The New Scofield Reference Bible, p. 1233.

[18] II Thessalonians 2:1-3.

indignation over this use of his name by one of the overzealous advocates of the view that Christ was coming at once.[19]

The glorious Day of Christ cannot come until two events occur: a falling away first, and that man of sin be revealed as the son of perdition. This is both good news and bad news. The good news is that once these events have taken place, believers will know the Lord Jesus will soon come for them. The bad news is that Christ cannot come until they happen. Clearly, these two events suggest hard times.

In this crucial passage, we see that the Thessalonians' troubled state of mind resulted from their believing that the Day of Christ was at hand. According to Green's Lexicon, the Greek word rendered "at hand" means, ". . . to impend . . . to stand by or near . . . be at hand . . . to be present . . . ."[20] A Greek scholar told the writer, "*at hand* means something is so near that you can reach out and touch it." The Thessalonian believers were shaken in mind and troubled, because they thought the coming of Christ was going to occur immediately. Robertson writes, "Paul broadens the warning to go beyond conversation and letter. He includes 'tricks' of any kind."[21]

Paul wrote the Thessalonians to calm them, so he said, ". . . that day [the Day of Christ] shall not come except there come a falling away first, and that man of sin be revealed, the son of perdition . . . ."[22] Paul taught them plainly that *two events must occur before the Day of*

---

[19] Robertson, p. 48.

[20] Thomas Green, *A Greek-English Lexicon to the New Testament* (New York: Harper and Bro., n.d.), p. 79.

[21] Robertson, p. 49.

[22] II Thessalonians 2:3.

Christ can come. Paul did *not* teach that the Day of Christ could come immediately or at any moment. Paul established the truth that two notable events must occur first. Let us now consider the two notable events that must occur before the Day of Christ can come.

First, *there must come a falling away.* During the writer's quarter of a century as a pretribulationist, the Bible scholars whom he heard and read taught that the "falling away" was the gradual spread of apostasy in Christendom. They gave notice of the establishment and aims of the National and World Councils of Churches. They warned of the growing ecumenical movement, and they sounded the alarm at the spread of theological liberalism. All of the above mentioned things reveal a growing apostasy, but *they are not the falling away* spoken of by Paul.

The apostasy of which Paul writes in this passage is not an ordinary apostasy. Paul identifies it as he apostasia, that is, *the apostasy.* The definite article he (the) is used before apostasia (falling away). This usage means that Paul is writing about a particular apostasy. When the Greek article is used before a noun, it denotes a particular thing in distinction from other things.

Apostasy has been occurring since the fall of man in the Garden of Eden. The antediluvian contemporaries of Noah were apostates. The Sodomites who were destroyed with Sodom and Gomorrah were apostates. Those responsible for the crucifixion of Christ were apostates. Moreover, church history is a history of apostasy.

However, *the apostasy* of which Paul speaks is *the falling away,* in distinction from all other apostasies. *The falling away* of which Paul speaks in II Thessalonians 2:3

is an event so noticeable, so conspicuous, that believers are able to know that *the Day of Christ cannot come until this notable event occurs first. The falling away* spoken of in this passage will occur when the world's inhabitants are faced with the choice of taking the mark of the beast to buy or sell.

When that time of testing comes, people will be forced to take the mark of the beast upon their foreheads or in their right hands in order to buy or sell. When the receiving of the mark is required by the beast, *a falling away* (he apostasia) such as the world has never before seen will occur. *That apostasy will be the falling away.* When they take the mark of the beast, many *professing* Christians who do not possess Christ, along with billions of others, will forsake the true and living God and His words. *This multitudinous religious defection* from Christ and His words by receiving the mark of the beast *will be the falling away.*

Second, the man of sin must be revealed as the son of perdition. Many Bible scholars believe that the man of sin will be slain and then revivified. The restoration to life of the beast who will be wounded to death seems to be taught by John, who writes, "And I saw one of his heads as it were wounded to death; and his deadly wound was healed; and all the world wondered after the beast."[23] When we hear that a man is stabbed to death or shot to death, we understand those expressions to mean that the man died. Furthermore, in the 1611 edition of the King James Version, the marginal reading of "wounded to death" is *slain.*

---

[23] Revelation 13:3.

The Bible also teaches that the beast will ascend out of the bottomless pit. The Scripture says, "And when they shall have finished their testimony, the beast that ascendeth out of the bottomless pit shall make war against them, and shall overcome them, and kill them."[24] The beast in this passage is the personal Antichrist, namely, the son of perdition. The view of many is that the man of sin will be wounded to death; then the beast will ascend out of the bottomless pit and enter into the slain man of sin. At that moment, the man of sin who will have been wounded to death will be revivified, and then he will be revealed as the son of perdition. This remarkable event, like the falling away, will be so conspicuous that it will be universally known.

According to the King James Version, these two highly noticeable events must occur *before* the Day of Christ can come. Therefore, if the Day of Christ begins with the rapture, which it does, and if the King James reading "the day of Christ" is correct, which it is, the rapture cannot be imminent. The rapture cannot be imminent, that is, it cannot occur at any moment; for it must be preceded by the two notable events. Furthermore, if the man of sin is revealed as the son of perdition in the midst of the Seventieth Week (when he breaks the covenant with many by causing the sacrifice and the oblation to cease in Daniel 9:27), the rapture cannot be pretribulational.

---

[24] Revelation 11:7.

HOW DO PRETRIBULATIONISTS EVADE II THESSALONIANS 2:3?

How do pretribulationists evade the clear teaching of Paul in II Thessalonians 2:3? In Ecclesiastes 7:29, the preacher says, "Lo, this only have I found, that God hath made man upright; but they have sought out many inventions." According to Webster, invention means "device." Let us consider some of the devices pretribulationists have used to evade the plain teaching of this Scripture.

Device One

One device is to attack the King James text. The King James Version teaches plainly that two events must occur before the Day of Christ can come. If the Day of Christ begins with the rapture, which it does, and if the King James Version is correct, which it is, the rapture can be neither imminent nor pretribulational.

Walvoord evades the obvious problem posed by the King James reading "the day of Christ" (II Thessalonians 2:2, 3) when he writes, "... *practically all manuscripts read 'LORD' instead of 'Christ.'*"[25] Would he have us believe that the King James reading is in error? Would he have us believe that the King James Version translators gave us the reading "day of Christ" with weak or little manuscript support? To which manuscripts is he referring?

Zane Hodges and Arthur Farstad, like Walvoord of Dallas Seminary, shed more light on this matter. They state that *only three Egyptian manuscripts contain II*

---

[25] John Walvoord, *The Rapture Question: Revised* (Grand Rapids, Mich.: Zondervan Publishing House, 1979), p. 238.

Thessalonians (Codex Sinaiticus, Codex Vaticanus, and Codex Alexandrinus). These three Egyptian manuscripts agree on the reading "Lord." Yet, the same footnote declares that *the majority reading "Christ" is "largely united . . . ."*[26] While the writer is not saying that all extant manuscripts contain II Thessalonians, one should keep in mind that there are more than 5,300 extant Greek manuscripts in museums and libraries around the world.

When faced with this easily understandable Scripture, pretribulationists must somehow evade its plain teaching if they are to salvage their "darling" doctrine. Pretribulationists have many motives for salvaging their pet *theory*, as Pentecost calls pretribulationism in *Things to Come*.[27]

Pretribulationism is a darling doctrine to some Christian college chiefs, because being pretribulational means enrollment, and enrollment means students. For example, about ten years ago, the writer was talking with a famous Baptist pastor and founder of a large Baptist college. This Baptist leader had publicly proclaimed that he believed the King James Version was without error. The writer asked this famous fundamentalist if he believed the Day of Christ begins with the rapture. He replied, "I certainly do." Then the writer asked him how he could hold the doctrines of imminency and pretribulationism in the light of II Thessalonians 2:2, 3. After a considerable period of deafening silence, the famous founder said, "You are playing with fire." The writer replied, "I know it," and dropped the subject. Notice that this famous head

---

[26] Zane Hodges and Arthur Farstad, *The Greek New Testament According to the Majority Text, Second Ed.* (Nashville, Tenn.: Thomas Nelson Publishers, 1985), p. 621.

[27] Pentecost, p. 193.

of a large Baptist college did not answer the writer's question; he just said, "You are playing with fire." After the conversation shifted to another subject, The writer remembered the word of Lord to Jeremiah, "Is not my word like as a fire? saith the Lord . . . ."[28] Another Baptist college president listened carefully to the writer explain his view of eschatology on more than one occasion. To this leader the writer said, "If you see anything in my position that is unscriptural, show me; for I am correctable by the Scriptures." He replied, "Your position is unanswerable." Yet, he continued to maintain his eschatological persuasion and his leadership position in that pretribulational Baptist college.

Pretribulationism is a darling doctrine to some evangelists, because being pretribulational means meetings. For instance, a pretribulational evangelist who had preached more than a hundred sermons in a church pastored by his friend who is a posttribulationist finally felt compelled to write the following letter:

Dear Brother — :

Greetings in the Name that is above every name! . . . You will recall that since you went public with your post-trib position-- some five or six years ago--I shared with you that I was getting a lot of flack from pastors I preach for who learned of your switch from the pre-trib position. None of them threatened to cancel me at that time, but did question how I could still go and preach at . . . [your church] since I am still a pre-tribber. I told them that I was your friend, and that I would keep preaching for you as long as it didn't come between us to the point where I couldn't do it anymore.

---

[28] Jeremiah 23:29.

You may recall that several times over the years, I told your
people from the pulpit that I bragged on them in other churches
across America because they always brought so many lost people
to the meetings. This, of course, established in the minds of
pastors and people that I was a 'regular' at . . . [your] Church.
When your post-trib position began to be known across the
country, the flack grew heavier . . . but still I stuck with you
because I love you and I am your friend.

Then last fall, you sent out, I suppose, hundreds of letters to
pastors across the country, inviting them to your post-trib
conference that was to be held in December. A pastor in
Southern California (who surrendered to preach under my
ministry in 1974) sent me your letter. I had heard about it, but I
had not seen it until that time. In his letter, he said, 'I know you
preach there every year in February. Have you gone along
with [that pastor] . . . in his post-trib view?'

I wrote back that I am still pre-trib, and explained why I still
preach for you. He canceled the meeting I had booked with him.
More preachers began to press me for my position on the
doctrine, knowing that I have continued to preach for you in
spite of our differences on the doctrine. The heat was on.
Pastors and people in the pews were wondering just where I
stood, in the light of your widespread letter and invitation to the
conference.

I was in a church . . . I preach in often--when the pastor stood in
the pulpit at announcement time and brought up your letter,
telling his people basically what it said. There I sat. People in
that church know I preach for you.

It continued to get worse, so I had no choice but to take my stand
and declare where I stood on the three basic things you said in
the letter. I had to let pastors and people in their church
. . . know that I have not moved from my pre-trib position by
answering your statements in the letter that came to their hands.
Hence, came the sermon you answered to your people from my
tape.

It has come to the place where I have no choice but to cancel the meetings you and I have scheduled in 1996 and 1997. I'm sure you can see that I cannot jeopardize my evangelistic ministry by keeping myself vulnerable to more cancellations, which will definitely come if I return to your pulpit . . . .

Yours for the Old Time Faith,

Pretribulationism is a darling doctrine to some pastors, because being pretribulational means open doors, pastorates, and members. This writer had been receiving invitations to speak in Bible conferences across America in the late nineteen eighties, but, as he knew would happen, the invitations stopped coming when he went public with his posttribulationism. The next-to-the-last pretribulational pastor who had invited the writer to speak at a Bible conference said to the writer, "You are going to be very lonely." The writer replied, "I know it."

Pretribulationism is a darling doctrine to some missionaries, because being pretribulational means meetings, and meetings mean support. The writer knows missionaries who were well on their way to the field; but when their posttribulationism was made known, their meetings were canceled. Yes, pretribulationists have many motives for salvaging their darling doctrine.

What motivated Walvoord to write, ". . . *practically all manuscripts read 'LORD' instead of 'Christ'?"* The truth is that practically all manuscripts of II Thessalonians read "Christ" instead of "Lord." His former colleagues at Dallas Seminary present solid evidence that *only three Egyptian manuscripts contain II Thessalonians.* Is this falsehood by Walvoord ("practically all manuscripts read 'LORD' instead of 'Christ') only poor scholarship, or is it a desperate attempt to evade a decisive verse which refutes his pet doctrines of imminency and pretribulationism? According to Walvoord, imminency is the central pillar upon which the theory of pretribulationism stands. Walvoord writes, "The *central feature* of pretribulationism . . . [is] the doctrine of imminency . . . ."[29]

The difference between the Day of Christ and the Day of the Lord is not nit-picking. They are, as Pentecost says, ". . . two separate programs." There is no problem with the reading "day of Christ." Even those who do not believe that the King James Version is without error must yield to the fact that "day of *Christ*" is the majority reading.

For those who follow the lightly supported Egyptian reading ("the day of the Lord"), there are still serious problems for the doctrines of imminency and pretribulationism in this verse if a pretribulational translation of the church marks the beginning of the Day of the Lord. And Walvoord writes, "The [pretribulational] translation of the church . . . marks the beginning of the day of the Lord."[30]

However, in *The Rapture Question: Revised*, Walvoord mentions the two events of II Thessalonians 2:3 and writes, ". . . *both of these* [the falling away and the man of sin revealed as the son of perdition] *would be necessary before the day of the Lord could really 'come.'*"[31] Walvoord apparently does not see the contradictory nature of his two statements. Since Walvoord believes the [pretribulational] translation of the church

---

[29] Walvoord, *The Rapture Question: Revised*, p. 51.

[30] John Walvoord, *The Thessalonian Epistles* (Findlay, Ohio: Dunham Publishing Co., 1955), p. 81.

[31] Walvoord. *Rapture Question: Revised*, p. 239.

marks the beginning of the Day of the Lord, he is egregiously inconsistent when, on the one hand, he teaches that Christ may come at any moment and then, on the other hand, teaches that "both of these would be necessary before the day of the Lord could really come."

First he says, "The translation of the church . . . marks the beginning of the day of the Lord." (If a pretribulational rapture of the church marks the beginning of the Day of the Lord, the rapture and the beginning of the Day of the Lord must, therefore, occur at the same time.) Then, he says, ". . . both of these [events] would be necessary before the day of the Lord could really come." Although Walvoord says, "The central feature of pretribulationism . . . [is] the doctrine of imminency . . . ," the rapture, according to his teaching, cannot be imminent, because ". . . both of these [events] would be necessary" before the rapture, which "marks the beginning of the day of the Lord," could really come.

Yes, there are very serious problems for pretribulationists who, like Walvoord, believe that the rapture marks the beginning of the Day of the Lord; for not only must "both of these [events]" occur, but also the sun and moon must be darkened (Joel 2:31) and Elijah must come (Malachi 4:5) before the Day of the Lord can really come. Elijah, if he is one of the two witnesses of Revelation eleven, as most pretribulationists believe, will prophesy until he is killed after the second woe, namely, the sixth trumpet judgment (Revelation 11:11-14). Furthermore, he will prophesy 1,260 days (Revelation 11:3). Since the sixth trumpet judgment will occur *after* the Great Tribulation is past (this fact will be explained in chapters three, eight, and nine), the coming of Elijah will be far too late to precede the beginning of a Day of the Lord which is

marked by a pretribulational translation of the church.
The Day of the Lord will not begin until after the sun and
moon are darkened immediately after the Great Tribulation (This truth will be proved in chapter three). Therefore, if "the translation of the church . . . marks the beginning of the day of the Lord," as Walvoord says, the
translation of the church cannot be pretribulational; it
must be posttribulational.

When you boil it down, what you have is Walvoord
admitting, seemingly without being aware of it, that two
events must precede the rapture. Even if the Egyptian
reading ("day of the Lord") is used, this passage still
destroys Walvoord's pretribulational concept of an imminent coming of Christ.

Furthermore, if the Day of the Lord begins concur-
rently with the rapture and with the beginning of the
Seventieth Week of Daniel, as most pretribulationists believe, both events (the falling away and the man of sin
revealed as the son of perdition) must occur before the
Seventieth Week can begin. This view would place the
falling away and the revealing of the man of sin as the son
of perdition prior to the beginning of the Seventieth
Week. The Bible disproves this fallacy, for it places the
revealing of the man of sin as the son of perdition in the
midst of the Seventieth Week, when he breaks the
covenant with many and causes the sacrifice and the
oblation to cease. The Bible says, ". . . *in the midst of the
week* he shall cause the sacrifice and the oblation to cease,
and for the overspreading of abominations, he shall make
it desolate."[32] At this time, not prior to the beginning of

---

[32] Daniel 9:27.

the Seventieth Week, the man of sin will be revealed as the son of perdition.

Device Two

A second device was proposed in 1952 by E. Schuyler English, who wrote *Rethinking the Rapture*. In this book, he set forth a new and novel idea. English suggested that *the falling away* could be the falling away of the saints from the earth to meet Christ in the air. This new idea was adopted by Kenneth Wuest, John R. Rice, John Walvoord, and others.

This view has no valid exegetical support. The Greek words for "a falling away," as we have mentioned, are <u>he</u> (the) <u>apostasia</u> (falling away). The only other time the word <u>apostasia</u> is used in the Greek New Testament is in Acts 21:21. Here Luke writes, "And they are informed of thee [Paul], that thou teachest all the Jews which are among the Gentiles to *forsake* Moses . . . ." The word <u>apostasia</u> in this verse is translated *forsake*. When this allegation was made by Paul's accusers, Moses had been dead for 1,500 years. Hence, the word "forsake" means the forsaking of the words of Moses. Therefore, what is referred to in II Thessalonians 2:3 is *a religious defection from God and His words of such great magnitude that the Scripture calls it the falling away*, namely, *the apostasy*. Gundry writes:

> The meaning and connotation of a New Testament word are determined from four sources: 1) other appearances in the New Testament; 2) the LXX [Septuagint]; 3) the Koine (of which New Testament Greek is a species); 4) classical Greek. The last makes the least important of all sources and, significantly, it is from this least important source that English draws his argu-

ment. But even in classical Greek simple departure by no means predominates.[33]

The falling away spoken of by Paul unquestionably refers to a particular religious defection. Greek scholar A.T. Robertson confirms this truth when he writes:

Apostasia is the late form of apostasis and is our word apostasy. Plutarch uses it of political revolt and it occurs in I Maccabees 2:15 about Antiochus Epiphanes who was enforcing the apostasy from Judaism to Hellenism.

In Joshua 22:22 it occurs for rebellion against the Lord. It seems clear that the word here means a religious revolt and the definite article (he) seems to mean that Paul had spoken to the Thessalonians about it. The only other New Testament use of the word is in Acts 21:21 where it means apostasy from Moses.[34]

The meaning of "falling away" is further confirmed by lexicographer Walter Bauer, who says that apostasia means, "rebellion, abandonment . . . *the rebellion caused by Antichrist in the last days 2 Th 2:3.*"[35] Bauer defines clearly the "falling away" as the religious rebellion caused by the son of perdition in the last days. There is no scriptural reason to claim that *a falling away* means the departure of the church from the earth.

---

[33] Robert Gundry, *The Church and the Tribulation* (Grand Rapids, Mich.: Zondervan Publishing House, 1973), p. 115.

[34] A.T. Robertson, *Word Pictures in the New Testament* (Nashville, Tenn.: Broadman Press, 1931), p. 49.

[35] Walter Bauer, *A Greek-English Lexicon of the New Testament and Other Early Christian Literature, Second Ed.* (Chicago, Ill.: The University of Chicago Press, 1958), p. 98.

Rather, three things prove that the falling away *cannot* be the departure of the saints from the earth, that is, the rapture.

First, *the meanings* of the terms "falling away" and "day of Christ" prove that the falling away cannot mean the rapture of the church. On the one hand, it has been shown that *the falling away* in II Thessalonians 2:3 means a religious defection or rebellion. Specifically, in this verse, the falling away means the religious defection or rebellion caused by the Antichrist in the last days. On the other hand, it has been demonstrated that *the Day of Christ* is a program that begins with the rapture of the church and includes the judgment seat of Christ and the marriage supper of the Lamb. Therefore, since *the Day of Christ* means one thing, and *the falling away* means another thing, *the falling away cannot be the rapture* of the church.

Second, *the different times* of the two events prove that the falling away cannot mean the rapture of the church. In II Thessalonians 2:3, Paul establishes the truth that *the falling away* and *the Day of Christ* will occur at *different times*. Paul says, ". . . that day [the Day of Christ] shall not come except there come *a falling away first* . . . ." A.T. Robertson confirms this truth when he writes, "It seems clear that the word [apostasia] here means a religious revolt and . . . it is to be *first* (proton) *before Christ comes again.*"[36] Therefore, since *the falling away must occur first*, that is, before the Day of Christ [which begins with the rapture], *the falling away cannot be the rapture* of the church.

---

[36] Robertson, p. 49.

Third, *the confirming* (sanctifying) work of Christ in believers, which will continue until the Day of Christ, proves that the falling away cannot be the rapture of the church. It has been shown that Christ will confirm (that is, progressively sanctify) believers unto the end and until the Day of Jesus Christ (I Corinthians 1:7, 8; Philippians 1:6).

It is helpful (but not necessary) to see that *the end* will occur at the close of the Great Tribulation. In the Olivet Discourse, Jesus said, ". . . he that shall endure unto the end, the same shall be saved" (Matthew 24:13). In this verse, Jesus teaches that the saints must endure the entire Great Tribulation, for the saving or delivering of the saints will not occur until the end. Hence, the end will not come until the close of the Great Tribulation.

This truth is further taught by Christ in the next verse of the Olivet Discourse, where He said, "And this gospel of the kingdom shall be preached in all the world for a witness unto all nations; and then shall the end come" (Matthew 24:14). Since *the gospel of the kingdom* must be preached in all the world for a witness unto all nations before the end comes, the end must be at the close of the Great Tribulation and immediately prior to the commencement of the millennial kingdom. That the end will occur at the close of the Great Tribulation is established by Christ in His letter to the church in Thyatira, where He said, ". . . *hold fast till I come*. And he that overcometh and keepeth my works *unto the end*, to him will I give power over the nations. And *he shall rule* them with a rod of iron . . ." (Revelation 2:25-27). Here Christ linked His coming with *the end* and with *ruling in the millennial kingdom*. Accordingly, the end will occur at the close of the Great Tribulation and immediately prior to the beginning of the millennial kingdom.

It has been established that believers will be wholly sanctified at the time of the rapture and not until, for John said, ". . . *when* he shall appear, we shall be like him; for we shall see him as he is" (I John 3:2). It has also been established that Christ will confirm believers until the Day of Christ (Phil. 1:6). Consequently, the rapture, at which time believers will be wholly sanctified, cannot occur until the Day of Christ. Therefore, *the falling away*, which must occur first, that is, before the Day of Christ, *cannot be the rapture of the church.*

Those who teach that *the falling away* is a pretribulational rapture must, accordingly, "divorce" the rapture from the Day of Christ. This thought leads us to our discussion of another device used by pretribulationists to evade Paul's plain teaching.

Device Three

The third device is used by many pretribulationists who believe the King James Version is without error. These pretribulationists dare not reject the reading "day of Christ" in II Thessalonians 2:2, 3, for they believe that this reading is the Word of God. Since they cannot deny that two events must occur before the Day of Christ, they evade the force of Paul's plain teaching by *divorcing the rapture from the Day of Christ.* Some of these pretribulationists teach that the Day of Christ is equivalent to the Day of the Lord. Further, they say that the rapture could occur fifty years more or less prior to the beginning of the Seventieth Week of Daniel.

Dr. Peter Ruckman, in his commentary *The Books of Galatians, Ephesians, Philippians, Colossians*, written in 1973, affirmed the biblical meaning of the Day of Christ. He wrote, ". . . 'the day of Christ' (as in II Thess 2) is NOT 'the day of the Lord' . . . ."[37]

However, in 1981, when this writer first realized the devastating impact that the King James reading "the day of Christ" has on the doctrines of imminency and pretribulationism, he called Dr. Ruckman and asked him how a pretribulationist could handle this passage.

Dr. Ruckman told the writer that the problem was easy to solve. He said that *the Day of Christ is equivalent to the Day of the Lord.* Compare carefully what Dr. Ruckman told the writer in 1981 with what he believed in 1973, when he wrote, ". . . 'the day of Christ' (as in II Thess 2) is NOT 'the day of the Lord' . . . ."[38] Why did Dr. Ruckman change his definition of the Day of Christ? Is it possible that he changed his definition in an attempt to salvage the doctrines of imminency and pretribulationism?

Dr. Ruckman teaches that the rapture could have taken place at any time since the time of the apostles. Accordingly, those who teach that the Day of Christ is equivalent to the Day of the Lord, and that the rapture could occur at any moment before the Day of Christ comes, must "divorce" the rapture from the Day of Christ. *The divorce view,* namely, the view that divorces the rapture from the Day of Christ, has several fatal flaws.

First, *the meaning* of "the day of Christ" is a fatal flaw in the divorce theory. It has been demonstrated from

---

[37] Ruckman, pp. 363, 364.
[38] Ibid.

the Scriptures that the Day of Christ, as most leading pretribulationists believe, is a program or a period of time that begins with the rapture of the church and includes the judgment seat of Christ and the marriage of the Lamb. Since the Day of Christ begins with the rapture, it is altogether unscriptural to divorce the rapture from the Day of Christ.

Second, *the time* of the Day of Christ is another fatal flaw in the divorce theory. According to the King James Version (and the overwhelming majority of Greek manuscripts), the Day of Christ cannot begin until the falling away comes first and the man of sin is revealed as the son of perdition. Most pretribulationists believe that the man of sin will be revealed *as the son of perdition* in the midst of the Seventieth Week, when he will cause the sacrifice and the oblation to cease, and the abomination of desolation will be caused to stand in the holy place (Matthew 24:15). Since Paul locates the Day of Christ after the midst of Daniel's Seventieth Week, a pretribulational rapture would *divorce* the rapture from the Day of Christ by no less than three and one-half years. The time flaw in the divorce theory becomes even more apparent when one sees that *Paul links the Day of Christ with the end* (I Corinthians 1:7, 8; Philippians 1:6). It has been shown that *the end* occurs at the close of the Great Tribulation. Consequently, *this variety of pretribulationism must divorce the rapture from the Day of Christ, which begins with the rapture, by seven or more years!* It is clearly unscriptural to claim that the rapture could occur seven or more years before the Day of Christ, which begins with the rapture.

Third, *the confirming* (sanctifying) work of Christ in believers until the Day of Christ is still another fatal flaw in the divorce theory. In this chapter, it has been demonstrated from the Scriptures that the Day of Christ begins with the rapture, when believers will be caught up to meet Christ in the air and be wholly sanctified. Paul said, "So that ye come behind in no gift, waiting for the coming of our Lord Jesus Christ: *who shall also confirm you unto the end*, that ye may be blameless in the day of our Lord Jesus Christ."[39] Again, Paul said, "Being confident of this very thing, that *he which hath begun a good work in you will perform it until the day of Jesus Christ . . . .*"[40] Moreover, the apostle John said, ". . . *when* he shall appear, we shall be like him; for we shall see him as he is."[41]

The divorce view teaches that the rapture may occur fifty years more or less before the Day of Christ, and when the rapture occurs, believers will be wholly sanctified, that is, the vile bodies of believers will be fashioned like unto His glorious body, and we shall be like Him; for we shall see Him as He is.

Now, if the rapture should occur fifty years (more or less) before the Day of Christ, what *confirming* work would Christ *continue* to perform in believers during the *interval* between a supposed pretribulational rapture and the Day of Christ, at which time believers will be wholly sanctified? The Scriptures teach that believers will be confirmed until the end (I Corinthians 1:7, 8) and until the Day of Jesus Christ (Philippians 1:6). *Consequently, believers cannot be wholly sanctified at a supposed pretribulational rapture that takes place fifty years (more or*

---

[39] I Corinthian 1:7. 8.
[40] Philippians 1:6.
[41] I John 3:2.

less) before the Day of Christ. Therefore, the divorce theory is unscriptural.

In conclusion, the following things must be emphasized:

First, as Pentecost says, "In each case in which Day of Christ is used, it is used specifically in reference to the expectation of the Church, her translation, *glorification,* and examination for reward."[42]

Second, the Day of Christ will be preceded by two notable events. The Scripture says, "Let no man deceive you by any means: for that day shall not come, except there come a falling away first, and that man of sin be revealed, the son of perdition . . . ."[43]

Third, the Day of Christ, which begins with the rapture, will not come until after the midst of the Seventieth Week, for the man of sin will not be revealed as the son of perdition until then. The Bible says, "And he shall confirm the covenant with many for one week: and in the midst of the week he shall cause the sacrifice and the oblation to cease . . . ,"[44] thereby breaking the covenant. At that time, the man of sin will be revealed as the son of perdition.

Fourth, since the Day of Christ must be preceded by the falling away and the man of sin being revealed as the son of perdition, the Day of Christ, which begins with the rapture, is not imminent, that is, it cannot occur at any moment.

Fifth, since the Day of Christ, which begins with the rapture, cannot come until after the man of sin is revealed

---

[42] Pentecost, p. 232.
[43] II Thessalonians 2:3.
[44] Daniel 9:27.

as the son of perdition in the midst of the Seventieth Week, the rapture cannot be pretribulational.

Sixth, since Paul linked the Day of Christ, which begins with the rapture, to "the end" (I Corinthians 1:7, 8), the rapture must be posttribulational.

THE DAY OF CHRIST

The Day of Christ begins with the Rapture

I Cor. 1:7, 8   Phil. 1:6
I Cor. 5:5   Phil. 1:10
II Cor. 1:14   Phil. 2:16
                II Thess. 2:2

The Day of Christ
Rapture I Cor. 1:7, 8
Judg. Seat of Christ
Rev. 11:15–18

Marriage of Lamb
Rev. 19:1–10

1. The *good work* (progressive sanctification) begun in believers will be performed until the day of Jesus Christ (Phil. 1:6).

2. Consequently, believers will be wholly sanctified at the day of Christ (Phil.1:6).

3. I John 3:2 teaches that believers will be wholly sanctified at the rapture ("...when he shall appear; we shall be like him...").

4. Therefore, *the Day of Christ begins with the rapture* (Phil. 1:6; I John 3:2).

5. I Cor. 1:7, 8 teaches that believers will be confirmed (progressively sanctified) unto "the end," that they may be blameless in the Day of Christ.

6. Accordingly, Paul taught that the Day of Christ, including the total sanctification of believers, will occur at the point in time called "the end" (I Cor. 1:7,8; Phil. 1:6).

7. Therefore, the rapture (which begins the Day of Christ) will occur at "the end" (I John 3:2; Phil. 1:6; I Cor. 1:7, 8).

CHART 2a

The seven New Testament references to the Day of Christ teach that this day is a day of blessing for believers, beginning with the rapture.

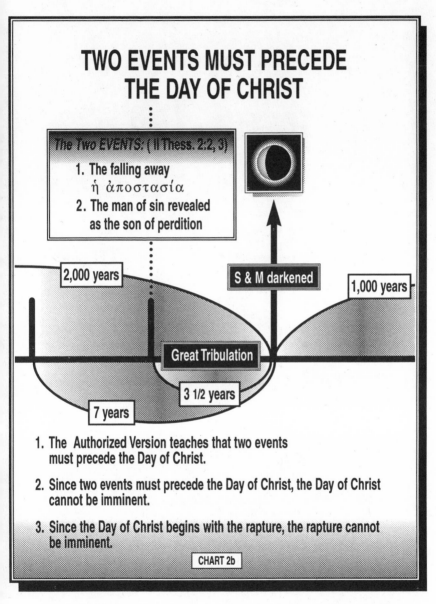

TWO EVENTS MUST PRECEDE
THE DAY OF CHRIST

The Two EVENTS: (II Thess. 2:2, 3)

1. The falling away
   ἡ ἀποστασία
2. The man of sin revealed
   as the son of perdition

2,000 years

S & M darkened

1,000 years

Great Tribulation

3 1/2 years

7 years

1. The Authorized Version teaches that two events
   must precede the Day of Christ.

2. Since two events must precede the Day of Christ, the Day of Christ
   cannot be imminent.

3. Since the Day of Christ begins with the rapture, the rapture cannot
   be imminent.

CHART 2b

The two events that must precede the Day of Christ will occur near the middle of the Seventieth Week of Daniel. In the K.J.V., II Thessalonians 2:3 disproves the doctrines of imminency and a pretribulation rapture.

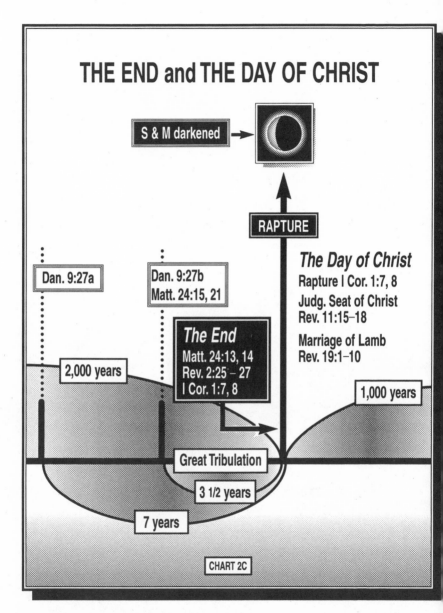

The Day of Christ begins with the rapture. In I Cor. 1:7, 8, Paul links the Day of Christ with "the end." Hence, the Bible does not teach a pretribulation or midtribulation rapture; it teaches a posttribulation rapture.

THREE

THE DAY OF THE LORD

"Behold, the day of the Lord cometh, cruel both with wrath and fierce anger, to lay the land desolate: and he shall destroy the sinners thereof out of it."

— Isaiah 13:9

Bible scholars hold different views regarding the Day of the Lord. Consequently, this writer determined to learn what the Bible itself says about this important day. In the light of Scripture, it is apparent that many are in egregious error in their understanding of the Day of the Lord. Understanding what the Bible says about the Day of the Lord is crucial to a clear comprehension of the order of events related to the second coming of Christ. In particular, this understanding is crucial to a correct conclusion regarding the time of the rapture.

WHAT IS THE DAY OF THE LORD?

Walvoord says, ". . . pretribulationists have identified *the Day of the Lord as the millennial kingdom including the judgments that introduce the kingdom.*"[1]

---

[1] Walvoord, *Rapture Question: Revised*, p. 213.

WHAT DO PRETRIBULATIONISTS SAY ABOUT THE DAY OF THE LORD?

Scofield said,

The day of Jehovah (called, also, 'that day,' and 'the great day,') is that lengthened period of time beginning with the return of the Lord in glory, and ending with the purgation of the heavens and the earth by fire preparatory to the new heavens and the new earth . . . .[2]

Ironside said:

. . . when at last the day of grace is ended the day of the Lord will succeed it . . . the day of the Lord follows. *It will be the time when the judgments of God are poured out upon the earth. It includes the descent of the Lord with all his saints to execute judgment on his foes and to take possession of the kingdom* . . . and to reign in righteousness for a thousand glorious years.[3]

Pentecost, commenting on Ironside's remarks, said:

This second view coincides with the previous one [that is, Scofield's] as to the terminus, but begins the Day of the Lord with the tribulation period so that the events of the tribulation, the second advent, and the millennium are all included within the scope of the Day of the Lord . . . .[4]

Walvoord says:

The significant truth revealed here is that *the Day of the Lord, which first inflicts terrible judgments, ends with an extended period of blessing on Israel*, and this will be fulfilled in the

---

[2] Pentecost, p. 229.
[3] Ibid., pp. 229, 230.
[4] Ibid., p. 230.

millennial kingdom. Based on the Old Testament revelation, *the Day of the Lord is a time of judgment, culminating in the second coming of Christ, and followed by a time of special divine blessing* to be fulfilled in the millennial kingdom.[5]

Stanton says:

. . . *The Day of the Lord*, in both Testaments, does not concern the Church but *is the time of God's wrath* and judgment upon the world. It is not a twenty-four hour day, or one single event, but a period of time which starts after the rapture of the church and incorporates the entirety of the Tribulation period.[6]

Pentecost said,

It is thus concluded that the Day of the Lord is that extended period of time beginning with God's dealing with Israel after the rapture at the beginning of the tribulation period and extending through the second advent and the millennial age unto the creation of the new heavens and new earth after the millennium.[7]

WHAT DOES THE BIBLE SAY ABOUT THE DAY OF THE LORD?

Isaiah says:

Enter into the rock, and hide thee in the dust, for fear of the LORD, and for the glory of his majesty. The lofty looks of man shall be humbled, and the haughtiness of men shall be bowed down, and the Lord alone shall be exalted in that day. For the day of the Lord of hosts shall be upon every one that is proud and lofty . . . and the LORD alone shall be exalted in that day. And the idols he shall utterly abolish. And *they shall go into the holes of the rocks, and into the caves of the earth, for fear of the*

---

[5] Walvoord, p. 218.

[6] Walvoord, *The Thessalonian Epistles*, p. 81.

[7] Pentecost, pp. 230, 231.

Lord, and for the glory of his majesty, when he ariseth to shake terribly the earth. In that day a man shall cast his idols of silver, and his idols of gold, which they made each one for himself to worship, to the moles and to the bats; To go into the clefts of the rocks, and into the tops of the ragged rocks, for fear of the Lord, and for the glory of his majesty, when he ariseth to shake terribly the earth.[8]

Again, Isaiah says:

Howl ye; for *the Day of the Lord* is at hand; it *shall come as a destruction from the Almighty.* Therefore shall all hands be faint, and every man's heart shall melt: And they shall be afraid: pangs and sorrows shall take hold of them; they shall be in pain as a woman that travaileth: they shall be amazed one at another; their faces shall be as flames. Behold, *the Day of the Lord cometh, cruel both with wrath and fierce anger, to lay the land desolate: and he shall destroy the sinners thereof out of it.* For the stars of heaven and the constellations thereof shall not give their light: *the sun shall be darkened* in his going forth, and the moon shall not cause her light to shine. *And I will punish the world for their evil, and the wicked for their iniquity*; and I will cause the arrogancy of the proud to cease, and will lay low the haughtiness of the terrible. I will make a man more precious than fine gold; even a man than the golden wedge of Ophir. Therefore I will shake the heavens, and the earth shall remove out of her place, in the wrath of the LORD of hosts, and *in the day of his fierce anger.*[9]

Once more, Isaiah says:

Come near, ye nations, to hear; and hearken, ye people: let the earth hear, and all that is therein; the world, and all things that come forth of it. *For the indignation of the LORD is upon all nations*, and his fury upon all their armies: he hath utterly

---

[8] Isaiah 2:10-21.
[9] Isaiah 13:6-13.

destroyed them, he hath delivered them to the slaughter. Their slain also shall be cast out, and their stink shall come up out of their carcases, *and the mountains shall be melted with their blood.* And all the host of heaven shall be dissolved, and the heavens shall be rolled together as a scroll: and all their host shall fall down, as the leaf falleth off from the vine, and as a falling fig from the fig tree.[10]

Zephaniah says:

The great day of the Lord is near, it is near, and hasteth greatly, even the voice of the day of the Lord: the mighty man shall cry there bitterly. *That day is a day of wrath, a day of trouble* and distress, a day of wasteness and desolation, a day of darkness and gloominess, a day of clouds and thick darkness, a day of the trumpet and alarm against the fenced cities, and against the high towers. *And I will bring distress upon men,* that they shall walk like blind men, *because they have sinned against the LORD:* and their blood shall be poured out as dust, and their flesh as the dung. Neither their silver nor their gold shall be able to deliver them *in the day of the Lord's wrath; but the whole land shall be devoured by the fire of his jealousy: for he shall make even a speedy riddance of all them that dwell in the land.*[11]

Zechariah says:

Behold, the day of the Lord cometh, and thy spoil shall be divided in the midst of thee. For I will gather all nations against Jerusalem to battle; and the city shall be taken, and the houses rifled, and the women ravished; and half of the city shall go forth into captivity, and the residue of the people shall not be cut off from the city. Then shall the LORD go forth, and fight against those nations, as when he fought in the day of battle. And his feet shall stand in that day upon the mount of Olives, which is before Jerusalem on the east, and the mount of Olives

---

[10] Isaiah 34:1-4.
[11] Zephaniah 1:14-18.

shall cleave in the midst thereof toward the east and toward the west, and there shall be a very great valley; and half of the mountain shall remove toward the north, and half of it toward the south. And ye shall flee to the valley of the mountains . . . and the LORD my God shall come, and all the saints with thee.[12]

These passages, as well as many others, reveal that there is a *"great and . . . terrible aspect"* of the Day of the Lord. The scriptures quoted above confirm that the divine judgments called *the wrath of the Lamb* will be poured out in the early part of the Day of the Lord.[13]

However, the major part of the Day of the Lord will be a time of special, divine blessing. This time of divine blessing is taught in Isaiah and other prophets.

Isaiah says:

And it shall come to pass *in the last days, that the mountain of the LORD'S house shall be established in the top of the mountains*, and shall be exalted above the hills; and all nations shall flow unto it. And many people shall go and say, come ye, and let us go up to the mountain of the Lord, to the house of the God of Jacob; and he will teach us of his ways, and we will walk in his paths: for out of Zion shall go forth the law, and the word of the Lord from Jerusalem. And he shall judge among the nations, and shall rebuke many people: *and they shall beat their swords into plowshares, and their spears into pruninghooks: nation shall not lift up sword against nation, neither shall they learn war any more.* O house of Jacob, come ye, and let us walk in the light of the LORD.[14]

---

[12] Zechariah 14:1-5.
[13] Revelation 6:15-17.
[14] Isaiah 2:2-9; cf. Revelation 12:9, 10.

Again, Isaiah says:

And *in that day* thou shalt say, O LORD, I will praise thee: though thou wast angry with me, thine anger is turned away, and thou comfortedst me. Behold, God is my salvation; I will trust, and not be afraid: for the Lord JEHOVAH is my strength and my song; he also is become my salvation. Therefore with joy shall ye draw water out of the wells of salvation. And *in that day* shall ye say, praise the LORD, call upon his name, declare his doings among the people, make mention that his name is exalted. Sing unto the LORD; for he hath done excellent things: this is known in all the earth. Cry out and shout, thou inhabitant of Zion: for great is the Holy One of Israel in the midst of thee.[15]

The blessings of the Day of the Lord are further described by Isaiah, who said:

And I will rejoice in Jerusalem, and joy in my people: and the voice of *weeping shall be no more heard in her,* nor the voice of crying. There shall be no more thence an infant of days, nor an old man that hath not filled his days: *for the child shall die an hundred years old;* but the sinner being an hundred years old shall be accursed. And they shall build houses, and inhabit them; and they shall plant vineyards, and eat the fruit of them. They shall not build, and another inhabit; they shall not plant, and another eat: *for as the days of a tree are the days of my people,* and mine elect shall long enjoy the work of their hands. They shall not labour in vain, nor bring forth for trouble; for they are the seed of the blessed of the LORD, and their offspring with them. And it shall come to pass, that before they call, I will answer; and while they are yet speaking, I will hear. *The wolf and the lamb shall feed together, and the lion shall eat straw like the bullock:* and dust shall be the serpent's meat. They shall not hurt nor destroy in all my holy mountain, saith the LORD.[16]

---

[15] Isaiah 12:1-6.
[16] Isaiah 65:19-25.

Scofield said:

> The moral characteristics of the kingdom are to be righteousness and peace. The meek, not the proud, will inherit the earth; longevity will be greatly increased; the knowledge of the Lord will be universal; beast ferocity will be removed; absolute equity will be enforced; and outbreaking sins visited with instant judgment; while the enormous majority of earth's inhabitants will be saved . . . The N.T. (Revelation 20:1-5) adds a detail of immense significance — the removal of Satan from the scene. It is impossible to conceive to what heights of spiritual, intellectual, and physical perfection humanity will attain in this, its coming age of righteousness and peace . . . .[17]

WHAT WILL OCCUR AT THE END OF THE DAY OF THE LORD?

There will be a final rebellion led by Satan, who will be loosed out of his prison. We read about this revolt in Revelation 20, which says:

> And when the thousand years are expired, Satan shall be loosed out of his prison, and shall go out to deceive the nations which are in the four quarters of the earth, Gog and Magog, to gather them together to battle: the number of whom is as the sand of the sea. And they went up on the breadth of the earth, and compassed the camp of the saints about, and the beloved city: and fire came down from God out of heaven, and devoured them.[18]

This revolt will occur *in the Day of the Lord.* One more awesome event follows the final revolt, and this event also takes place *in* the Day of the Lord. Peter said:

---

[17] The New Scofield Reference Bible, p. 977.
[18] Revelation 20:7-9.

But the day of the Lord will come as a thief in the night; *in the which* the heavens shall pass away with a great noise, and the elements shall melt with fervent heat, the earth also and the works that are therein shall be burned up.[19]

Peter continued:

Looking for and hasting unto the coming of the day of God, *wherein* the heavens being on fire shall be dissolved, and the elements shall melt with fervent heat? Nevertheless we, according to his promise, look for new heavens and a new earth, wherein dwelleth righteousness.[20]

These statements by Peter teach plainly that the heavens will pass away with a great noise, the elements will melt with fervent heat, and the earth will be burned up *in* the Day of the Lord. Peter further revealed that the very day on which these stupendous events will occur is "the Day of God."[21]

WHEN DOES THE DAY OF THE LORD END?

We have seen that the Day of the Lord includes a period of divine wrath upon the wicked who worship the beast and his image. Walvoord said correctly, "Pretribulationists have identified the Day of the Lord as *the millennial kingdom including the judgments that introduce the kingdom.*"[22] After the short time during which God's wrath will be poured out *in an unparalleled way*, there will be an extended time of divine blessing during

---

[19] II Peter 3:10.

[20] II Peter 3:12, 13.

[21] II Peter 3:12.

[22] Walvoord, *Rapture Question: Revised*, p. 213.

the Day of the Lord. At the end of the one thousand years, Satan will be released from the bottomless pit, and he will lead the final revolt against the city of the saints.

The Day of the Lord, Pentecost said, ". . . will include all the events of the millennial age, with the final revolt of Satan . . . and the purging of the earth."[23] Stanton says, "Peter . . . gives a good indication that the day of the Lord . . . includes the entire millennial kingdom, up to the creation of the new heaven and the new earth."[24] These leading pretribulationists agree that the Day of the Lord comes to a close after the one thousand years. There is no disagreement between leading pretribulationists and the Bible when it comes to the terminus, that is, the end of the Day of the Lord.

WHEN DOES THE DAY OF THE LORD BEGIN?

The question that must be answered correctly is, "When does the Day of the Lord begin?" To quote Hamlet, "That is the question."

First, let us see when the *new* pretribulationists say the Day of the Lord begins.

Ironside said, ". . . when at last the day of grace is ended the day of the Lord will succeed it . . . . It will be the time when the judgments of God are poured out upon the earth."[25]

Regarding Ironside's remarks, Pentecost said, "This . . . view . . . begins the Day of the Lord with the tribulation period so that *the events of the tribulation . . . are all*

---

[23] Pentecost, p. 231; II Peter 3:10-13.

[24] Stanton, p. 81.

[25] Pentecost, pp. 229, 230.

included within the scope of the day of the Lord."[26]

Walvoord says, "The [pretribulational] translation of the church . . . marks the beginning of the Day of the Lord."[27]

Stanton says, ". . . *the day of the Lord* . . . is the time of God's wrath . . . a period of time which starts after the rapture of the church and *incorporates the entirety of the tribulation period.*" [By tribulation, Stanton and other pretribulationists mean Daniel's Seventieth Week.][28]

Pentecost said, ". . . The day of the Lord is that *extended period of time beginning* with God's dealing with Israel *after the rapture at the beginning of the trib-ulation* period . . . ."[29]

The New Scofield Reference Bible notes read, "The order of events appears to be . . . the [pretribulational] rapture of the church just preceding the beginning of the day of the Lord . . . ."[30]

Hence, we see that *new* pretribulationists are in agreement about what *they believe* is the beginning point of the Day of the Lord. They teach that a pretribulational rapture will occur "just preceding the beginning of the day of the Lord."[31] They also teach that the Day of the Lord "incorporates the entirety of the tribulation period."

Second, let us see when the *old* pretribulationists say the Day of the Lord begins.

The *old pretribulationists did not teach what the new pretribulationists teach* regarding the beginning point of

---

[26] Ibid, p. 230.

[27] Walvoord, *The Thessalonian Epistles*, p. 81.

[28] Stanton, pp. 75, 76.

[29] Pentecost, p. 230.

[30] The New Scofield Reference Bible, p. 1372.

[31] Ibid.

the Day of the Lord. There is a whale of a difference between the two views. Darby, an old pretribulationist, said there are "two proofs that the day of the Lord had not come . . . first, the day could not be already come, since Christians were not yet gathered to the Lord, and . . . second, *the wicked one [Antichrist]* who has then to be judged *had not yet appeared . . . .*"[32] Did you get that? Darby said that the Day of the Lord could not come until the wicked one [the son of perdition] had appeared.

Scofield, an *old* pretribulationist, said,

> The day of the Lord is preceded by seven signs: *the sending of Elijah* (Malachi 4:5 . . .) . . . *cosmical disturbances* (Joel 2:1-12; Matthew 24:29; Acts 2:19, 20; Revelation 6:12-17) . . . *the apostasy* [namely, the 'falling away'] of the professing church (II Thessalonians 2:3) . . . *the manifestation of 'the man of sin,'* the Beast [II Thessalonians 2:3].[33]

Therefore, we see that *the old pretribulationists taught that the Day of the Lord will not begin until after the manifestation of the man of sin and after the cosmical disturbances* mentioned in Matthew 24:29 and Revelation 6:12, 13.

Walvoord, a *new* pretribulationist, sees clearly the difference between the views of the old pretribulationists and the new pretribulationists, so he writes:

> Pretribulationists have identified the day of the Lord as *the millennial kingdom including the judgments that introduce the kingdom.* This view was popularized by the 1917 edition of the

---

[32] John N. Darby, *Synopsis of the Books of the Bible*, Volume V (New York: Loizeaux Bro., 1942), pp. 132, 133.

[33] The New Scofield Reference Bible, p. 1349.

Scofield Reference Bible. In this interpretation . . . *the day of the Lord begins* at the end of or *after the great tribulation.*[34]

Here Walvoord states clearly the view of the *old* pre-tribulationists. Remember, in *The Thessalonian Epistles*, Walvoord says, "The [pretribulational] translation of the church . . . marks the beginning of the Day of the Lord."[35]

Therefore, we see that *new* pretribulationists have forsaken the position of the *old* pretribulationists regarding the beginning point of the Day of the Lord.

Why did the *new* pretribulationists depart from the view of the *old* pretribulationists? Why did the *new* pretribulationists move the beginning point of the Day of the Lord from *after* the Great Tribulation to just after a pretribulational rapture? What motivated them to forsake the position of their eschatological heroes Darby and Scofield? Did Walvoord let the cat out of the bag when he wrote, "*Pretribulationists* who see the day of the Lord beginning at the end of the Tribulation *have difficulty harmonizing this with the pretribulational rapture*"?[36] Think about that for five minutes.

The truth is that it is so difficult to harmonize the Day of the Lord beginning *after* the Great Tribulation with a pretribulational rapture, that Walvoord does an absolutely incredible thing. In *Rapture Question: Revised*, Walvoord quoted Joel 2:31, which says, "The sun shall be turned into darkness, and the moon into blood, *before* the great and terrible day of the Lord come." Then, shockingly, Walvoord wrote, "What is meant here is *not* that the day of the Lord will begin after these wonders in

---

[34] Walvoord, *Rapture Question: Revised*, p. 213.
[35] Walvoord, *The Thessalonian Epistles*, p. 81.
[36] Walvoord, *Rapture Question: Revised*, p. 213.

heaven . . . ."[37] There it is like a dead skunk. What Walvoord did with Joel 2:31 is like quoting John 3:16, which says, "For God so loved the world," and then saying *what is meant here is not that God so loved the world.*

Despite Walvoord's *incredible twisting of the Scripture* in Joel 2:31, Joel proclaims that the Day of the Lord will *not* begin until *after* these wonders in heaven which will occur *after* the Great Tribulation. Joel 2:31 says, "The sun shall be turned into darkness, and the moon into blood, *before* the great and the terrible day of the Lord come." The theological necessity of having a pretribulational translation of the church mark the beginning of the Day of the Lord is so great for pretribulationism that Walvoord flagrantly wrested Scripture. Think about that for another five minutes.

Walvoord and other pretribulationists have a theological necessity to place *the wrath of the Lamb*, which will be poured out *in* the Day of the Lord, in the Seventieth Week. By believing that "the [pretribulational] translation of the church . . . marks the beginning of the Day of the Lord,"[38] *new* pretribulationists can then believe that the wrath of the Lamb, which will be poured out *in* the Day of the Lord, will accordingly be poured out in the Seventieth Week.

It is pure theological necessity that motivates many *new* pretribulationists to move the beginning of the Day of the Lord to a point seven years earlier than the Bible teaches. They can then smuggle the trumpet judgments, the vial judgments, and the Battle of Armageddon into Daniel's Seventieth Week. By this clever eschatological

---

[37] Walvoord, *Rapture Question: Revised*, p. 218.
[38] Walvoord, *The Thessalonian Epistles*, p. 81.

bootlegging, *they advance, by violating the Scriptures, the beginning of the Day of the Lord seven years,* and they place the wrath of the Lamb in the Seventieth Week.

WHEN DOES THE BIBLE SAY THE DAY OF THE LORD BEGINS?

The Bible is crystal-clear about the commencement of the Day of the Lord. Joel says, *"the sun shall be turned into darkness, and the moon into blood, before the great and the terrible Day of the Lord come."*[39] Then Jesus, in His Olivet Discourse as recorded in Matthew, said, *"immediately after the tribulation [the Great Tribulation] of those days shall the sun be darkened,* and the moon shall not give her light, and the stars shall fall from heaven, and the power of the heavens shall be shaken."[40] Did you get that? Joel says, "The sun shall be turned into darkness . . . *before* the great and the terrible day of the Lord come." Then Jesus said, "Immediately *after* the tribulation of those days shall the sun be darkened . . . ."

Therefore, *the Bible teaches that the Day of the Lord will not begin until after the sun and moon are darkened immediately after the Great Tribulation.* Why, it is as simple as two plus two equals four. Even Scofield said, *"The day of the Lord is preceded by . . . cosmical disturbances* (Joel 2:1-12; Matthew 24:29; Acts 2:19, 20; Revelation 6:12-17)."[41] Isn't that amazing!

It is also crucial to observe that *the darkening of the sun and moon will occur with the opening of the sixth seal.* Revelation 6:12 says, "And I beheld *when he had*

---

[39] Joel 2:31.

[40] Matthew 24:29.

[41] The New Scofield Reference Bible, p. 1349.

opened the sixth seal, and, lo, there was a great earth-quake; and *the sun became black as sackcloth of hair, and the moon became as blood*." Therefore, the Day of the Lord will not begin until after the sixth seal is opened. (This truth will be further confirmed later.)

After the opening of the sixth seal, the seventh seal will be opened, and the first trumpet judgment will begin. John says:

> And when he had opened the seventh seal, there was silence in heaven about the space of half an hour. And . . . *the first angel sounded*, and there followed hail and fire mingled with blood, and they were cast upon the earth: and the third part of trees was burnt up, and all green grass was burnt up.[42]

After the first six trumpet judgments are poured out, the Bible then says:

> And the seventh angel sounded; and there were great voices in heaven, saying, The kingdoms of this world are become the kingdoms of our Lord and of his Christ; and he shall reign for ever and ever . . . And the nations were angry, *and thy wrath is come* . . . .[43]

When the first angel sounds his trumpet, divine wrath will be poured out. Furthermore, divine wrath will continue to be poured out through the remainder of the trumpet judgments, through the seven vials of wrath, and through the Battle of Armageddon.

To make it really clear, the trumpet judgments, the vial judgments, and Armageddon *will not occur during Daniel's Seventieth Week; they will occur in the Day of*

---

[42] Revelation 8:1, 2, 7.
[43] Revelation 11:15, 18.

the Lord after the sixth seal is opened and after the sun and moon are darkened, immediately after the Great Tribulation.

Describing the events which will take place after the opening of the sixth seal and the darkening of the sun and moon, John writes,

> And the kings of the earth, and the great men, and the rich men, and the chief captains, and the mighty men, and every bondman, and every free man, hid themselves in the dens and in the rocks of the mountains; and said to the mountains and rocks, Fall on us, and hide us from the face of him that sitteth on the throne, and from *the wrath of the Lamb*: for the great day of *his* wrath *is come*; and who shall be able to stand?[44]

It is not until *after* the sun and moon are darkened that men will hide themselves in the dens and in the rocks of the mountains. While they are hiding, they will say to the rocks and the mountains, "Fall on us, and hide us from the face of him that sitteth on the throne, and from the *wrath of the Lamb*; for the great day of *his* wrath *is come*, and who shall be able to stand?" Now, notice carefully Revelation 6:17, which says, "For the great day of *his* wrath *is come* . . . ." The two words "*is come*" are translated from the Greek word <u>elthen</u>, which is a second aorist *indicative*. In the Greek, the aorist *indicative* denotes *action that occurred in past time.*[45]

Since the verb <u>elthen</u> ("is come") is an aorist *indicative*, it denotes that *when* the declaration ("the great day of his wrath is come") is made, *the action of entrance* into the condition of "the great day of his wrath" had *occurred*

---

[44] Revelation 6:15-17.
[45] See Appendix B.

in past time, that is, prior to the declaration. Accordingly, *the time of entrance* into the condition of the great day of his wrath will be *before* the declaration ("the great day of his wrath is come"), but it will be *after* the Great Tribulation. The people crying to the rocks and the mountains to fall upon them will already be *in the great day of His wrath*. They will know that they are *in the great day of His wrath* and that *the wrath of the Lamb* is about to fall upon them. Consequently, they are crying to the rocks and the mountains to fall upon them to hide them from the wrath of the Lamb.

Although some pretribulationists attempt to do so, there is no exegetical basis for placing the commencement of the great day of his wrath or the Day of the Lord back far enough to include the first five seals of Revelation 6:1-11. To do so is actually unscriptural, for Joel 2:31 and Matthew 24:29 teach that the Day of the Lord cannot begin until *after* the sun and moon are darkened, immediately after the Great Tribulation. Dr. Arnold Fruchtenbaum admitted, ". . . there is no grammatical reason to make the aorist tense of the sixth seal [Revelation 6:17] retroactive . . . ."[46]

If Joel and Jesus are correct, and they are, *Walvoord's statement* "the translation of the church . . . marks the beginning of the Day of the Lord," *can only be true if the rapture is posttribulational.*

In conclusion, the Bible teaches plainly that *the Day of the Lord cannot begin until after* the sun and moon are darkened, immediately *after the Great Tribulation.*

---

[46] Dr. Arnold Fruchtenbaum, "Problems with the Pre-Wrath Rapture," Tape on file at Post-Trib Research Center.

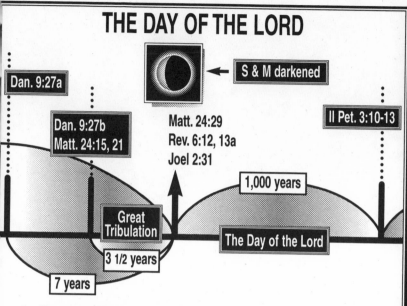

THE DAY OF THE LORD

Dan. 9:27a

S & M darkened

Dan. 9:27b
Matt. 24:15, 21

Matt. 24:29
Rev. 6:12, 13a
Joel 2:31

II Pet. 3:10-13

1,000 years

Great
Tribulation

The Day of the Lord

3 1/2 years

7 years

1. The sun and the moon are darkened immediately AFTER the Great Tribulation (Matt. 24:29; Rev. 6:12, 13a).

2. The Day of the Lord cannot begin until AFTER the sun and the moon are darkened (Joel 2:31).

3. Therefore, the Day of the Lord cannot begin until AFTER the Great Tribulation.

4. Since God's unparalleled wrath will be poured out IN the Day of the Lord (Isa. 13:6-13; Isa. 34:1-8; Zeph. 1:14-18; Zech. 14:1-5; Rev. 6:17-19: 20), this wrath will NOT be poured out IN the Seventieth Week.

5. Therefore, when the church goes through the Great Tribulation, it will NOT experience God's unparalleled wrath (I Thess. 5:9; Rev. 6:16,17).

CHART 3

Pretribulationists claim that the beginning of the Day of the Lord coincides with the beginning of the Seventieth Week of Daniel; however, the Bible teaches that the Day of the Lord cannot begin until seven years later, immediately after the Great Tribulation.

FOUR

THE SEVENTIETH WEEK
OF DANIEL

*"And he shall confirm the covenant with many for
one week . . . ."*

— *Daniel 9:27*

The preeminent prophecy of Daniel 9:24-27 reads as follows:

Seventy weeks are determined upon thy people and upon thy holy city, to finish the transgression, and to make an end of sins, and to make reconciliation for iniquity, and to bring in everlasting righteousness, and to seal up the vision and prophecy, and to anoint the most Holy.   Know therefore and understand, that from the going forth of the commandment to restore and to build Jerusalem unto the Messiah the Prince shall be *seven weeks, and threescore and two weeks:* the street shall be built again, and the wall, even in troublous times.   And after *threescore and two weeks* shall Messiah be cut off, but not for himself: and the people of the prince that shall come shall destroy the city and the sanctuary;   and the end thereof shall be with a flood, and unto the end of the war desolations are determined.   And he shall confirm the covenant with many for *one week:*   and *in the midst of the week* he shall cause the sacrifice and oblation to cease, and for the overspreading of abominations he shall make it desolate, even until the consummation, and that determined shall be poured upon the desolate.

THE DURATION OF EACH WEEK

If we are to interpret correctly this crucial prophecy, the first thing that we must ascertain is the duration of each week. The word rendered "week" is <u>shabua</u>, and this Hebrew word simply means "seven." The word <u>shabua</u> (week) is like the English word "dozen."

Hence, we must determine whether the weeks are weeks of days, weeks, months, or years. The Israelites had *a week of days* with a sabbath day of rest, and they also had *a week of years* with a sabbath year of rest for the land.[1]

In the first two verses of chapter nine, Daniel says,

> In the first year of Darius . . . king over the realm of the Chaldeans . . . I Daniel understood by books *the number of the years*, whereof the word of the LORD came to Jeremiah the prophet, *that he would accomplish seventy years* in the desolations of Jerusalem.[2]

The above passage reveals that Daniel was thinking in terms of *years*--seventy years, to be explicit. Furthermore, the Bible says, "To fulfil the word of the Lord by the mouth of Jeremiah, *until the land had enjoyed her sabbaths*: for *as long as she lay desolate she kept sabbath*, to fulfil threescore and ten *years*."[3] These three verses (Daniel 9:1, 2; II Chronicles 36:21) teach that the Lord would accomplish seventy years of sabbath rest for the land during the desolations of Jerusalem. Israel had not observed the sabbath year of rest for the land for 490 years or seventy weeks of years. Consequently, Jerusalem

---

[1] Leviticus 25:3, 4.
[2] Daniel 9:1, 2.
[3] II Chronicles 36:21.

would have to lie in desolations for seventy years in order for the land to enjoy her sabbaths. Accordingly, one week equals seven years, and seventy weeks equals 490 years.

The seventy weeks of years was to begin with the going forth of the commandment to restore and to build Jerusalem. Daniel says,

> Know therefore and understand, that *from the going forth of the commandment* to restore and to build Jerusalem unto the Messiah the Prince shall be *seven weeks, and threescore and two weeks*: the street shall be built again, and the wall, even in troublous times.[4]

If the seventy weeks were seventy weeks of days, the total time would have been 490 days. The great blessings which God promised to Jerusalem and Daniel's people listed in Daniel 9:24 ("to finish the transgression, and to make an end of sins, and to make reconciliation for iniquity, and to bring in everlasting righteousness, and to seal up the vision and prophecy, and to anoint the most Holy") did not come at the end of 490 days from the going forth of the commandment to restore and to build Jerusalem referred to in Nehemiah (March 14, 445 B.C.).[5] Neither did the great blessings promised to Jerusalem and Israel come at the end of seventy weeks of weeks nor at the end of seventy weeks of months from the going forth of the commandment. Therefore, it must be concluded that the "seventy weeks" are weeks of years.

The only commandment in Scripture pertaining to the building of the city of Jerusalem and its walls is the commandment of Artaxerxes mentioned in Nehemiah 2:4-8.

---

[4] Daniel 9:25.
[5] Nehemiah 2:6-9.

The decrees or commandments mentioned in Ezra relate to the rebuilding of the temple--not to the building of the city and the walls.

THE DURATION OF THE YEARS

There are solar years; there are lunar years; and there are Bible years. A Bible year has 360 days. For example, Genesis teaches that the flood began on the seventeenth day of the second month.[6] Genesis also teaches that the flood ended on the seventeenth day of the seventh month.[7] The period of time between the beginning of the flood and the end of the flood was exactly five months. Furthermore, Genesis gives the same time period in days, and the number was 150 days.[8] Hence, the five months equal 150 days. The months were months of 30 days each, and a year of 30-day months had 360 days.

In addition to the facts found in the flood account, we have the evidence of Bible prophecy confirming that the weeks are weeks of years. For instance, the Seventieth Week will be divided in the midst by Antichrist's causing the sacrifice and the oblation to cease. Daniel 9:27 says, "And he shall confirm the covenant with many for one week: and *in the midst of the week* he shall cause the sacrifice and oblation to cease, and for the overspreading of abominations he shall make it desolate . . . ." Referring to Daniel 9:27, the Lord said,

> When ye therefore shall see *the abomination of desolation, spoken of by Daniel the prophet*, stand in the holy place (whoso

---

[6] Genesis 7:11.
[7] Genesis 7:24; 8:3.
[8] Ibid.

readeth, let him understand:) . . . For *then* shall be great tribulation, such as was not since the beginning of the world to this
time, no, nor ever shall be.[9]

In short, when the abomination of desolation stands in
the holy place, the Great Tribulation will begin. According to Daniel, the duration of the Great Tribulation will be
exactly three and one-half years, for Daniel says, "And he
shall speak great words against the most High, and shall
wear out the saints of the most High . . . and *they shall be
given into his hand until a time and times and the dividing of time.*"[10]

McClain writes:

Although the Aramaic word translated 'times' in Daniel 7:25 is
not dual, but plural in form, *undoubtedly the plural is here used
with a dual significance* (see Barnes, Com., Keil, Com.; also
Gesenius, Lex.). *This is confirmed by the parallel expression
which occurs in Daniel 12:7,* 'a time, times, and an half,' *where
the word 'times' is a dual form in the Hebrew original.*[11]

Accordingly, Daniel 7:25 reveals that the length of the
Great Tribulation, during which the little horn will wear
out the saints, will be exactly three and one-half years.
Because the Great Tribulation of *three and one-half years
will be the last half of the Seventieth Week, the whole
Seventieth Week will be a period of seven years.*
Furthermore, the Bible teaches plainly that a time,
times, and half a time is 1,260 days. This fact is estab-

---

[9] Matthew 24:15, 21.

[10] Daniel 7:25.

[11] Alva J. McClain, *Daniel's Prophecy of the 70 Weeks* (Grand
Rapids, Mich.: Zondervan Publishing House, 1940), p. 71.

lished by John, who writes, "And the *woman* fled into the wilderness, where she hath a place prepared of God, that they should feed her there *a thousand two hundred and threescore days.*"[12] John continues, "And to the *woman* were given two wings of a great eagle, that she might fly into the wilderness, into her place, where she is nourished *for a time, and times, and half a time,* from the face of the serpent."[13] Again, we see that a time, times, and half a time is 1,260 days or three and one-half years.

Because Bible years have 360 days, the duration of each of Daniel's seventy weeks is seven years of 360 days each.

THE BEGINNING POINT OF THE SEVENTY WEEKS

What was the beginning point of the seventy weeks? Daniel 9:25 teaches that the seventy weeks began with the going forth of the commandment to restore and to build Jerusalem. Daniel says, "Know therefore and understand, that from the going forth of the commandment to restore and to build Jerusalem unto the Messiah the Prince shall be seven weeks, and threescore and two weeks . . . ."[14] There was to be a period of seven weeks plus sixty-two weeks, a total of sixty-nine weeks, from the going forth of the commandment to restore and to build Jerusalem unto the Messiah the Prince. In his book entitled, *The Coming Prince*, Sir Robert Anderson, with the aid of the Astronomer Royal of Great Britain, found the date of the commandment to be March 14, 445 B.C.

[12] Revelation 12:6.
[13] Revelation 12:14.
[14] Daniel 9:25.

THE TERMINATION OF THE SIXTY-NINTH WEEK

Beginning with March 14, 445 B.C., 69 weeks or 483 years (69 weeks x 7 years) or 173,880 days (483 years x 360 days) later the date was April 6, A.D. 32. Did anything of importance happen on April 6, A.D. 32? One of history's most important events did indeed occur on that day. In fulfillment of Zechariah's prophecy regarding the coming of Israel's King, the Lord Jesus Christ rode into Jerusalem on a colt and offered Himself as King to Israel on that very day, which is called the day of Triumphal Entry. Zechariah had written, "Rejoice greatly, O daughter of Zion; shout, O daughter of Jerusalem: behold, thy King cometh unto thee: he is just, and having salvation; lowly, and riding upon an ass, and upon a colt the foal of an ass."[15]

The Bible says:

And they that were sent went their way, and found even as he had said unto them. And as they were loosing the colt, the owners thereof said unto them, Why loose ye the colt? And they said, The Lord hath need of him. And they brought him to Jesus: and they cast their garments upon the colt, and they set Jesus thereon. And as he went, they spread their clothes in the way. And when he was come nigh, even now at the descent of the mount of Olives, the whole multitude of the disciples began to rejoice and praise God with a loud voice for all the mighty works that they had seen; Saying, Blessed be *the King that cometh* in the name of the Lord: peace in heaven, and glory in the highest. And some of the Pharisees from among the multitude said unto him, Master, rebuke thy disciples. And he an-

---

[15] Zechariah 9:9, 10.

swered and said unto them, I tell you that, if these should hold
their peace, the stones would immediately cry out. And when he
was come near, he beheld the city, and wept over it, Saying, *if
thou hadst known,* even thou, at least *in this thy day*, the things
which belong unto thy peace! but now they are hid from thine
eyes. For the days shall come upon thee, that thine enemies
shall cast a trench about thee, and compass thee round, and keep
thee in on every side, And shall lay thee even with the ground,
and thy children within thee; and they shall not leave in thee
one stone upon another; because thou knewest not *the time of
thy visitation.*[16]

Notice carefully Luke 19:41, which says, "And when he
was come near, he beheld the city, and wept over it,
Saying, *if thou hadst known*, even thou, at least *in this thy
day*, the things which belong unto thy peace! but now
they are hid from thine eyes."

The day of the Triumphal Entry was the day the Lord
Jesus referred to as *"this thy day."* It was the very day
that had been prophesied in the book of Daniel more than
five hundred years before. That day was the terminus,
that is, the termination point of the seven weeks plus
threescore and two weeks or sixty-nine weeks of years.
From the going forth of the decree to restore and to build
Jerusalem unto the day of the Triumphal Entry was exactly 173,880 days or sixty-nine weeks of years. *This
amazing fact proves* not only that the weeks of Daniel's
prophecy are weeks of years, but it also proves *that the
Bible is the very Word of God.*

---

[16] Luke 19:32-44.

IS THERE A GAP BETWEEN THE SIXTY-NINTH AND SEVENTIETH WEEKS?

Do the seventy weeks run consecutively, or is there a gap between the Sixty-Ninth and the Seventieth Weeks? It is important to observe that gaps are not uncommon in Bible prophecy. For example, Isaiah writes, "For unto us a child is born . . . and the government shall be upon his shoulder . . . ."[17] While Christ presently reigns over His people who have been born again and translated into His kingdom,[18] there will be a future eschatological aspect of the kingdom when the kingdoms of this world will become the kingdoms of our Lord and of His Christ.[19] At that time, Christ will not only govern his people, but He will also govern the kingdoms of this world, which will have become His kingdoms. There has already been a gap of nearly two thousand years between the fulfilled part and the yet unfulfilled part of this prophecy.

Again, Isaiah writes, ". . . the LORD hath anointed me to preach good tidings unto the meek . . . to proclaim . . . the day of vengeance of our God . . . ."[20] According to Luke 4:18-21, the first part of this prophecy was fulfilled when Jesus stood and read from the book of Isaiah in the synagogue in Nazareth. The latter part of the prophecy will not be fulfilled until the Day of the Lord. Other examples are found in Joel 2:28-31 and Zechariah 9:9, 10.

The above scriptures show that gaps are often found in prophetic portions of the Word of God. There must be a gap between the end of the Sixty-Ninth Week and

---

[17] Isaiah 9:6.
[18] John 3:3, 5; Colossians 1:13.
[19] Revelation 11:15.
[20] Isaiah 61:1, 2.

the beginning of the Seventieth Week, for the blessings of Daniel 9:24 *did not* come to Daniel's "people" and his "holy city" seven years (one week) after the day that Jesus Christ presented Himself as King to Israel on the day of the Triumphal Entry. If the seventy weeks ran continuously, the seventy weeks would have ended in March of A.D. 39.

If you start the Seventieth Week with the baptism of the Lord, as some do erroneously, and place Christ's crucifixion in the midst of the Seventieth Week, then the seventy weeks would have ended three and a half years after the crucifixion in the year A.D. 35. The great blessings promised to Daniel's "people" and to his "holy city" did not come in either A.D. 39 or in A.D. 35.

Moreover, the Lord Jesus placed the Seventieth Week at the end of the age, when He said, "*When* ye therefore shall see *the abomination of desolation, spoken of by Daniel the prophet,* stand in the holy place . . . For *then* shall be great tribulation."[21] In this passage, Christ identified the *"overspreading of abominations"* in Daniel 9:27 with the *"abomination of desolation"* of which He spoke in Matthew 24:15. When the abomination stands in the holy place, the Great Tribulation will begin; and it will last 1,260 days. In Matthew 24:29 Jesus said, *"Immediately after* the tribulation of those days *shall the sun be darkened,* and the moon shall not give her light . . . ."[22] The darkening of the sun and the moon will occur just before the coming of the Day of the Lord, for Joel says, "The sun shall be turned into darkness, and the moon into

---

[21] Matthew 24:15, 21.
[22] Matthew 24:29.

blood, *before* the great and the terrible day of the Lord come."[23]

Therefore, the Lord Jesus places *the Great Tribulation immediately before* the darkening of the sun and the moon *just before* the Day of the Lord comes.

Because *the Great Tribulation is the last half of Daniel's Seventieth Week*, there must, therefore, be a large gap of time between the Sixty-Ninth and Seventieth Weeks. An amillennial Baptist pastor told the writer that he believed the Seventieth Week ended with the destruction of Jerusalem in A.D. 70. The writer asked, "Were the sun and moon darkened immediately after the destruction of Jerusalem in A.D. 70?" The preacher replied, *"That is a problem for us."*

The Seventieth Week will begin when the "prince that shall come," that is, the Antichrist "shall confirm the covenant with many for one week."[24]

A SUMMARY OF THE SEVENTIETH WEEK

Let us keep in mind the following:

1. The Seventieth Week will be a week of years, with each year having 360 days.

2. The Seventieth Week will begin when the Antichrist " . . . shall confirm the covenant with many . . . ."[25]

---

[23] Joel 2:31.
[24] Daniel 9:26, 27.
[25] Daniel 9:27.

3. In the midst of the week, the Antichrist ". . . shall cause the sacrifice and the oblation to cease . . . ."[26]

4. In the midst of the week, the abomination of desolation will stand in the holy place. This event will mark the beginning of the Great Tribulation, which will last 1,260 days.[27]

5. Immediately after the Great Tribulation, the end of which will mark the end of the Seventieth Week, the sun and moon will be darkened.[28]

6. The Seventieth Week must run its full course before the blessings promised in Daniel 9:24 will be realized by Israel and Jerusalem.

---

[26] Ibid.

[27] Daniel 9:27; Matthew 24:15, 21.

[28] Matthew 24:29.

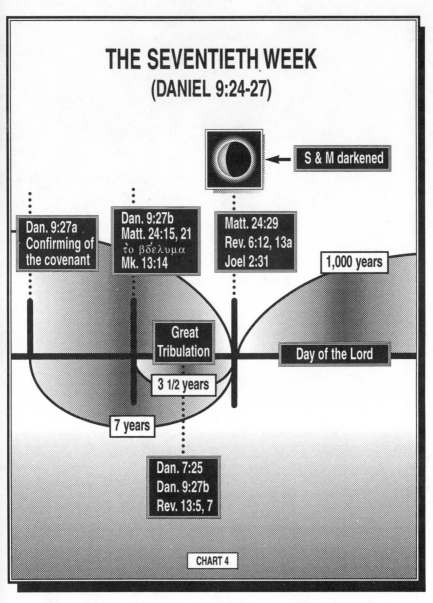

The Seventieth Week begins with the "confirming of the covenant." In the midst of the Week, the abomination of desolation will stand in the holy place. This event marks the beginning of the Great Tribulation, which will occur during the last half of the Week.

FIVE

THE "TRIBULATION"

"When ye therefore shall see the abomination of desolation, spoken of by Daniel the prophet, stand in the holy place . . . then shall be great tribulation . . . "

— *Matthew 24:15, 21*

The Lord Jesus informed His disciples of a truly trying truth. To them He said, *"In the world ye shall have tribulation . . . ."*[1] Paul further said, ". . . all that will live godly in Christ Jesus shall suffer persecution."[2] These are prophetic statements. Therefore, in the world believers will have tribulation.

History documents plainly that Christians down through the ages have experienced tribulation in varying degrees. A galaxy of God's saints have suffered severe tribulation and even martyrdom. For example, all of the apostles except John suffered martyrs' deaths.

The Lord's prophetic warning, *"In the world ye shall have tribulation . . . ,"* has been fulfilled in the lives of saints from the earliest days of the church until the present time. Tribulation for the believer is a certainty, the variable being merely the degree. Foxe wrote, "The history of the church may be said to be a history of the trials and

---

[1] John 16:33.
[2] II Timothy 3:12.

sufferings of its members, as *experienced at the hands of wicked men.*"[3]

WHAT IS TRIBULATION?

The word "tribulation" is from the Greek word <u>thlipsis</u>. According to Green, <u>thlipsis</u> means, "pressure, compression . . . distress of mind, distressing circumstances, trial, affliction."[4] The verbal cognate of <u>thlipsis</u> is <u>thlibo</u>, and according to Green, <u>thlibo</u> means, "to squeeze, press; to press upon, throng, crowd . . . metaphorically to distress, afflict . . . [in the passive voice] to be compressed, narrowed . . . ."[5] The definitions of the words <u>thlipsis</u> and <u>thlibo</u> show plainly that *tribulation does not mean wrath.*

In the Authorized Version, eight different words are used to translate these Greek words in their fifty-five occurrences. They are as follows: tribulation, affliction, persecution, trouble, anguish, burden, throng, and narrow. *Tribulation* is found twenty-two times. Affliction is found twenty-one times. Trouble is found seven times. Each of the others is found only once.

EXAMPLES OF TRIBULATION IN THE NEW TESTAMENT

In Matthew's account of the parable of the sower, Jesus says:

But he that received the seed into stony places, the same is he

---

[3] *Foxe's Book of Martyrs* (Philadelphia, Pa.: John D. Winston Co., n.d.), p. 15.
[4] Green, p. 85.
[5] Ibid.

that heareth the word, and anon with joy receiveth it; yet hath he not root in himself, but dureth for a while: for when *tribulation* or persecution *ariseth because of the word*, by and by he is offended.[6]

Here Christ teaches plainly that tribulation arises because of the Word; that is, *tribulation has its source in those who are the enemies of God's Word.*

In Mark's account of the same parable, Jesus says:

And these are they likewise which are sown on stony ground; who, when they have heard the word, immediately receive it with gladness; and have no root in themselves, and so endure but for a time: afterward, when *affliction* or *persecution ariseth for the word's sake*, immediately they are offended.[7]

In this passage, <u>thlipsis</u> is translated *affliction.* We see again that "affliction . . . ariseth for the word's sake."

In Mark 13:19 (the parallel verse to Matthew 24:21), Jesus says, "For in those days shall be affliction, such as was not from the beginning of the creation which God created unto this time, neither shall be." In this verse, <u>thlipsis</u> is translated *affliction.* The context reveals that this affliction will have its source in the Antichrist and his worshipers during the Great Tribulation.

To His disciples, Jesus said, "In the world ye shall have *tribulation . . . .*"[8] Here Jesus taught that believers are to expect tribulation as a normal occurrence in this present evil world, which is itself a source of tribulation. Jesus also said, "If ye were of the world, the world would love his own: but because ye are not of the world, but I

---

[6] Matthew 13:20, 21.
[7] Mark 4:16, 17.
[8] John 16:33.

have chosen you out of the world, therefore the world hateth you."[9]

In Acts, Luke writes, "Now they which were scattered abroad upon the *persecution* [thlipsis] that arose about Stephen travelled as far as Phenice, and Cyprus, and Antioch, preaching the word . . . ."[10] In this case, the persecution of the saints came from those who murdered Stephen and hated the preaching of God's Word.

Luke again writes:

> And there came thither certain Jews from Antioch and Iconium, who persuaded the people, and, *having stoned Paul*, drew him out of the city, supposing he had been dead. Howbeit, as the disciples stood round about him, he rose up, and came into the city: and the next day he departed with Barnabus to Derbe. And when they had preached the gospel to that city, and had taught many, they returned again to Lystra, and to Iconium, and Antioch, confirming the souls of the disciples, and exhorting them to continue in the faith, and that *we must through much tribulation enter into the kingdom of God.*[11]

Upon rising up, after being stoned by those who hated the gospel that he was preaching, Paul said, ". . . *we must through much tribulation enter into the kingdom of God.*" Again, the Bible teaches that tribulation for God's elect has its source in the enemies of God and His Word.

In his epistle to the Romans, Paul said, ". . . we glory in *tribulations* also: knowing that tribulation worketh patience; and patience, experience; and experience, hope: and hope maketh not ashamed . . . ."[12]

---

[9] John 15:19.
[10] Acts 11:19.
[11] Acts 14:19-22.
[12] Romans 5:3-5.

Paul gloried in tribulations because he knew that he was suffering for righteousness' sake, and that his reward would be great in heaven. In the Sermon on the Mount, Jesus said:

> Blessed are they which are persecuted for righteousness' sake, for theirs is the kingdom of heaven. Blessed are ye, when men shall revile you, and persecute you, and shall say all manner of evil against you falsely, for my sake. Rejoice, and be exceeding glad: for great is your reward in heaven: for so persecuted they the prophets which were before you.[13]

In his letter to the Corinthians, Paul wrote, "For our light *affliction* [thlipsis] which is but for a moment, worketh for us a far more exceeding and eternal weight of glory . . . ."[14] This passage teaches clearly the glorious truth that believers who endure tribulation will enjoy a better resurrection.

To the Thessalonians, Paul wrote, ". . . ye became followers of us, and of the Lord, having received the word in much *affliction* . . . ."[15]

This Scripture teaches plainly that *affliction* came upon the Thessalonian saints because *of their having received the Word.*

In Revelation, John wrote, "I John, who also am your brother, and companion in *tribulation* . . . was in the isle that is called Patmos, *for the word of God, and for the testimony of Jesus Christ.*"[16] This Scripture teaches unquestionably that John, the aged apostle, was suffering tribulation for the Word of God and for the testimony of

---

[13] Matthew 5:10-12.

[14] II Corinthians 4:17.

[15] I Thessalonians 1:6.

[16] Revelation 1:9, 10.

Jesus Christ. In short, his tribulation came from the enemies of Christ.

In Revelation, to the church at Smyrna, Jesus said:

> I know thy works, and *tribulation* . . . . Fear none of those things
> which thou shalt suffer: behold, *the devil shall cast some of you
> into prison, that ye may be tried; and ye shall have tribulation
> ten days*: be thou faithful unto death, and I will give thee a
> crown of life.[17]

Nothing could be clearer. The tribulation suffered by
the church in Smyrna came from the Devil.

There are only three cases in the Authorized Version
in which the word "tribulation" is used with reference to
evildoers being afflicted by God. In each of these cases,
either God afflicted the evildoers in the past, or He will
afflict them in the future. Let us consider these three
cases.

First, to the church in Rome, Paul wrote, *"Tribulation
and anguish, upon every soul of man that doeth
evil . . . ."*[18] This verse pertains either to God's afflicting
evildoers with His wrath in the present (as He did in the
case of the sodomites in Sodom and Gomorrah), or it
pertains to God's afflicting evildoers with His wrath in the
future (either in the Day of the Lord or in hell).

Second, to the Thessalonians, Paul wrote:

> Seeing it is a righteous thing with God to recompense *tribulation*
> to them that *trouble* you; and to you who are troubled rest with
> us, when the Lord Jesus shall be revealed from heaven with his
> mighty angels, In flaming fire taking vengeance on them that
> know not God, and that obey not the gospel of our Lord Jesus

---

[17] Revelation 2:9, 10.
[18] Romans 2:9.

Christ: who shall be punished with everlasting destruction from the presence of the Lord, and from the glory of his power . . . .[19]

This passage is crystal-clear; it teaches that those who know not God and that bring trouble upon believers will be recompensed with tribulation from God.

Third, to the church in Thyatira, Jesus said:

Notwithstanding, I have a few things against thee, because thou sufferest that woman Jezebel, which calleth herself a prophetess, to teach and to seduce my servants to commit fornication, and to eat things sacrificed unto idols. And I gave her space to repent of her fornication; and she repented not. Behold, I will cast *her* into a bed, *and them* that commit adultery with her *into great tribulation, except they repent* of their deeds. And I will kill her children with death; and all the churches shall know that I am he which searcheth the reins and hearts . . . .[20]

It is imperative to observe that this passage does *not* refer to *the* Great Tribulation of the future. It refers to great tribulation that God said He would bring upon *those who were committing adultery with Jezebel,* when John wrote to the church in Thyatira nearly two thousand years ago. In the Greek, the phrase "them that commit adultery" is a present participle with the article. The *present* denotes that those about whom Christ was speaking at the time were guilty of continuous adultery *when* John wrote. In this letter, Jesus warned those who were continuously committing adultery at that time that they would be cast into great tribulation if they did not repent.

Accordingly, "great tribulation" in this passage does not refer to *the* Great Tribulation which will occur during

---

[19] II Thessalonians 1:6-9.
[20] Revelation 2:20-23.

the last half of Daniel's Seventieth Week. This truth is confirmed by the fact that a person could escape *that* great tribulation (that is, great affliction from God) by repentance.[21]

It will not be possible to escape *the* Great Tribulation of the future (that is, affliction from Antichrist) by repentance, for Jesus said, ". . . he that shall endure unto the end, the same shall be saved (that is, delivered from danger or from harm)."[22] This deliverance of those that endure unto the end will be by the posttribulation rapture of the church.

Therefore, it is established by the Scriptures that *tribulation for the saints of God comes from the Devil, the Antichrist, and wicked men* who hate Christ, His Word, and His people.

IS TRIBULATION EQUIVALENT TO THE WRATH OF GOD?

It has been shown from the Scriptures that the tribulation which comes upon the saints comes as a result of their testimony for Christ and His Word. Furthermore, it has been demonstrated from the Bible that tribulation for believers comes from the Devil, his people, and the world. Therefore, *tribulation for the saints is not equivalent to divine wrath upon the wicked.* Divine wrath comes from God, and it is poured out upon the wicked, not the saints.

There are two Greek words that are translated *wrath*. The first is <u>thumos</u>. According to Green, <u>thumos</u> means,

---

[21] Revelation 2:22.
[22] Matthew 24:13.

"a strong passion or emotion of the mind; anger, wrath . . . swellings of anger . . . ."[23] Gundry says:

> Thumos, a violent outburst of anger, represents God's wrath in nine out of eighteen occurrences in the New Testament, all nine in Revelation. *A survey of these occurrences shows that the divine wrath strikes only the wicked* (14:8--Babylon; 14:10--worshippers of the beast; 14:19--the armies at Armageddon; 18:3--fornicators with Babylon; 19:15--the armies at Armageddon).[24]

Observe carefully that in the nine occurrences in which thumos means God's wrath, all nine are in Revelation in which the divine wrath is poured out upon the wicked *in* the Day of the Lord.

The second Greek word translated "wrath" is the word orge. Green defines orge as follows: ". . . mental bent, impulse; anger, indignation, wrath . . . vengeance, punishment . . . ."[25] Gundry says:

> Orge, the settled state of wrath, stands for God's anger about twenty-seven times in the New Testament. Paul clearly states that believers are 'saved from the wrath of God through him:' (Rom 5:9), '. . . delivered . . . from the wrath to come.' . . . the divine orge falls only upon the wicked (Rev. 6:16, 17; 14:10; 16:19; 19:15).[26]

Neither thumos (wrath) nor orge (wrath) is used to refer to tribulation experienced by the saints. Therefore, *tribulation* (thlipsis) *for believers is not synonymous with wrath* (thumos *and* orge). While the *saints will have trib-*

---

[23] Green, p. 86.

[24] Gundry, pp. 48, 49.

[25] Green, p. 130.

[26] Gundry, p. 49.

ulation in the world, they will not experience God's wrath, for Paul wrote, ". . . God hath not appointed us to wrath, but to obtain salvation by our Lord Jesus Christ."[27]

There is a great gulf fixed between the tribulation which will be experienced by the saints during the Great Tribulation and the wrath of the Lamb which will be poured out upon the wicked in the Day of the Lord. Remember, the Day of the Lord cannot begin until *after* the sun and moon are darkened, immediately *after* the Great Tribulation. Therefore, the unparalleled wrath of the Lamb, which will be poured out in the Day of the Lord *after* the Great Tribulation, cannot be equivalent to the tribulation which will be experienced by the saints *during* the Great Tribulation.

WHAT IS "THE TRIBULATION"?

Will there be a future period called "the Tribulation"? The Bible teaches that the Seventieth Week of Daniel's prophecy will occur in the future, and evidence for the futurity of the week was given in chapter four. The Seventieth Week of Daniel is commonly called "the Tribulation," but it should be noted that the Bible speaks only of the last half of the Seventieth Week as *"great tribulation."*

The Seventieth Week will begin with the confirming of the covenant by the Antichrist with many. The confirming of this covenant will be followed by the reinstituting of the Jewish sacrificial system and the building of the third temple.

---

[27] I Thessalonians 5:9.

Daniel 9:27 says,

> And he shall confirm the covenant with many for one week: and
> in the midst of the week he shall cause the sacrifice and the obla-
> tion to cease, and for the overspreading of abominations he shall
> make it desolate, even until the consummation, and that deter-
> mined shall be poured upon the desolate.

"The Tribulation," namely, the Seventieth Week of
Daniel, will be divided into two equal parts by the placing
of the "abomination of desolation" in the holy place of the
third temple.[28] This event will occur in the midst of the
week, and it will mark the beginning of the Great Tribulation. Jesus said:

> When ye therefore shall see the abomination of desolation,
> spoken of by Daniel the prophet, stand in the holy place, (whoso
> readeth, let him understand:) . . . For *then* shall be great trib-
> ulation, such as was not since the beginning of the world to this
> time, no, nor ever shall be.[29]

The Great Tribulation will take place during the last
half of the Seventieth Week. The end of the Seventieth
Week will be marked by the darkening of the sun and
moon immediately after the Great Tribulation, and this
event will be coincident with the opening of the sixth
seal.[30] After the conclusion of the Seventieth Week, the
blessings promised to Israel in Daniel 9:24 will be realized.

---

[28] Matthew 24:15; Daniel 9:27.

[29] Matthew 24:15, 21.

[30] Matthew 24:29; Revelation 6:12, 13.

WHAT DO PRETRIBULATIONISTS SAY ABOUT "THE TRIBULATION"?

Stanton writes:

> . . . the distinctive character of *the tribulation* period is that *it is a time of divine wrath.* Satan may be given a little leeway before he is chained, but *the primary source of wrath in the tribulation is neither Satan nor wicked men, but God.* He pours it out 'without mixture.' There is not a drop of water to cool its heat. It is not blended with hope or grace. It is undiluted wrath on a world that has rejected His own glorious son . . . It is here maintained that persecutions of this age are the endeavors of wicked men to exterminate the Church, while *the tribulation of the future period will be primarily the wrath and judgment of an angry God upon Christ-rejectors.*[31]

Notice carefully that Stanton says, ". . . *the distinctive character of the tribulation period is that it is a time of divine wrath.*" Stanton's view regarding "the tribulation" is the standard pretribulational position, but Stanton is guilty of teaching egregious error regarding "the Tribulation." Like Stanton, other pretribulationists teach that God's unparalleled wrath will be poured out upon Christ-rejectors *during* the Seventieth Week.

WHAT DO POSTTRIBULATIONISTS SAY ABOUT "THE TRIBULATION"?

Reese writes, "According to the Scripture *it is the Devil's wrath against the saints* for their rejection of Antichrist, and adherence to Christ."[32]

---

[31] Stanton, p. 42.

[32] Alexander Reese, *The Approaching Advent of Christ* (London: Marshall, Morgan and Scott Co., n.d.), p. 284.

Fraser writes, *"The great tribulation is not judgment, but persecution."*[33]

Frost says,

"For the church, therefore, to go into the days of Antichrist, and to be called upon to endure his hatred and harassments, is but for her to pass from one phase of an experience into another, the difference being, not in kind, but in degree."[34]

It is clear, therefore, that pretribulationists and post-tribulationists have dramatically different views of "the Tribulation." Pretribulationists see "the Tribulation" as a time of unparalleled wrath from God upon Christ-rejectors. Posttribulationists see "the Tribulation" as a time of great persecution for the saints.

WHAT IS THE GREAT TRIBULATION?

In the Olivet Discourse Jesus said:

When ye therefore shall see the abomination of desolation, spoken of by Daniel the prophet, stand in the holy place . . . *then shall be great tribulation*, such as was not since the beginning of the world to this time, no, nor ever shall be. And except those days should be shortened, there should no flesh be saved: but for the elect's sake those days shall be shortened.[35]

Here, the Lord reveals that the Great Tribulation will be unparalleled either in the past or in the future. In Revelation, John writes:

---

[33] Alexander Fraser, *Is There but One Return of Christ?* (Pittsburgh, Pa.: Evangelical Fellowship, 1947), p. 63.

[34] Henry W. Frost, *The Second Coming of Christ* (Grand Rapids, Mich.: Wm. B. Eerdmans Publishing Co., 1934), p. 64.

[35] Matthew 24:15, 21, 22.

And there was given unto him [namely, the beast] a mouth speaking great things and blasphemies; and power was given unto him to continue forty and two months . . . And it was given unto him to make war with the saints, and to overcome them: and *power was given him over all kindreds, and tongues, and nations.*[36]

This passage discloses that the power of Antichrist will be global and that he will use his power to make war with the saints and overcome them. The coming tribulation will be great because of its universality and its severity.

In Revelation, John also writes:

And he [namely, the beast out of the earth] had power to give life unto the image of the beast, that the image of the beast should both speak, and cause that as many as would not worship the image of the beast should be killed. And he causeth all, both small and great, rich and poor, free and bond, to receive a mark in their right hand, or in their foreheads . . . .[37]

This passage predicts clearly the severity of the Great Tribulation for the saints of God.

It must be emphasized vigorously that Stanton is outrageously wrong when he says, ". . . the distinctive character of the tribulation period is that it is a time of divine wrath." Stanton is in great darkness, for the unparalleled wrath of the Lamb will *not* be poured out in the Seventieth Week. It will be poured out *in* the Day of the Lord, which will not begin until *after* the sun and moon are darkened immediately *after* the Great Tribulation.

---

[36] Revelation 13:5-7.
[37] Revelation 13:15, 16.

WHEN WILL THE GREAT TRIBULATION BEGIN?

In the Olivet Discourse, our Lord revealed that the Great Tribulation will begin when the abomination of desolation stands in the holy place of the third temple. Jesus said,

> When ye therefore shall see the abomination of desolation, spoken of by Daniel the prophet, stand in the holy place . . . *then* shall be great tribulation, such as was not since the beginning of the world to this time, no, nor ever shall be.[38]

More than half a millennium before Christ disclosed the event that will mark the beginning of the Great Tribulation, Gabriel said to Daniel, "And he [namely, the Antichrist] shall confirm the covenant with many for one week: and *in the midst of the week he shall cause the sacrifice and the oblation to cease*, and for the overspreading of abominations he shall make it desolate . . . ."[39]

Accordingly, it was revealed to Daniel that, in the midst of the Seventieth Week, the Antichrist would make the third temple desolate because of the overspreading of abominations. In Matthew 24:15, when He mentioned the abomination of desolation spoken of by Daniel the prophet, Jesus linked *the moment* the abomination of desolation will stand in the holy place *with the midst of the Seventieth Week* mentioned in Daniel's prophecy. Therefore, the Great Tribulation will begin in the midst of the Seventieth Week of Daniel, when the abomination of desolation stands in the holy place.

---

[38] Matthew 24:15, 21.
[39] Daniel 9:27.

HOW LONG WILL THE GREAT TRIBULATION LAST?

The Great Tribulation will last for exactly three and one-half years. This truth is taught in the Bible. While considering the little horn, namely, the Antichrist (Daniel 7:8), Daniel was told, "And *he* shall speak great words against the most High, and *shall wear out the saints* of the most High . . . *and they shall be given into his hand until a time and times and the dividing of time.*"[40]

Following are a few of the many Bible scholars who have taught that the three and one-half *times* mentioned in Daniel seven are three and one-half *years*: John Peter Lange, Samuel P. Tregelles, Robert Jamison, A.R. Fausset, David Brown, Adam Clarke, James Gray, Albert Barnes, F.L. Godet, Alfred Martin, G. Coleman Luck, Robert Culver, and Harry Ironside. Commenting on Daniel 7:25, Biederwolf writes:

> According to frequent Chaldee usage the plural is put for the dual, and 'times' means 'two times,' and the whole is equivalent to three and one-half . . . *the only satisfactory explanation of the expression is to take it in a literal sense, as meaning three years and a half* . . . applied, as we think it should be, to the suffering under the Antichrist of the end-time. The reference is to be explained in harmony with the same expression in the twelfth chapter [where the Hebrew dual is used].[41]

In Revelation, John confirms that the Great Tribulation is three and one-half years in duration, when he

---

[40] Daniel 7:25.

[41] William E. Biederwolf, *The Second Coming Bible Commentary* (Grand Rapids, Mich.: Baker Book House, 1985), pp. 211, 212.

writes, ". . . and power was given unto him *to continue forty and two months . . . and* it was given unto him *to make war with the saints, and to overcome them.*"[42] After the Great Tribulation has run its course of three and one-half years or forty-two months or 1,260 days, it will come to a close at the moment Jesus called "the end." When warning of the Great Tribulation to come, Jesus said, "But he that shall endure unto *the end*, the same shall be saved."[43]

Therefore, the Bible teaches unmistakably that the Great Tribulation, which will begin when the abomination of desolation stands in the holy place in the midst of the Seventieth Week, will continue for exactly three and one-half years.

WHO WILL SUFFER DURING THE GREAT TRIBULATION?

The Bible teaches clearly that the *saints* will suffer tribulation during the Great Tribulation. Daniel was told, "And he shall speak words against the most High, and shall wear out the *saints* of the most High . . . and they shall be given into his hand until a time and times and the dividing of time."[44] John confirms that the *saints* will suffer at the hand of the Antichrist during the Great Tribulation, for he writes, ". . . and power was given unto him to continue forty and two months . . . And it was given unto him to make war with the *saints*, and to overcome them . . . ."[45]

---

[42] Revelation 13:5-7.
[43] Matthew 24:13.
[44] Daniel 7:25.
[45] Revelation 13:5, 7.

At this point, we need to answer a crucial question. Who are the *saints*? The English word "saint" comes from the Greek word hagios. According to Green, hagios means, "separate from common condition and use; dedicated . . . hallowed; used of things . . . and of persons, saints, e.g. *members of the first Christian communities . . . .*"[46] Aaron is called a saint in the book of Psalms, and Daniel heard one saint talking with another saint. The word "saint" is used elsewhere in the Old Testament, mostly in the Psalms.

With only two exceptions in the Authorized Version of the New Testament, *the word "saints" means believers who constitute the church.*

The first exception is Matthew 27:52, which speaks of the bodies of the *saints* rising just after the resurrection of our Lord Jesus Christ. This writer believes that the saints who rose just after Christ's resurrection were Old Testament saints who experienced the first phase of the first resurrection (cf. I Corinthians 15:22-24).

The second exception is found in Revelation 20:9, which speaks of Satan, loosed from the bottomless pit, leading an army in the final revolt against the camp of the *saints*. The saints mentioned in this passage are obviously millennial saints.

To confirm the truth that saints in the New Testament are believers who constitute the membership of the churches, one can check carefully every use of the word "saint" or "saints" in the New Testament by simply using Strong's Concordance.

Now, let us consider just a few examples. Paul addressed his epistle to the Romans as follows, "To all that

---

[46] Green, p. 2.

be in Rome, beloved of God, called to be *saints* . . . ."[47] The church in Rome consisted of saints. Paul addressed his epistle to the Corinthians as follows, "Unto the church of God which is at Corinth, to them that are sanctified in Christ Jesus, called to be *saints* . . . ."[48] The Corinthian church consisted of saints. Paul addressed his second epistle to the Corinthians as follows, ". . . unto the church of God which is at Corinth, with all the *saints* . . . ."[49] Again, it is clear that the church in Corinth was made up of saints. Paul addressed his epistle to the Ephesians as follows, "Paul, an apostle of Jesus Christ by the will of God, to the *saints* which are at Ephesus . . . ."[50]

The Ephesian church consisted of saints. Paul addressed his letter to the Philippians as follows, "Paul and Timotheus, the servants of Jesus Christ, to all the *saints* in Christ Jesus which are at Philippi . . . ."[51] The church in Philippi consisted of saints. Paul addressed his epistle to the Colossians as follows, "Paul, an apostle of Jesus Christ by the will of God, and Timotheus our brother, to the *saints* and faithful brethren in Christ which are at Colosse . . . ."[52] The church at Colosse consisted of saints. Accordingly, the Scriptures teach unmistakably that *the believers who constitute the membership of the churches are called saints.* Therefore, since the Bible speaks of no other body of saints who are part of a separate program prior to the millennial saints, it must be concluded that it will be the saints who constitute the

---

[47] Romans 1:7.
[48] I Corinthians 1:2.
[49] II Corinthians 1:1.
[50] Ephesians 1:1.
[51] Philippians 1:1.
[52] Colossians 1:1, 2.

membership of the church who will suffer great tribulation at the hand of Antichrist.

The Bible also teaches plainly that the *elect* will suffer persecution during the Great Tribulation. In the Olivet Discourse, Jesus said:

> When ye therefore shall see the abomination of desolation, spoken of by Daniel the prophet, stand in the holy place . . . *then shall be great tribulation, such as was not since the beginning of the world to this time, no, nor ever shall be. And except those days should be shortened, there should no flesh be saved: but for the elect's sake those days shall be shortened.*[53]

Here Jesus says that the elect will experience tribulation so great that except those days should be shortened, no flesh will be saved.

The word "elect" is from the Greek word <u>eklektos</u>. According to Green, <u>eklektos</u> means: "Chosen out, selected; in N.T., chosen as a recipient of special privilege, *elect, Colossians 3:12* . . . ."[54] In his letter to the church at Colosse, Paul wrote: "To the saints and faithful brethren in Christ . . . . Put on therefore, as the *elect* of God, holy and beloved, bowels of mercies, kindness, humbleness of mind, meekness, longsuffering . . . ."[55] It is apparent that the elect here are the saints and faithful brethren who constituted the membership of the church.

In the Old Testament, the word "elect" is used four times. The word "elect" occurs in Isaiah 42:1, where it refers to Christ, as Scofield notes in his reference Bible. *The Liberty Annotated Study Bible* says of this verse:

---

[53] Matthew 24:15, 21, 22.
[54] Green, p. 57.
[55] Colossians 1:2; 3:12.

My *servant* is identified here as a person rather than a personification of the nation of Israel. With all the traits of a King, Prophet, and High Priest, he is none other than the Messiah, Jesus Christ Himself. He is also called *mine elect* (bechiri, 'set apart for a divine purpose') and the One in whom *I have put my Spirit.* The New Testament quotes this prophecy as being fulfilled in the Lord Jesus Christ (Matt. 12:18-21).[56]

The word "elect" is found again in Isaiah 45:4, where the Bible says, "For Jacob my servant's sake, and Israel mine elect . . . ." Here "Jacob" my servant is equivalent to "Israel mine elect." This phrase is found in Isaiah 45:1-4, which says:

Thus saith the Lord to his anointed to Cyrus, whose right hand I have holden, to subdue nations before him . . . And I will give thee the treasures of darkness, and hidden riches of secret places, that thou mayest know that I, the Lord, which call thee by thy name, am the God of Israel. For Jacob my servant's sake, and Israel mine elect, I have even called thee by thy name: I have surnamed thee, though thou hast not known me.

Commenting on this passage, *The Liberty Annotated Study Bible* says:

Yahweh Himself has set an open door of conquest before Cyrus. The Persian king is called by the designation *anointed* (meshiach, messiah). This is the only place in Scripture where a Gentile is so designated. The term originated with the Israelite custom of anointing kings and leaders. Cyrus is given this title only in the sense that he will deliver the Jews from Babylonian bondage.[57]

---

[56] *The Liberty Annotated Study Bible* (Lynchburg: Liberty University, 1988), p. 1069.

[57] Ibid., p. 1074.

Ten years before this prophecy was given to Isaiah in 712 B.C., Israel, which had become apostate, was judged by God, who gave the kingdom of Israel to the Assyrians. After a three-year siege, Samaria, the capital of the kingdom of Israel, fell in 722 B.C. By 606 B.C., the kingdom of Judah was so apostate that God gave Judah to the Babylonians for judgment. By 586 B.C., the destruction of Jerusalem was completed, and both the Northern and Southern Kingdoms were in captivity. Only a small remnant would return to the land of Israel, and Cyrus was anointed by God to deliver the small remnant from Babylonian captivity.

Previously, when Israel arrived at Sinai, God had said to Israel through Moses:

> Now therefore, if ye will obey my voice indeed, and keep my covenant, then ye shall be a peculiar treasure unto me above all people; for all the earth is mine: And ye shall be unto me a kingdom of priests, and an holy nation. These are the words which thou shalt speak unto the children of Israel.[58]

However, instead of obeying God's voice and keeping His covenant, the nation of Israel went into apostasy. Even the descendants of the remnant that returned from the captivity went into apostasy. Israel, as a nation, turned its back on God, and she failed to bring forth fruit as God's vineyard should have done. When Jesus came, the Bible says, "He came unto his own, and his own received him not."[59] To the leaders of the nation of Israel, which rejected Him, Jesus said, "Therefore I say

---

[58] Exodus 19:5, 6.
[59] John 1:11.

unto you, the kingdom of God shall be taken from you, and given to a nation bringing forth the fruits thereof."[60]

The kingdom of God was taken from that Israel, and it was given to the church. To the *elect* that constitute the church, Peter wrote, "But *ye are* a chosen generation, *a royal priesthood, an holy nation,* a peculiar people; that ye should shew forth the praises of him who hath called you out of darkness into his marvelous light: which in time past were not a people, but are now the people of God . . . ."[61]

Again examining the phrase ("For Jacob my servant's sake, for Israel mine elect . . . ."), it seems that in this verse the word "elect" refers to that small remnant of Israel which had not bowed the knee to Baal. After Christ founded His church, elect Israelites trusted Christ and were added to the church, as were the apostles and those saved on the day of Pentecost.

The word "elect" is used twice in Isaiah 65. In this chapter, the word "elect" refers to Israelites who will enter the millennial kingdom unsaved and then be saved after the kingdom has begun. This truth will be explained later.

The word "elect" occurs sixteen times in the New Testament. However, it is used only in thirteen separate cases, for it occurs three times in Matthew's version of the Olivet Discourse and three times in Mark's version of the same discourse. Accordingly, Christ actually used the word "elect" only three times in the Olivet Discourse.

In I Timothy 5:21, the word "elect" is used as follows: "I charge thee before God . . . and the *elect* angels." Here

---

[60] Matthew 21:43.
[61] I Peter 2:9, 10.

Paul uses the word "elect" to modify "angels." In I Peter 2:6, the word "elect" is used in the following sentence: "Behold, I lay in Sion a chief corner stone, *elect*, precious: and he that believeth on him shall not be confounded." Here Peter uses the word "elect" to modify "cornerstone." Christ, of course, is the cornerstone, elect, precious.

The word "elect" occurs in eight other New Testament references. In all eight of the other references, the word "elect" means those who were saved (or those who would be saved) and who constituted the membership of the churches. The eight references are the following: Luke 18:7; Romans 8:33; Colossians 3:12; II Timothy 2:10; Titus 1:1; I Peter 1:2; and II John 1, 13. Regarding Luke 18:7, it should be noted that Jesus' words ("And shall not God avenge his own *elect*, which cry day and night unto him . . . .") were spoken to the apostles (Luke 17:22-18:8), who were set first in the church (I Corinthians 12:28), who were the foundation of the church (Ephesians 2:20), and in whose doctrine the church continued (Acts 2:42). The truth that the apostles were part of the church will be explained more fully later.

Accordingly, with the exception of the three cases where the word "elect" was used by Christ in His Olivet Discourse (and with the exception of I Timothy 5:21 and I Peter 2:6), every other usage of the word "elect" means those who were saved (or those who would be saved) and who composed the membership of the churches.

Neither Jesus, nor Paul, nor any other New Testament writer gave any hint or indication that the word "elect" in the Olivet Discourse means something different than what it means in the rest of the New Testament. Therefore, since the word "elect" in the entire New Testament (except the noted exceptions) means saved persons who form the membership of the churches, the only scriptural conclusion that can be drawn is that the "elect" referred to by Christ in the Olivet Discourse must also mean saved persons who constitute the membership of the churches. Consequently, it is easily understandable why Green, the lexicographer, in order to illustrate the meaning of "elect," gave the reference Colossians 3:12, which says, "Put on therefore, as the elect of God, holy and beloved, bowels of mercies, kindness, humbleness of mind, meekness, longsuffering . . . ."

Therefore, since the elect are saints or brethren who constitute the membership of the churches, it must be concluded that the church will go through the Great Tribulation and be tried by the Devil at the hand of Antichrist.

WHY WILL GOD ALLOW THE CHURCH TO GO THROUGH GREAT TRIBULATION?

God's purpose for allowing the saints to experience tribulation is seen in Christ's letter to the church in Smyrna. In the letter, Jesus said:

> I know thy works, and tribulation . . . Fear none of those things which thou shalt suffer: behold, the devil shall cast some of you into prison, *that ye may be tried*; and ye shall have tribulation ten days: *be thou faithful unto death, and I will give thee a crown of life.*[62]

From this passage, we learn that God allows Satan to bring tribulation upon the saints to try them. The trying of the saints will be very evident during the Great Trib-

---

[62] Revelation 2:9, 10.

ulation. In the Smyrna letter, Christ warned the saints of
the coming persecution and tribulation that would come
from the Devil. Further, the Lord exhorted the church to
fear none of the things it would suffer, and *He promised
them a crown of life in return for their being faithful unto
death.*

God tried Abraham on Mount Moriah when He commanded him to offer his beloved son Isaac for a burnt
offering. Abraham passed his test, proving his fear of
God, and because of his obedience, he was blessed by the
Lord. The trying of saints is a doctrine that is woven into
the very fabric of Scripture. Yes, God tries His saints.
The three Hebrew children were tried when they were
threatened with the burning fiery furnace. They stood
true and were blessed. Daniel was tried when he was
threatened with the lions' den. He stood true and was
blessed. The Bible says:

> . . . others were tortured, not accepting deliverance; *that they
> might obtain a better resurrection*: And others had trial of cruel
> mockings and scourgings, yea, moreover of bonds and imprison-
> ment: They were stoned, they were sawn asunder, were tempted,
> were slain with the sword: they wandered about in sheepskins
> and goatskins; being destitute, afflicted, tormented; (of whom the
> world was not worthy:) they wandered in deserts, and in moun-
> tains, and in dens and caves of the earth. And these all, having
> obtained a good report through faith . . . .[63]

In his Book of Martyrs, Foxe writes:

> Stephen's . . . death was occasioned by the faithful manner in
> which he preached the Gospel to the betrayers and murderers of

---

[63] Hebrews 11:35-39.

Christ. To such a degree of madness were they excited, that they cast him out of the city and stoned him to death . . . .

The next martyr we meet with . . . was James the son of Zebedee, the elder brother of John . . . as James was led to the place of martyrdom, his accuser was brought to repent of his conduct by the apostle's extraordinary courage . . . and fell down at his feet to request his pardon, professing himself a Christian, and resolving that James should not receive the crown of martyrdom alone. Hence they were both beheaded at the same time.

Philip . . . labored diligently in Upper Asia, and suffered martyrdom at Heliopolis, in Phrygia. He was scourged, thrown into prison, and afterwards crucified A. D. 54.

. . . The scene of [Matthew's] labors was Parthia, and Ethiopia, in which latter country he suffered martyrdom, being slain with a halberd in the city of Nadabah, A. D. 60.

James the Less . . . was the author of the Epistle ascribed to James . . . . At the age of ninety-four he was beat and stoned by the Jews; and finally had his brains dashed out with a fuller's club.

Matthias . . . was elected to fill the vacant place of Judas. He was stoned at Jerusalem and then beheaded.

Andrew . . . preached the gospel to many Asiatic nations; but on his arrival at Edessa he was taken and crucified on a cross, the two ends of which were fixed transversely in the ground.

. . . Mark was dragged to pieces by the people of Alexandria, at the great solemnity of Serapis their idol, ending his life under their merciless hands.

. . . Peter was condemned to death, and crucified . . . . Jerome saith that he was crucified, his head being down and his feet upward, himself so requiring, because he was (he said) unworthy to be crucified after the same form and manner as the Lord was.

Paul . . . suffered also in this first persecution under Nero . . . .
Nero sent . . . Ferega and Parthemius, to bring him word of his
death . . . . This done, the soldiers came and led him out of the
city to the place of execution, where he, after his prayers made,
gave his neck to the sword.

Jude . . . was crucified at Edessa, A. D. 72.

Bartholomew . . . having translated the Gospel of Matthew into
the language of India, propagated it in that country. He was at
length cruelly beaten and then crucified by the impatient idolaters.

Thomas . . . preached the Gospel in Parthia and India, where
exciting the rage of the pagan priests, he was martyred by being
thrust through with a spear.

Luke . . . travelled with Paul through various countries, and is
supposed to have been hanged on an olive tree, by the idolatrous
priests of Greece.

John the 'beloved disciple,' was brother to James . . . . The
churches of Smyrna, Pergamos, Thyatira, Sardis, Philadelphia,
and Laodicea were founded by him. From Ephesus he was
ordered to be sent to Rome where it is affirmed he was cast into a
cauldron of boiling oil. He escaped by miracle without injury.
Domitian afterwards banished him to the Isle of Patmos.

. . . And yet, notwithstanding all these continual persecutions
and horrible punishments, the Church daily increased, deeply
rooted in the doctrine of the apostles and of men apostolical, and
watered plenteously with the blood of saints.[64]

With the Great Tribulation rapidly approaching, believers should remember the words of James, who wrote,

---

[64] William Forbush, ed., *Foxe's Book of Martyrs* (Philadelphia, Pa.: The John C. Winston Co., 1926), pp. 2-5.

"Blessed is the man that endureth temptation: *for when he is tried, he shall receive the crown of life, which the Lord hath promised to them that love him.*"[65]

Believers should also recall the words of Paul, who wrote:

> *Blessed be God,* even the Father of our Lord Jesus Christ, the Father of mercies, and the God of all comfort; *who comforteth us in all our tribulation* [thlipsis], that we may be able to comfort them which are in any trouble, by the comfort wherewith we ourselves are comforted of God. *For as the sufferings of Christ abound in us, so our consolation also aboundeth by Christ.*[66]

In his great hymn, George Keith wrote,

> When through fiery trials thy pathway shall lie,
> My grace, all sufficient, shall be thy supply . . . .[67]

John, who was on the isle that is called Patmos, for the Word of God, and for the testimony of Jesus Christ, wrote,

> . . . and *I saw the souls of them that were beheaded for the witness of Jesus, and for the word of God,* and which had not worshipped the beast, neither his image, neither had received his mark upon their foreheads, or in their hands; *and they lived and reigned with Christ for a thousand years.*[68]

---

[65] James 1:12.

[66] II Corinthians 1:3-5.

[67] George Keith, "How Firm a Foundation." *Soul Stirring Songs and Hymns: Revised* (Murfreesburo, Tenn.: Sword of the Lord, 1986), p. 153.

[68] Revelation 20:4.

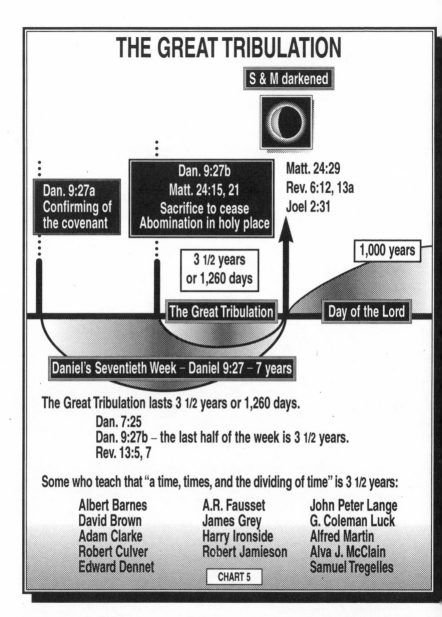

THE GREAT TRIBULATION

S & M darkened

Dan. 9:27a
Confirming of
the covenant

Dan. 9:27b
Matt. 24:15, 21
Sacrifice to cease
Abomination in holy place

Matt. 24:29
Rev. 6:12, 13a
Joel 2:31

1,000 years

3 1/2 years
or 1,260 days

The Great Tribulation

Day of the Lord

Daniel's Seventieth Week – Daniel 9:27 – 7 years

The Great Tribulation lasts 3 1/2 years or 1,260 days.
        Dan. 7:25
        Dan. 9:27b – the last half of the week is 3 1/2 years.
        Rev. 13:5, 7

Some who teach that "a time, times, and the dividing of time" is 3 1/2 years:

Albert Barnes	A.R. Fausset	John Peter Lange
David Brown	James Grey	G. Coleman Luck
Adam Clarke	Harry Ironside	Alfred Martin
Robert Culver	Robert Jamieson	Alva J. McClain
Edward Dennet		Samuel Tregelles

CHART 5

*The Great Tribulation lasts 3 1/2 years. It begins in the midst of
the Seventieth Week. It is to be characterized by tribulation upon
saints, not divine wrath upon unbelievers.*

THE COMING OF CHRIST IN THE CLOUDS

"Immediately after the tribulation of those days shall the sun be darkened, and the moon shall not give her light . . . and they shall see the Son of man coming in the clouds of heaven with power and great glory."

— *Matthew 24:29, 30*

The coming of Christ in the clouds with power and great glory is the supreme event discussed by Jesus in His great prophecy called the Olivet Discourse. Describing the scene that became the occasion of this great prophetic dissertation, Matthew writes:

> And Jesus went out, and departed from the temple: and his disciples came to him for to shew him the buildings of the temple. And Jesus said unto them, See ye not all these things? verily I say unto you, *There shall not be left here one stone upon another, that shall not be thrown down.*[1]

As Jesus and His disciples were departing from the temple, He made His remarkable statement about the approaching destruction of Jerusalem which would occur

---

[1] Matthew 24:1, 2.

in A.D. 70. Jesus' prophecy evoked two questions from the disciples.

"WHEN SHALL THESE THINGS BE?"

Matthew continues his description of the scene: "And as he sat upon the mount of Olives, the disciples came unto him privately, saying, Tell us, *when shall these things be*? and *what shall be the sign of thy coming, and of the end of the world?*"[2] These two questions by the disciples were the occasion of the Olivet Discourse, which is found in Matthew 24 and 25, Mark 13, and Luke 21. As Jesus and His disciples departed from the temple, He said to them, "See ye not all these things? verily I say unto you, there shall not be left one stone upon another, that shall not be thrown down."[3]

The answer to the disciples' *first question* pertaining to the destruction of the temple is not given in either Matthew's or Mark's account of the Olivet Discourse. The answer to the disciples' first question is given only in Luke's version. In Luke's account, we read:

> And when ye shall see Jerusalem compassed with armies, then know that the *desolation* thereof is nigh. Then let them which are in Judea flee to the mountains; and let them which are in the midst of it depart out; and let not them that are in the countries enter thereinto. For these be the days of vengeance, that all things which are written may be fulfilled. But woe unto them that are with child, and to them that give suck, in those days! for there shall be great distress in *the* land, and *wrath* upon *this people*. And *they* shall fall by the edge of the sword, and *shall be led away captive into all nations: and Jerusalem shall be*

---

[2] Matthew 24:3.
[3] Matthew 24:2.

trodden down of the Gentiles, until the times of the Gentiles be fulfilled.[4]

The Lukian account of Jesus' answer to the disciples' first question deals with the desolation and destruction of the second temple in A.D. 70. This fact is confirmed by Jesus, Who said, "*. . . this people . . . shall be led away captive into all nations: and Jerusalem shall be trodden down of the Gentiles, until the times of the Gentiles be fulfilled.*" This people, namely, Israel, was led away captive after the Romans destroyed Jerusalem in A.D. 70. However, they will *not* be led away captive into all nations at the time of the end. Rather, they will be gathered from all nations into the land of Israel.

"WHAT SHALL BE THE SIGN OF THY COMING?"

Now let us consider the disciples' *second question.* The disciples asked, "*. . . what shall be the sign of thy coming, and of the end* of the world?"[5] The disciples did not ask, "What shall be the signs [plural] of thy coming, and of the end of the world?" They asked, ". . . what shall be *the sign* [singular] of thy coming, and of the end of the world?" The Greek word for "sign" is <u>semeion</u>. According to Green's lexicon, <u>semeion</u> means "*. . . a sign, a mark . . . token, by which any thing* is known or distinguished . . . in N.T., *a sign, wonder, remarkable event . . . extraordinary phenomenon . . . a portent . . . .*"[6]

---

[4] Luke 21:20-24.
[5] Matthew 24:3.
[6] Green, p. 167.

Hence, we see that *a sign calls attention to the thing* which is signified by the sign. For example, God said to Noah, "I do set my *bow* in the cloud, and *it* shall be for a *token* [that is, a sign] of a covenant between me and the earth."[7] The rainbow was not the Noahic Covenant; *the rainbow was a token* or sign of the covenant God made with the earth. The rainbow simply signifies the covenant.

There are many examples of a sign calling attention to something in Scripture. Notice, for instance, that the Lord said to Abraham, "And ye shall circumcise the flesh of your foreskin; and *it* shall be a *token* of the covenant betwixt me and you."[8] In this particular case, circumcision was not the Abrahamic Covenant; *circumcision was a token* or sign of the Abrahamic Covenant. Once again, the sign is not the thing; *the sign signifies the thing*.

WHAT IS "THE SIGN" OF HIS COMING?

Biederwolf writes:

Perhaps this sign cannot be imagined until it comes, but among the varied views the following will be of interest:

1. The star of the Messiah

2. The rending of heaven and the appearing of angels

3. A cross

4. A lightning flash[9]

---

[7] Genesis 9:13.
[8] Genesis 17:11.
[9] Biederwolf, p. 343.

B.H. Carroll writes, "The sign is nothing other than the great white throne, coming out of the darkness of space."[10] If any of the above is the sign of Christ's coming, Jesus did not answer the disciples' question, for none of the views listed above are mentioned in the answer Jesus gave to His disciples in the Olivet Discourse.

Margaret Macdonald, a fifteen-year-old Scottish lassie from Port Glasgow, Scotland, had a vision between February 1 and April 14, 1830. In her vision, Margaret declared that "*the sign*" of His coming *was the Lord Jesus Himself* descending from heaven.

Margaret is the first person (of whom the writer knows) *to teach that believers would be caught up* to meet Christ in the air *prior to* the emergence of the Antichrist. During her vision, Margaret was given a revelation of pretribulationism which was combined with partial rapturism. The crucial part of *her vision teaches that believers who are filled with "the light of God" will be caught up to meet Christ* in the air before the Antichrist begins his persecution of the church. In part of her own account of her vision, Margaret wrote:

Now there is distress of nations, with perplexity, the seas and the waves roaring, men's hearts failing them for fear--now look out for *the sign* of the Son of man. Here I was made to stop and cry out, O, it is not known what *the sign* of the Son of man is; the people of God think they are waiting, but they know not what it is. I felt this needed to be revealed, and that there was great darkness and error about it, but suddenly what it was burst upon me with a glorious light. *I saw it was just the Lord Himself*

---

[10] B.H. Carroll, *An Interpretation of the English Bible, Volume 4* (Westwood, N.J.: Fleming Revell Co., 1913), pp. 269, 270.

descending from heaven with a shout, just the glorified man, even Jesus .... [11]

There you have it, right from the horse's mouth, or rather, right from Margaret's vision. However, Margaret Macdonald's vision regarding *the sign* of Christ's coming and of the end of the world is false. It is false, in part, because *a sign is not the thing itself*; rather, a sign calls attention to the thing signified by the sign.

After the disciples asked their two questions, the Scripture says:

> And Jesus answered and said unto them, Take heed that no man deceive you. For many shall come in my name, saying, I am Christ; and shall deceive many. And ye shall hear of wars and rumours of wars: see that ye be not troubled: for all these things must come to pass, but the end is not yet. For nation shall rise against nation, and kingdom against kingdom: and there shall be famines, and pestilences, and earthquakes, in divers places. All these are the beginning of sorrows. Then shall they deliver you up to be afflicted, and shall kill you: and ye shall be hated of all nations for my name's sake. And then shall many be offended, and shall betray one another, and shall hate one another. And many false prophets shall rise, and shall deceive many. And because iniquity shall abound, the love of many shall wax cold. But he that shall endure unto the end, the same shall be saved. And this gospel of the kingdom shall be preached in all the world for a witness unto all nations; and then shall the end come. [12]

As Jesus laid the foundation for His answer to the disciples' second question (*What shall be the sign of*

---

[11] Dave MacPherson, *The Incredible Cover-Up* (Medford, Oreg.: Omega Publications, 1975), p. 151.

[12] Matthew 24:4-14.

thy coming, and of the end of the world?), He gave us a prophecy not to be overlooked.

"WHEN YE THEREFORE SHALL SEE THE ABOMINATION OF DESOLATION"

Jesus said,

> *When ye therefore shall see the abomination of desolation*, spoken of by Daniel the prophet, *stand in the holy place*, (whoso readeth, let him understand:) ... For *then shall* be *great tribulation*, such as was not since the beginning of the world to this time, no, nor ever shall be.[13]

Here Jesus prophesied plainly that when the abomination of desolation stands in the holy place, the Great Tribulation will begin. It will last exactly three and one-half years or forty-two months or twelve hundred sixty days.

IMMEDIATELY AFTER THE TRIBULATION OF THOSE DAYS

In Matthew, Jesus continued, *"Immediately after* the tribulation of those days *shall the sun be darkened*, and the moon shall not give her light . . . ." The darkening of the sun and moon must be "the sign" of Christ's coming in the clouds,[14] for the darkening of the sun and moon is the only thing mentioned by Jesus in the Olivet Discourse that could possibly be "the sign," that is, the remarkable event or portent of His coming. It is vital to see that *when* the sun and moon are darkened, *then the Son of Man will come* in the clouds with great power and

---

[13] Matthew 24:15, 21.
[14] Matthew 24:29.

glory.[15] Here is the order of events as they are given by Jesus in the Olivet Discourse:

1. The abomination of desolation will stand in the holy place (Matthew 24:15).

2. *"Then* shall be great tribulation" (Matthew 24:21).

3. "Immediately *after the tribulation* of those days *shall the sun be darkened,* and the moon shall not give her light" (Matthew 24:29).

4. *"Then* [at that time] shall appear the sign of the Son of Man in heaven" (Matthew 24:30).

5. *"Then* [at that time] shall all the tribes of the earth mourn" (Matthew 24:30).

6. *"Then* [at that time] shall they see the Son of man coming in the clouds with great power and glory" (Mark 13:26).

7. *"Then* [at that time] shall He send His angels and shall gather together His elect" (Mark 13:27).

What could be clearer? *First,* the sun and moon will be darkened; *then,* they will see the Son of Man coming in the clouds. According to Webster's 1828, "then" means, *"at that time;* the Canaanite was *then* in the land . . . ." In Matthew 24:29, we have *the darkening of the sun and moon; then* we have *the coming of the Son of Man* "in the

---

[15] Mark 13:26.

clouds with great power and glory."[16] *The only possible sign Jesus gave in answer to the disciples' request for* "the sign of His coming, and of the end of the world" *is the darkening of the sun and moon.* You can be assured that when the sun and moon are darkened, every person on planet earth will sit up and take notice of this remarkable event. This effect is precisely what "the sign" is intended to accomplish.

THE STARS WILL FALL FROM HEAVEN

Now let us consider the stars that will fall from heaven unto the earth. In Matthew, Jesus said, "Immediately *after* the tribulation of those days shall the sun be darkened, and the moon shall not give her light, and *the stars* shall fall from heaven . . . ."[17] In the *Second Coming Bible*, Biederwolf lists the following views regarding the stars that will fall from heaven:

1. The downfall of the Jewish commonwealth.

2. The downfall of heathen star worship.

3. The downfall of those who have shone brightly in the church.

4. Stars literally falling, according to the notion that they were fixed in the heavens.

5. Phenomenal appearances, shooting stars and meteors popularly mistaken for real stars.[18]

---

[16] Ibid.
[17] Matthew 24:29.
[18] Biederwolf, pp. 342, 343.

Here the "doctors" disagree, but Peter informs us "that no prophecy of the Scripture is of any private interpretation."[19] The Bible is its own interpreter. Notice that these stars do not merely fall from heaven; they fall to the earth. John writes,

> And I beheld when he had opened the sixth seal, and, lo, there was a great earthquake; and the sun became black as sackcloth of hair; and the moon became as blood; *and the stars of heaven fell unto the earth . . . .*[20]

For those who take the Bible literally, every view listed by Biederwolf, except "stars literally falling," is eliminated, because all of the other interpretations are symbolic. Furthermore, the stars cannot be stars like the sun in our solar system. The sun is large enough to contain a million earths inside its sphere; consequently, if the sun in our solar system should fall to the earth, all of earth's inhabitants, not to mention the earth itself, would be burned to a crisp. If stars like our sun are not meant, there must be other literal stars mentioned in the Bible. Indeed there are, for *literal angels called stars* are mentioned in the Bible; and there will be a time when they will fall to the earth. Job says, "When *the morning stars* sang together, and all *the sons of God* shouted for joy . . . ."[21]

This statement by Job is from one of the five Old Testament books of Hebrew poetry. The key characteristic of Hebrew poetry is its use of parallelism in the expression of ideas. In Job 38:7, there are two members in the parallelism. "The morning stars" in the first mem-

---

[19] II Peter 1:19-21.
[20] Revelation 6:12, 13.
[21] Job 38:7.

ber of the parallelism are equivalent to "the sons of God" in the second member of the parallelism. The nature of Hebrew poetry interprets the verse for us. "The morning stars" are "the sons of God," that is, they are angels.

Now, notice the New Testament to see how the word "stars" is used there. In Revelation, Jesus said, "The mystery of the seven *stars* which thou sawest in my right hand, and the seven golden candlesticks. The seven *stars are the angels* of the seven churches . . . ."[22] *Here, stars are angels.* Again, in Revelation, the Scripture says:

> And the fifth angel sounded, and I saw a *star* fall from heaven unto the earth: and to *him* was given the key to the bottomless pit. And *he* opened the bottomless pit; and there arose a smoke out of the pit, as the smoke of a great furnace . . . .[23]

This star is a person and is identified as a person by the personal pronouns *"him"* in verse one and *"he"* in verse two; furthermore, this *star is a personal being* with the intelligence to take the key of the bottomless pit and to use it to open the bottomless pit. *This star is an angel*--a very powerful angel--an angel fallen from heaven.

Now, look at Revelation 12:3, 4. Here the Bible says:

> And there appeared another wonder in heaven; and behold a great red dragon, having seven heads and ten horns, and seven crowns upon his heads. And his tail drew the third part of *the stars of heaven*, and did cast *them* to the earth . . . .

In Revelation 12:9, we are given the interpretation of the dragon and the stars. This Scripture says, "And the great dragon was cast out, that old serpent, called the

---

[22] Revelation 1:20.
[23] Revelation 9:1, 2.

Devil, and Satan, which deceiveth the whole world: *he was cast out into the earth, and his angels were cast out with him.*" So, in Revelation twelve we see again that angels are called stars. Therefore, a literal interpretation of the Bible requires us to believe that *the stars* which fall from heaven to the earth in Matthew 24:29, Mark 13:25, and Revelation 6:12, 13 *are angels called stars.*

Immediately after Jesus speaks of the *stars* falling from heaven, He further says, ". . . and *the powers of the heavens* shall be shaken."[24] Paul reveals that evil angels constitute the *powers* of darkness, for he writes, ". . . we wrestle not against flesh and blood, but against principalities, against *powers*, against the rulers of the darkness of this world, against spiritual wickedness in high places."[25] When Satan and his angels are cast out of heaven into the earth at the darkening of the sun and moon, *"the powers of the heavens shall be shaken."*

THEN WILL ALL THE TRIBES OF THE EARTH MOURN

Inasmuch as all the tribes of the earth will mourn, the twelve tribes of Israel will also be among those that mourn. The fact that they will be among the mourners raises a question: "When will the 144,000 Israelites be called servants and sealed?" Many commentators put the sealing of the 144,000 Israelites *in* the Seventieth Week of Daniel, but to do so is to overlook the clear teaching of Scripture. The 144,000 Israelites (Revelation 7:1-8) will not be called servants and sealed until *after* the coming of

---

[24] Matthew 24:24.
[25] Ephesians 6:12.

Christ in the clouds to rapture the church following the Great Tribulation. The Bible says that it will be *"after these things,"* that is, *after* the first six seals are opened and *after* the darkening of the sun and moon, that the 144,000 Israelites will be called servants and sealed.

Because the darkening of the sun and moon at the opening of the sixth seal is coincident with the rapture taught in Matthew 24:29-31, the sealing of the 144,000 must occur *after* a posttribulational rapture. The rapture in Matthew 24:31 will be established later in this chapter. Paul says,

> . . . blindness in part is happened to Israel, *until* the fulness of the Gentiles be come in. And so all Israel shall be saved: as it is written, There shall come out of Sion the Deliverer, and shall turn away ungodliness from Jacob . . . .[26]

The 144,000 will not be raptured with the elect as described in Matthew 24:31, at the darkening of the sun and moon, for they are not called servants and sealed *until after* the opening of the sixth seal. Furthermore, if the 144,000 were saved before the coming of Christ in the clouds (Matthew 24:30), they would be part of the church, and they would be raptured with the church at the posttribulational rapture.

Revelation 7:1-3 says:

> And *after these things* I saw four angels standing on the four corners of the earth, holding the four winds of the earth, that the wind should not blow on the earth, nor on the sea, nor on any tree. And I saw another angel ascending from the east, having the seal of the living God: and he cried with a loud voice to the four angels, to whom it was given to hurt the earth and the sea,

---

[26] Romans 10:25, 26.

saying, Hurt not the earth, neither the sea, nor the trees, till we have *sealed* the *servants* of our God in their foreheads.

The 144,000 are sealed at this time for protection from *the wrath of the Lamb* that is about to fall upon those who have received the mark of the beast. The 144,000 will enter the millennial kingdom because they will not be saved, neither will they be called servants nor be sealed *until after* the Great Tribulation and *after* the posttribulational rapture.

This fact is confirmed by the first phrase in Revelation 7:1, which says, "And after these things . . . ." The words *"after these things"* come from two Greek words (meta tauta). *These two Greek words in Revelation 7:1 mean "after these things" or "after this," just as they do in Revelation 4:1,* where the same two Greek words are used. Notice how these two Greek words are used elsewhere in the New Testament. In John 3:22, following Jesus' discourse with Nicodemus, we read these words, "And *after these things* [meta tauta] came Jesus and His disciples into the land of Judea . . . ." The meaning is obvious. First, Jesus had His encounter with Nicodemus; then, after those things, Jesus and His disciples went into the land of Judea. Again, in the latter part of John four, we read of Jesus' healing the nobleman's son in Cana of Galilee. Then John 5:1 says, *"After this* [meta tauta] there was a feast of the Jews; and Jesus went up to Jerusalem." The meaning again is perfectly clear. First, Jesus healed the nobleman's son in Cana of Galilee; then, after this miracle, He went up to Jerusalem. How could anything be clearer? The words "after this" or "after these things" in the above scriptures are used to show that the events happened sequentially.

The words "after these things" in Revelation 7:1 *follow* the opening of the sixth seal and the darkening of the sun and moon.[27] Accordingly, the sealing of the 144,000 will take place *after* the opening of the sixth seal and the darkening of the sun and moon. Hence, if we take the Bible literally, the sealing of the 144,000 will not occur *in* the Seventieth Week. Rather, the sealing of the 144,000 will occur *after* the Seventieth Week ends and *after* the opening of the sixth seal. This sealing will occur very early *in* the millennial kingdom before the seventh seal is opened.

Pretribulationists are correct in saying that *Revelation chapters four and five*, which describe the throne scene in heaven, *follow chapters two and three* (which contain the seven letters which John was commanded to write, and which were dictated to him by Christ), because they follow the words "after this" (Revelation 4:1). In short, they are correct in saying that "after this" means "after this." Now, if the Greek words (<u>meta</u> <u>tauta</u>) mean "after this" in Revelation 4:1, then those same Greek words (<u>meta</u> <u>tauta</u>) mean "after this" or "after these things" in Revelation 7:1. As Stewart Custer says, "If the sauce is good for the goose, it is good for the gander."

THEY WILL SEE THE SON OF MAN COMING IN THE CLOUDS

There are several things that we should notice about the coming of Christ in the clouds with great power and glory. First, it is not a secret coming, for "then shall appear the sign of the Son of man in heaven: and then

---

[27] Revelation 6:12-7:1.

shall *all the tribes of the earth* mourn, and *they shall see the Son of man coming in the clouds of heaven . . . .*"[28] Second, when Christ comes in the clouds, there is no mention of a white horse, and there is no mention of an army on white horses coming with Him. Third, *the coming of Christ in the clouds is not His coming to the earth*, for the Scripture says He comes in the clouds, that is, He comes in the air. Here the Bible says nothing about His coming to the earth. His coming to the earth on the white horse will occur at the end of the "the great day of his wrath," *in* the Day of the Lord. This truth will be explained in chapter nine.

Therefore, the coming of Christ in the clouds is not the coming of Christ for the Battle of Armageddon. In the Olivet Discourse, Jesus described His coming in the clouds, and this coming will occur *when* the sun and moon are darkened immediately *after* the Great Tribulation. In Revelation 6:12, 13, we see that the sun and moon will be darkened *when* the sixth seal is opened. Armageddon will not occur *until after* the seventh seal is opened, and *after* the seven trumpet judgments and *after* the seven vial judgments are poured out, and *after* the whore of Revelation 17 and 18 is destroyed. Then, and *not until then, will Christ descend on a white horse* with His army on white horses for the Battle of Armageddon, which is described in Revelation 19:11-20.

---

[28] Matthew 24:30.

WHEN THE SUN IS DARKENED, TWO MOMENTOUS EVENTS WILL OCCUR

First, Mark says, "And *then shall they see the Son of man coming in the clouds* with great power and glory."[29] When the sun and moon are darkened immediately *after* the Great Tribulation, the Son of Man will come in the clouds of heaven with great power and glory.

Second, when the sun and moon are darkened and *the stars fall from heaven unto the earth, the millennial kingdom will begin.* This truth is confirmed by Revelation 12:4, 9, 10, which say:

> *And his tail drew the third part of the stars of heaven, and did cast them to the earth* . . . . And the great dragon was cast out, that old serpent, called the Devil, and Satan, which deceiveth the whole world: *he was cast out into the earth, and his angels were cast out with him.* And I heard a loud voice saying in heaven, *now is come . . . the kingdom of our God,* and the power of his Christ: *for the accuser of our brethren is cast down* . . . .

Did you get that? *When the stars, namely, Satan and his angels,* are cast out of heaven into the earth *when* the sun and moon are darkened, immediately *after* the Great Tribulation, *then (at that time) will come the kingdom of our God,* and the power of his Christ. What could be clearer? Why, it's as plain as the nose on your face. Armerding, a pretribulationalist, saw that the falling of the stars and shaking of the powers of the heavens pertain to

---

[29] Mark 13:26.

Satan and his angels, so he wrote, ". . . the *powers of the heavens*, [are] a reference to Satan and his hosts . . . ."[30]

HE WILL GATHER TOGETHER HIS ELECT

Now, notice the verb "gather together" used in both Matthew 24:31 and Mark 13:27. The words "gather together" are translated from the Greek word <u>episunago.</u> According to Green, <u>episunago</u> means, ". . . *to gather to a place*; to gather together, assemble, convene . . . ."[31]

In Matthew 24:31, Jesus says, "And *he* [the Son of man] shall send his angels with a great sound of a trumpet, and *they shall gather together his elect* from the four winds, from one end of heaven to the other." In verse 31, we have the words, "gather together." The Greek word <u>episunago</u> ("gather together") in this verse is in the third person *plural*. The subject of this verb is the pronoun "they," and the antecedent of the pronoun "they" is the word "angels." According to this verse, *the angels will gather together the elect.*

Now look at Mark 13:26, 27. In this passage, Jesus said,

> And *then* shall they see the Son of man coming in the clouds with great power and glory. And *then* shall *he* send his angels, and shall gather together his elect from the four winds, from the uttermost part of the earth to the uttermost part of heaven.

---

[30] Carl Amerding , "The Coming of the Son of Man," *Moody Monthly*, Volume 51, pp. 788, 809; cited by Rand Bibliotheca Sacra, Volume 113, p. 201.

[31] Green, p. 73.

The words "gather together" in Mark 13:27 are also translated from the Greek word <u>episunago</u>. This is the same word used in Matthew 24:31, but here in Mark, it is in the third person *singular* instead of the third person plural, as in Matthew. In Mark, the verb is in the third person singular because its subject is the pronoun "he," and the antecedent of the pronoun "he" is "the Son of man" in verse 26.

According to this verse, the one who gathers together the elect is none other than the Son of Man Himself. There is, of course, no contradiction between Matthew 24:31 and Mark 13:27. The Bible never contradicts itself. This difficulty is cleared up by an understanding of Semitic thought. Relevant to this, Gundry writes:

> Equation of the rapture with the gathering of the elect after the tribulation immediately runs into the objection that angels gather them in the Olivet Discourse, but Jesus Himself does so in Paul's description of the rapture (I Thessalonians 4:16). However, it is a genius of semitic thought that the medium or agency through which an action is accomplished often drops out of sight. *The ultimate cause then appears as the direct cause.*[32]

In a footnote to his statement above, Gundry says:

> Cf. Matthew 8:5-13, where the *centurion* appears to beseech Christ personally to heal his servant. But Luke's account shows that the centurion was doing it through *a delegation of Jewish elders* and a further delegation of *'friends'* (Luke 7:1-10).[33]

Reese, a posttribulationist, writes, "Now, concerning the rapture there are only three undisputed texts in the

---

[32] Gundry, pp. 135, 136.
[33] Ibid., p. 136.

Bible that deal with it, namely: John 14:3; I Thessalonians 4:17; II Thessalonians 2:1 . . . ."[34]

These three passages do deal with the rapture, but many outstanding scholars of the past have also identified Matthew 24:31 and Mark 13:27 as rapture passages. For instance, commenting on Matthew 24:31, Biederwolf writes, "*Most premillennial expositors* . . . say that this passage refers to the time of the resurrection of believers, commonly called the First Resurrection, and they refer the trumpet to the one blown in I Thessalonians 4:16."[35] Biederwolf mentions the following scholars who held that viewpoint: Meyer, Alford, Godet, Lange, and Ellicott. Then Biederwolf writes, "Meyer and Lange identify this trumpet also with that of I Corinthians 15:52 . . . ."[36] Incidentally, I Corinthians 15:51, 52, is another passage that deals with the resurrection and the rapture.

In their vain attempt to show that the coming of Christ in the clouds in Matthew 24:30, 31 is not the same as the coming of Christ in I Thessalonians 4:16, 17, some pretribulationalists point out differences between Matthew 24 and I Thessalonians 4. Then they conclude erroneously that Matthew 24 does not refer to the same event, namely, the rapture described by Paul in I Thessalonians 4. Relevant to this issue, Gundry writes:

> In Matthew 24, signs precede the coming, but not in I Thessalonians 4. But, to quote one writer against himself, '*There is no need that all the accompaniments of the rapture be restated at every mention of the event.*'[37] Paul does imply that signs will

---

[34] Reese, p. 34.
[35] Biederwolf, p. 345.
[36] Ibid.
[37] Stanton, p. 199.

precede the second coming and that the Thessalonians already knew them (5:1ff.). And in 2 Thessalonians 2:1-5 he reiterates two of the outstanding signs.

In Matthew 24 the Son of Man comes, in I Thessalonians the Lord Himself. Are we then to infer a different event every time a different title for Jesus is used? Is the glorious appearing 'of our great God and Saviour, Christ Jesus' (Titus 2:13) to be distinguished from the coming of 'the Lord Himself' (I Thessalonians 4:16)?

In I Thessalonians we read of the trumpet of God, but in Matthew 24 of the trumpet of the angels. However, Jesus does not identify the one who will blow the 'great trumpet.' Even did an angel blow it, it might still be the trumpet of God. 'The sword of the Lord' was also called 'the sword of Gideon.' 'The rod of God' was Moses' rod.

Jesus baptized, yet not Jesus, but His disciples (John 4:1, 2). *Similarly, there is no problem in the gathering of the elect by angels.*[38]

There is a law of biblical interpretation which the writer calls the law of supplementation. Others call it the hermeneutical law of unity. This law of interpretation must be carefully followed in order to correctly interpret the Bible. Many of us take vitamins and minerals to supplement the food we eat. The vitamin and mineral supplements are not in contradiction to the food we eat; they are in supplementation to the food we eat. The importance of this interpretative law is seen clearly when we read the separate accounts of the Olivet Discourse in Matthew, Mark, and Luke. For instance, in Mark, Jesus says, ". . . *after* that tribulation, the sun shall be darkened,

---

[38] Gundry, p. 160.

and the moon shall not give her light . . . ."[39] In Matthew's account of the same event, Jesus says, *"Immediately after* the tribulation of those days shall the sun be darkened . . . ."[40]

Obviously, these are not accounts of two separate events. *Matthew gives us a supplementary word*; that word is *"immediately."* We see the same thing in the verses dealing with the Son of Man coming in the clouds and in the gathering together of His elect. In Matthew, Jesus says, ". . . and they shall see the Son of man coming in the clouds of heaven . . . ."[41] In Mark, Jesus said, "And *then* shall they see the Son of man coming in the clouds . . . ."[42] Once again, these passages do not refer to two separate events; Mark gives us the word "then," whereas Matthew does not.

Again, we see the need for using the interpretative law of supplementation regarding the stars' falling from heaven. In Matthew, Jesus says, "Immediately after the tribulation of those days shall the sun be darkened, and the moon shall not give her light, and *the stars shall fall from heaven*, and the powers of the heavens shall be shaken."[43] In Revelation, John writes, "And I beheld when he had opened the sixth seal, and, lo, there was a great earthquake; and the sun became black as sackcloth of hair, and the moon became as blood; And *the stars of heaven fell unto the earth* . . . ."[44] Jesus and John were not referring to two separate events; rather, Revelation 6:13 gives

---

[39] Mark 13:24.

[40] Matthew 24:29.

[41] Matthew 24:30.

[42] Mark 13:26.

[43] Matthew 24:29.

[44] Revelation 6:12, 13.

information that Matthew does not give us. Revelation 6:13 not only tells us that the stars fall from heaven, but also that *the stars fall to the earth.*

The hermeneutical law of unity explains why the account of the resurrection and rapture in I Thessalonians 4:16, 17 is not precisely the same as the account given in Matthew 24:31. The interpretative law of supplementation must be applied as we study these separate passages. Why did God give the Scriptures in this manner? Could it be that He desires His people *to study to show themselves approved?*

Some pretribulationalists argue that I Thessalonians 4:16, 17 cannot refer to the same event as Matthew 24:31. They say that in I Thessalonians, the Lord Himself descends from heaven, but in Matthew 24:31, the Son of Man sends His angels who gather together the elect. *A little serious Bible study solves the problem.* All pretribulationalists need to do is to read Mark's version of Jesus' statement in Mark 13:26, 27, for it teaches that *the Son of Man Himself* will gather together His elect. In Mark 13:27, the Greek verb "gather together" is in the third person singular, and the third person singular means that the subject is "he." The antecedent of "he" is "the Son of man" in Mark 13:26. In short, Christ Himself will gather together His elect, according to Mark's version. So much for the pretribulationists who vainly attempt to remove the rapture from Matthew 24:30, 31 by pointing out differences between I Thessalonians 4:16, 17 and Matthew 24:30, 31.

One should consider the word for "gather together" in that great rapture text--II Thessalonians 2:1. The verse reads, "Now we beseech you, brethren, by the coming of our Lord Jesus Christ, and by our *gathering together* unto him." The words "gathering together" are from the Greek word <u>episunagoge</u>. This word, according to Green, means, *"The act of being gathered together or assembled,* II Thessalonians 2:1 . . . ."[45] <u>Episunagoge</u> is the noun of which the verb used in Matthew 24:31 and Mark 13:27 is the verbal cognate. According to Webster, cognate means, ". . . words having in common the same original word or root . . . ." In short, the noun in II Thessalonians 2:1 describes the result of the action of the verbs used in Matthew 24:31 and Mark 13:27.

Did you get that? In Matthew 24:31 and Mark 13:27, the Bible teaches that the elect are gathered together, that is, taken *out of* the earth and *from* one end of heaven. Then they are taken *to* the other end of heaven, namely, to the uttermost part of heaven where they are assembled. Yes, Virginia, the rapture of the church is taught plainly by Jesus Christ in Matthew 24:31 and Mark 13:27.

WHO ARE THE ELECT IN MATTHEW 24:31 AND MARK 13:27?

The correct answer to this question is decisive. In Mark's version of the Olivet Discourse, Jesus says:

> *And then shall they see the Son of man coming in the clouds with great power and glory. And then shall he send his angels, and shall gather together his elect from the four winds, from the uttermost part of the earth to the uttermost part of heaven.*[46]

Regarding the parallel passage in Matthew 24:30, 31,

---

[45] Green, p. 73.
[46] Mark 13:26, 27.

Biederwolf writes,

> Most premillennial expositors . . . say that this passage (Matthew
> 24:31) refers to the time of the resurrection of believers, com-
> monly called the First Resurrection, and they refer the trumpet to
> the one blown in I Thes. 4:16.[47]

Biederwolf continues, "These elect are, of course,
according to the authorities just quoted [Alford, Godet,
Lange, Ellicott], the chosen of God of all ages who are
caught up at the coming of the Lord . . . ."[48]

In the postapostolic writing *The Teaching of the
Twelve Apostles*, Matthew 24:31 (which concerns the
gathering of the elect) is quoted with the substitution of
"church" for "elect," and Christians are urged to be faithful to Christ during the reign of the Antichrist until the
posttribulational coming of Christ and the resurrection.

In the Scofield Reference Bible, the note in the center
column relevant to Matthew 24:31 says that "elect"
means Israel. John R. Rice, a pretribulationist, writes:

> Then 'he shall send his angels with a great sound of a trumpet,
> and they shall gather together *His elect (Israel, the chosen
> nation, all the Jews left alive in the world)* from the four winds,
> from one end of heaven to the other.' Note that this regathering
> is to be miraculous, is to be done by the angels of God, and is to
> be complete. *Every Jew scattered throughout the world will be
> miraculously regathered to Palestine.*[49]

Gundry writes, "Most pretribulationists refer the gathering of the elect in the tribulation to the gathering of the

---

[47] Biederwolf, p. 345.
[48] Ibid.
[49] John R. Rice, "No Signs of Christ's Coming," *The Sword of
the Lord*, Volume 55, 29 September 1989, Number 20, p. 21.

remaining dispersed Jews into the promised land."[50]
Because of theological necessity, pretribulationists cannot
afford to admit that the "elect" in Matthew 24:31 means
the church. If the elect in Matthew 24:31 and Mark 13:27
means the saints who constitute the church, then we have
explicit proof of a posttribulational rapture.

When the doctors disagree, as they do on the definition of the word "elect" in Matthew 24 and Mark 13,
what shall we do? There is only one place to find the
answer, and that place is the Bible. In chapter five, it was
pointed out that of the sixteen occurrences of the word
"elect" in the New Testament, the word is actually used in
only thirteen separate situations. It occurs in the same
three situations in both Matthew's and Mark's versions of
the Olivet Discourse. Hence, Christ really used the word
"elect" only three times in the discourse.

We noticed that I Timothy 5:21 and I Peter 2:6
contain uses of the word "elect" that are exceptions to
what we see in the other New Testament passages. In
I Timothy 5:21, the word "elect" modifies the word
"angels," and in I Peter 2:6, the word "elect" modifies the
word "cornerstone." We noticed also that Jesus used the
word "elect" in Luke 18:7. In this parable, the word
"elect" means believers, for Jesus spoke this parable to
the apostles, who were members of the church as, will be
shown shortly.

Holding in abeyance the three times Jesus used the
word "elect" in the Olivet Discourse, and with the exceptions of I Timothy 5:21 and I Peter 2:6, all other seven
times the word "elect" is used in the New Testament, it
means persons who were saved (or would be saved--

---

[50] Gundry, p. 135.

II Timothy 2:10) in this age and, accordingly, were members of the church. For example, Paul addressed his letter to the church in Colosse as follows, "Paul . . . to the *saints* and faithful *brethren in Christ* which are at Colosse . . ." (Colossians 1:1, 2). Then, Paul said to them, "Put on therefore, as *the elect* of God, holy and beloved, bowels of mercies . . ." (Colossians 3:12). Accordingly, in his other epistles, when Paul used the word "elect," the word always means the saints or brethren who form the church.

There are seven verses in the New Testament in which the word "elect" means believers who constitute the church. Therefore, these verses determine the meaning of the word "elect" in the three instances in which it is used by Jesus in the Olivet Discourse. Accordingly, based on the usage of the word by Paul, Peter, and John, the word "elect" in Matthew 24:31 and Mark 13:27 means the church. This constitutes solid biblical evidence that Matthew 24:31 and Mark 13:27 are proof texts for the post-tribulational rapture of the church.

This truth becomes more obvious when we understand that the apostles to whom the Olivet Discourse was given were members of the church. Gundry writes:

> Pretribulationists regard the apostles to whom Jesus delivered the Olivet Discourse as representative of the Jewish remnant belonging to redeemed Israel. Posttribulationists regard the apostles as representative of the Jewish remnant belonging to the churches of Jerusalem and Judea and in turn to the Church at large. If we may determine from other Scriptures whether the apostles usually represent Israel or the Church, we shall have data for a decision concerning the group to which the Jewish remnant belongs and therefore to which Jesus addresses the Olivet Discourse. The purpose of the enquiry is almost to answer it.

The apostles had previously received instruction concerning ecclesiastical discipline (Matthew 18:15-18). Only two days later they were to receive the Upper Room Discourse (including the promise of the rapture, John 14:1-3) and participate in the institution of the Lord's Supper, an ordinance of the Church. A few weeks following they were to be baptized in the Holy Spirit and form the nucleus of the first church of Jerusalem. The apostles were the foundation of the Church (Ephesians 2:20). Their doctrine was that of the Church (Acts 2:42). They were God's gift to the Church (Ephesians 4:11) and the highest offices in the Church (I Corinthians 12:28). They were the recipients of distinctly ecclesiological truth (Ephesians 3:5, 6). And their names will be inscribed on the foundations of the New Jerusalem in contradistinction to the names of the tribes of Israel (Revelation 21:12-14). Clearly, the apostles stand as representatives of the Church, not of Israel. Hence, their representative role in the Olivet Discourse leads to the conclusion that the tribulational saints [the elect] addressed through them belong to the Church.[51]

Neither C.I. Scofield nor John R. Rice has the authority to change the definition of the word "elect" from what it means in the New Testament to what they *need* it to mean to meet their theological necessity. They say that the word "elect" means "elect Jews" or "elect Israelites" by adding the words "Jews" or "Israelites" to the word "elect." They do this because of theological necessity. The Bible forbids the adding of words to Scripture. It is neither right nor safe for any teacher of the Bible to add words to Scripture, *even if he adds them only in the minds of his readers or listeners.*

The place to which the elect will be gathered together reveals that Scofield and Rice are in egregious error when they say that the "elect" means "Israel" or "all Jews left alive in the world." The "elect" are not gathered to the

---

[51] Gundry, pp. 133, 134.

land of Israel or to Jerusalem. The "elect" of Matthew 24:31 and Mark 13:27 are taken "to the uttermost part of heaven," that is, to the end or extremity of heaven. This is what the Bible says, and it is always safest to go by what the Bible says rather than what teachers like Scofield or Rice say the Bible means.

FROM WHERE ARE THE ELECT GATHERED?

Christ said that the elect will be gathered *from the earth and from heaven.* When Christ comes in the clouds, ". . . the dead in Christ shall rise first: Then we which are alive and remain shall be caught up together with them in the clouds to meet the Lord in the air: and so shall we ever be with the Lord."[52] The elect gathered from the earth will meet in the air the elect who have gone to heaven before, that is, the spirits of just men made perfect. The previously perfected spirits of saints will at that time receive their glorified resurrection bodies. The spirits of just men made perfect (reunited with their resurrected and glorified bodies), along with the saints resurrected just after Christ's resurrection (Matt. 27:52, 53), who are already in heaven, will be gathered *from one end of heaven.* Those gathered *from earth* and *from heaven,* after meeting in the air, will then be gathered together to the uttermost part of heaven. Paul writes:

Behold, I shew you a mystery; *we shall not all sleep, but we shall all be changed,* In a moment, in the twinkling of an eye, at the last trump: for the trumpet shall sound, and the dead shall be raised incorruptible, and we shall be changed. For *this cor-*

---

[52] I Thessalonians 4:16, 17.

ruptible must put on incorruption, and this mortal must put on immortality.[53]

Yes, there will be a meeting in the air. Moreover, the Bible says, ". . . we look for the Saviour, the Lord Jesus Christ: *who shall change our vile body*, that it may be fashioned *like unto his glorious body . . . .*"[54] At the time of the rapture, the believer will experience total sanctification, even the sanctification of the body, for the Bible says, "Beloved, now are we the sons of God, and it doth not yet appear what we shall be: but we know that, *when he shall appear, we shall be like him*; for we shall see him as he is."[55]

In Matthew, we see that *the elect are gathered from "the four winds."*[56] In Mark, we read that *the elect are gathered "from the four winds, from the uttermost part of the earth . . . ."*[57] Winds relate to the earth. For instance, in Revelation, John writes, "And after these things I saw four angels standing on the four corners of the earth, holding *the four winds of the earth, that the wind should not blow on the earth, nor on the sea, nor on any tree.*"[58] In Ezekiel, the Lord says,

A third part of thee shall die with the pestilence, and with famine shall they be consumed in the midst of thee: and a third part shall fall by the sword round about thee; and *I will scatter a third part into all the winds*, and I will draw out a sword after them.[59]

---

[53] I Corinthians 15:51, 52.
[54] Philippians 3:20, 21.
[55] I John 3:2.
[56] Matthew 24:31.
[57] Mark 13:27.
[58] Revelation 7:1-3.
[59] Ezekiel 5:12.

Therefore, we see that the elect are gathered *from the four winds, that is, from the earth.* This is made clear in Mark's account of the Olivet Discourse, for there Jesus says, "And then shall he send his angels, and shall gather together his elect from the four winds, *from the uttermost part of the earth* to the uttermost part of heaven."[60] The precise definitions of the two different Greek words translated *"from"* in both Matthew 24:31 and Mark 13:27 are determinative (decisive) definitions. In the phrase *"from the four winds"* in both Matthew 24:31 and Mark 13:27, the word "from" is from the Greek word <u>ek</u>. According to Green, <u>ek</u> means, *"from, out of,* denoting origin or source . . . ."[61]

An example of the meaning of <u>ek</u>, understood by all Baptists, is found in the book of Acts. Luke writes, ". . . they went down both into the water, both Philip and the eunuch; and he baptized him. And when they were come up *out of* [<u>ek</u>] the water, the Spirit of the Lord caught away Philip . . . ."[62] Gundry says:

> Our first major question concerns the exact force of the Greek preposition <u>ek</u>, translated 'from.' Essentially, <u>ek</u>, a preposition of motion concerning thought or physical direction, means *out from within.* <u>Ek</u> does not denote a stationary position outside its object . . . *the basic idea of emergence from within* is illustrated in usages in other verses of similar expression. The large host of tribulational saints will be 'they which came *out of* the great tribulation' (Revelation 7:14). 'The Lord knoweth how to deliver the godly *out of* temptation' (II Peter 2:9).[63]

---

[60] Mark 13:27.
[61] Green, p. 55.
[62] Acts 8:38, 39.
[63] Gundry, p. 55.

Robertson says, "The word means *'out of,'* *'from within,'* ...."[64] Again, Gundry says:

> ... the preposition <u>ek</u> appears in John's writings approximately 336 times, far more often than in the writings of any other NT author. *There is not a single instance where the primary thought of emergence*, or origin, cannot fit, indeed, *does not best fit the thought of the context.*[65]

The primary sense of *emergence* in the meaning of <u>ek</u> devastates the pretribulational interpretation. Their interpretation is that the elect are gathered to the Promised Land for entrance into the millennial kingdom. The truth is that *the elect are gathered out of the four winds, that is, out of the earth, even out of the uttermost part of the earth.*

Next, let us consider the phrase "from one end."[66] In this phrase, the word "from" is translated from the Greek word <u>apo</u> in its contracted form. Its contracted form, which is found in both Matthew 24:31 and Mark 13:27, is <u>ap'</u>. According to Green, <u>apo</u> means, "forth from, away from; *hence it signifies departure*; distance or time of place...."[67] Robertson says, "<u>Ek</u> means 'from within' while <u>apo</u> is merely the general starting-point.... [Apo] does not deny the 'within-ness'; *it simply does not assert it* as <u>ek</u> does."[68]

---

[64] A.T. Robertson, *A Grammar of the Greek New Testament in Light of Historical Research* (Nashville, Tenn.: Broadman Press, 1934), p. 596.

[65] Gundry, p. 57.

[66] Matthew 24:31.

[67] Green, p. 17.

[68] Robertson, *A Grammar of the Greek New Testament in Light of Historical Research*, p. 577.

Bearing in mind the definition of <u>apo</u>, let us consider Matthew 24:31 again. Jesus said, "And he shall send his angels with a great sound of a trumpet, and they shall gather together his elect from the four winds, *from* [ap'] one end of heaven to the other." Here the meaning is obvious. *The elect who are in heaven*, that is, "*the spirits of just men made perfect*"[69] (now in their resurrection bodies) and the previously resurrected saints (Matt. 27:52, 53) are gathered *from* (here the word "from" signifies departure) *one end of heaven.*

One must remember that Robertson said that the word <u>ap'</u> (from) "*does not assert*" the thought of emergence. The elect who are in heaven will not emerge from heaven; *they will be taken from one end of heaven.* They will meet in the air *the elect who will be gathered from the four winds, that is, from the uttermost part of the earth.* At this time, the elect who will be resurrected and raptured will experience total sanctification and will receive their glorified resurrection bodies. They will remain with Christ *in heaven* until they return *with* Christ on white horses for the Battle of Armageddon. This truth will be explained later.

Notice the word for "gather together" in that great rapture text--II Thessalonians 2:1. The verse reads, "Now we beseech you, brethren, by the coming of our Lord Jesus Christ, and by our gathering together unto him." The words "gathering together" are from the Greek word <u>episunagoge</u>. According to Green, this word means, ". . . *the act of being gathered together or assembled*, II Thessalonians 2:1 . . . ."[70]

---

[69] Hebrews 12:22.
[70] Green, p. 73.

TO WHERE WILL THE ELECT BE GATHERED?

The Bible reveals plainly where the elect will be taken when they are gathered together at the coming of Christ in the clouds. *The elect will be taken "to the uttermost part of heaven;" they will not be taken to the promised land or to Jerusalem.* John R. Rice wrote:

> Then 'he shall send his angels with a great sound of a trumpet, and they shall gather together *his elect (Israel, the chosen nation, all the Jews left alive in the world)* from the four winds, from one end of heaven to the other.' . . . *Every Jew scattered throughout the world will be miraculously regathered to Palestine.*[71]

The above is what John R. Rice taught in one of his sermons on the second coming of Christ. Furthermore, the above is what most pretribulationists teach. We must always beware of believing what people say the Bible *means*; rather, we must believe what the Bible *says*. *The Bible says that the elect will be gathered together to "the uttermost part* [that is, the extremity or end] *of heaven."* In Mark's version of the Olivet Discourse, Jesus said, "And *then* shall they see the Son of man coming in the clouds with great power and glory. And *then* shall he send his angels, and shall gather together his elect from the four winds, from the uttermost part of the earth *to the uttermost part of heaven*."[72]

The words "uttermost part" are from the Greek word akron. According to Green, the word akron means, "the

---

[71] Rice, "No Signs of Christ's Coming," p. 21.
[72] Mark 13:27.

top, tip, *end, extremity*, Matthew 24:31 . . . ."[73] The Bible teaches plainly that *the elect are gathered together from the four winds* (which pertain to the earth) and *from the uttermost part of the earth to the uttermost part of heaven*. Despite this clear teaching by Christ in the Olivet Discourse, pretribulationists cannot admit the possibility of the church's being caught up immediately after the Great Tribulation. Hence, they say that these elect are elect *Jews* or *Israelites gathered to Palestine or Jerusalem*. Pretribulationists must add "Jews" or "Israelites" to the elect due to their own theological necessity.

Another important word in this verse is the word "to" in the phrase "*to* the uttermost part of heaven." This word "to" is from the Greek word <u>heos</u>. <u>Heos</u> can be either a preposition of time or *a preposition of place*.[74] In Mark 13:27 there is no possible way <u>heos</u> can be a preposition of time; *in this verse, it must be a preposition of place*. Did you get that? The word <u>heos</u> in this verse is a preposition of place, and it denotes *the place to which the elect are gathered together*. The place is *the uttermost part of heaven*, that is, the *extremity* of heaven.

Prior to His coming in the clouds, the Lord Jesus Christ sits at the right hand of the Father making intercession for believers. When Christ comes in the clouds with great power and glory, He will gather together His elect and take them *to the uttermost part,* that is, the extremity *of heaven*. Jesus said, ". . . I will come again and receive you unto myself; that where I am, there ye may be also."[75] The church will remain with Christ *in the utter-*

---

[73] Green, p. 6.
[74] Green, p. 80.
[75] John 14:3.

most part of heaven until He returns for the Battle of Armageddon. During this time, the judgment seat of Christ and the marriage of the Lamb will take place. Then the church will return with Christ for the Battle of Armageddon. The church's return to the earth with Christ on white horses will occur *after* the seven trumpet judgments, and *after* the seven vials of God's wrath are poured out upon the earth, and *after* the destruction of the great whore.

Remember, the coming of Christ in the clouds with great power and glory *occurs just after the darkening of the sun and moon when the sixth seal is opened* (Matthew 24:29-31; Revelation 6:12, 13). The coming of Christ in the clouds will occur a considerable period of time *before* the trumpet judgments, the vial judgments, the destruction of the whore, and the Battle of Armageddon have been completed. This truth will be explained later.

Admitting that Matthew 24:30, 31 and Mark 13:26, 27 refer to the rapture would be devastating to pretribulationism, for there is *no explicit reference* to a pretribulational rapture of the church in the Bible. Pentecost admits that no single reference proves pretribulationism, for he writes,

> The pretribulation doctrine is not based on these arguments *singly*, but rather they are considered as cumulative evidence that the church will be delivered by rapture before the inception of Daniel's seventieth week.[76]

One must remember that Pentecost himself admitted that the pretribulation doctrine is not based on any of his arguments *singly*. *Singly* means single-handedly or indi-

---

[76] Pentecost, p. 218.

vidually. In short, *Pentecost admitted* that not one of his arguments by itself proves pretribulationism. Just one clear verse teaching a pretribulational rapture is all a Bible believer needs. One explicit proof text is all a Bible believer needs to believe in the virgin birth, the sinlessness of Christ, the deity of Christ, the bodily resurrection of Christ, or any other Bible doctrine.

Not only does Pentecost make this amazing admission, but Walvoord also confesses the same thing. Walvoord concedes, *"One of the problems that faces both pretribulationism and posttribulationism is the fact that their point of view is an induction based on scriptural facts rather than an explicit statement of the Bible."*[77] *Posttribulationism,* however, is not an induction; it is based on the clear teaching of the Bible. Ponder Walvoord's amazing admission once again; he writes, *". . . pretribulationism . . . is an induction . . . rather than an explicit statement of the Bible."*[78] There it is--like a dead fish. Walvoord continues, *"While both pretribulationists* and posttribulationists *have strained to find some specific reference in support of their views, most adherents* of either view usually *concede that there is no explicit reference . . . ."*[79]

The two leading proponents of modern pretribulationism concede that no single scripture or explicit reference exists that proves a pretribulation rapture. *There are, however, explicit references in the Bible to a posttribulational rapture.* It has just been demonstrated that

---

[77] Walvoord, *Rapture Question: Revised,* p. 182.
[78] Ibid.
[79] Ibid.

Matthew 24:31 and Mark 13:27 are indeed explicit references to a posttribulational rapture.

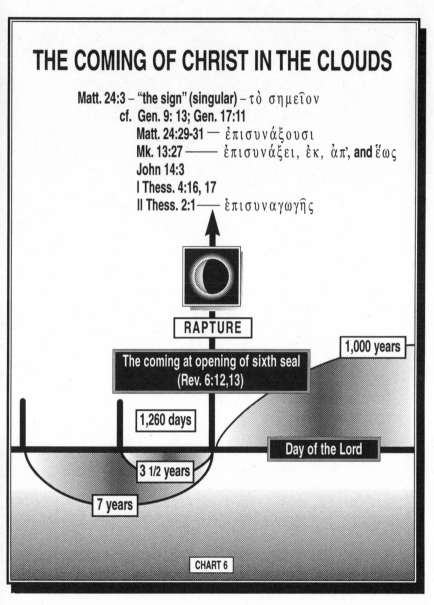

THE COMING OF CHRIST IN THE CLOUDS

Matt. 24:3 – "the sign" (singular) – τὸ σημεῖον
cf. Gen. 9: 13; Gen. 17:11
Matt. 24:29-31 — ἐπισυνάξουσι
Mk. 13:27 —— ἐπισυνάξει, ἐκ, ἀπ', **and** ἕως
John 14:3
I Thess. 4:16, 17
II Thess. 2:1 —— ἐπισυναγωγῆς

RAPTURE

**The coming at opening of sixth seal
(Rev. 6:12,13)**

1,000 years

1,260 days

Day of the Lord

3 1/2 years

7 years

CHART 6

The coming of Christ in the clouds to rapture the church occurs at the opening of the sixth seal immediately after the Great Tribulation.

SEVEN

THE ENLIGHTENING EIGHTH CHAPTER OF DANIEL

"The entrance of thy words giveth light. . . .
— Psalm 119:130

A clear understanding of the eighth chapter of Daniel is essential to a correct comprehension of end-time events. End-time events include the emerging of the Antichrist, his confirming the covenant with many, his causing the sacrifice and the oblation to cease, the placing of the abomination of desolation in the holy place, the beginning of the Great Tribulation, the coming of Christ in the clouds, and the pouring out of God's wrath upon the wicked in an unparalleled way during *the great day of His wrath.*

Larkin writes:

This Vision of the *'ram'* and the *'he-goat'* occurred in the 'third year' of the reign of Belshazzar . . . *its purpose was* to inform Daniel what Empires were to succeed the Babylonian, and *to further trace the little horn*, for it is worthy of note that while the prophecies of Isaiah relate mainly to the 'Christ,' the visions of Daniel are for the purpose of unveiling the Anti-Christ.[1]

THE VISION OF THE RAM

Daniel says:

And I saw in a vision . . . a ram which had two horns: and . . . I saw the ram pushing westward, and northward, and southward; so that no beasts might stand before him, neither was there any that could deliver out of his hand; but he did according to his will, and became great.[2]

The interpretation of the first part of Daniel's vision is given in Daniel 8:20, which says, "The ram which thou sawest having two horns are the kings of Media and Persia."

THE VISION OF THE HE GOAT

Daniel continues:

And as I was considering, behold, an he goat came from the west on the face of the whole earth, and touched not the ground: and the goat had a notable horn between his eyes. And he came to the ram that had two horns, which I had seen standing before the river, and ran unto him in the fury of his power. And I saw him come close unto the ram, and he was moved with choler against him, and smote the ram, and brake his two horns: and there was no power in the ram to stand before him, but he cast him down to the ground, and stamped upon him: and there was none that could deliver the ram out of his hand.[3]

---

[1] Clarence Larkin, *The Book of Daniel* (Philadelphia, Pa.: Erwin W. Mover Co., 1929), p. 155.

[2] Daniel 8:2.

[3] Daniel 8:5-7.

The interpretation for this part of the vision is found in Daniel 8:21, which says, "And the rough goat is the king of Grecia: and the great horn that is between his eyes is the first king."

Larkin, commenting on the "he goat" with the great horn, writes:

> We are told by Gabriel that the 'Great Horn' that was between the eyes of the 'He-Goat' represented the First King (of Greece). Now this King, as all historians know, was *Alexander the Great* (B.C. 356-323, the son of Philip of Macedon), who became King of Greece when but twenty years of age, B.C. 336. Two years later (B.C. 334), in goat-like fashion, he leaped the Hellespont, and with an army of 30,000 infantry, and 5,000 cavalry, he defeated a Persian force on the banks of the Granicus. By a swift advance eastward he, in the following year, B.C. 333, defeated at Issus a Persian army of 600,000 men, commanded by the Persian King, Darius. After minor conquests in Phoenicia and Egypt, he returned to Syria, where on the banks of the Tigris River he defeated an enormous army led by Darius. This is known as the Battle of Arbela, B.C. 331.[4]

THE VISION OF THE FOUR HORNS

Moreover, Daniel says, "Therefore the he goat waxed very great: and when he was strong, the great horn was broken; and for it came up four notable ones toward the four winds of heaven."[5]

The interpretation for this part of the vision is given in Daniel 8:22, which says, "Now that [great horn on the he goat] being broken, whereas four stood up for it, four kingdoms shall stand up out of the nation, but not in his power."

---

[4] Larkin, p. 182.
[5] Daniel 8:8.

Larkin writes:

> From B.C. 330 to 327, Alexander was engaged in subjugating the outlying provinces of the Persian Empire [*which includes territory that is now Pakistan, the land from which Maitreya, who claims he is the Christ, comes*]. Later he returned to Babylon, where, at the climax of his glory, he died of marsh fever and intemperance in June, B.C. 323, in his thirty-third year. After the death of Alexander . . . four of his Generals divided the territory of the Empire among themselves. *Gassander* took Macedonia, *Lysimachus* took Thrace. *Seleucus* took Syria [Syria at that time included all of the middle east including what is today Syria, Jordan, Iraq, Iran, *Pakistan*, and east and north of the Indus River]. *Ptolemy* took Egypt.[6]

The division of Alexander's empire into four parts, ruled by four of his generals and their successors was prophesied in Daniel 11:4, which says, "And when he [Alexander the Great] shall stand up, his kingdom shall be broken, and shall be divided toward the four winds of heaven; and *not to his posterity* . . . ."

THE VISION OF THE LITTLE HORN

The last and most important part of this vision given to Daniel pertains to *the "little horn,"* which is mentioned in Daniel 8:9-12. This Scripture says:

> And out of one of them [that is, out of one of the four notable horns namely, kingdoms of Daniel 8:8, 22] came forth a little horn, which waxed exceeding great, toward the south, and toward the east, and toward the pleasant land. And it waxed great, even to the host of heaven; and it cast down some of the host and of the stars to the ground, and stamped upon them. Yea, he magnified himself even to the prince of the host, and by

---

[6] Larkin, p. 163.

him the daily sacrifice was taken away, and the place of his sanctuary was cast down. And an host was given him against the daily sacrifice by reason of transgression, and it cast down the truth to the ground; and it practised, and prospered.

At this point, we must watch our step. Bob Jones, Sr. enjoyed telling his story about rabbit-chasers. Where he grew up in Alabama, the men enjoyed hunting 'possums. In tracking 'possums, the hunters used 'possum dogs. Dr. Bob said that some dogs would leave the 'possum trail if a rabbit had crossed the trail, and the dog would then follow the rabbit trail and lose the 'possum. Dr. Bob said that some hunters would shoot those worthless dogs, because they were rabbit-chasers.

While tracking the little horn of Daniel 8:9-14, many expositors have left the 'possum trail and followed a rabbit trail. They have become rabbit-chasers. The rabbit they have followed is Antiochus Epiphanes, a Seleucid king, who at one time ruled the Syrian part of Alexander's divided empire.

Antiochus Epiphanes was the eighth in a succession of twenty-six Seleucid kings. After launching an invasion against his Ptolemaic adversaries in Egypt, he was ordered by Rome to return to his own land. Ruling only a third-rate kingdom in comparison with Rome, he yielded to the power of Rome and ordered his army away from Egypt. He made his homeward march through Judea. This thwarted tyrant desecrated the second temple in Jerusalem by stopping the appointed sacrifices and by setting up a statue of Zeus in the sanctuary. He further defiled the sanctuary by sacrificing a swine and sprinkling its blood throughout the temple.

Historians have established that this desecration by Antiochus began on December 25, 168 B.C., and continued through December 25, 165 B.C. On this very day, December 25, 165 B.C., the second temple was delivered by Judas Maccabeus and his followers. The Maccabees cleansed the temple, and they established the festival of lights, called Hanukkah, in celebration of the cleansing of the temple.

As mentioned above, it is at this point that we must be extremely careful. As a result of believing the prophecy of the little horn of Daniel 8:9-14 was fulfilled by Antiochus Epiphanes, many Bible teachers have followed a rabbit trail, and they have misled multitudes of Bible students.

For example, the Scofield Reference Bible, in its note on Daniel 8:10-14, says, "This passage is confessedly the most difficult in prophecy, a difficulty increased by the present state of the text." First, notice that Scofield did not have the foggiest idea what this passage means. Second, observe that Scofield, in substance, said that the Bible is all "messed up" in this passage when he said the "difficulty [is] increased by the present state of the text."

Now, if one wants to believe the interpretation of Scofield, who believed the Bible is all "messed up" here, that is his choice. However, it is beyond this writer how any genuine Bible believer can accept such a footnote. In that Bible-bashing note, Scofield further said, "Historically, this [prophecy] was fulfilled in and by Antiochus Epiphanes . . . ." It is amazing to see how quickly Scofield overcame his uncertainty and took off on the rabbit trail.

The first commentator, of whom this writer knows, who led Bible believers onto the rabbit trail of Antiochus

Epiphanes was an unconverted Jew. His name was Josephus, a Jewish historian, who wrote around A.D. 100. Josephus gave to Daniel 8:9-14 the interpretation that *the little horn was Antiochus Epiphanes.* It is shocking that the vast majority of Christian commentators have followed the view set forth by an unconverted Jew.

Let us examine the weighty evidence which proves that the little horn of Daniel 8:9-14 could not have been Antiochus Epiphanes.

First, notice the evidence from I Maccabees. I Maccabees 1:54 says, "Now the fifteenth day of the month Casleu, *in the hundredth forty and fifth year, they set up the abomination of desolation upon the altar . . . .*" Then I Maccabees 1:59 says, "*Now the five and twentieth day of the month, they did sacrifice upon the idol altar, which was upon the altar of God.*" That is, they sacrificed upon the idol altar on December 25, 168 B.C. Next, note I Maccabees 6:1, 3-8, 16, which says:

About that time King Antiochus traveling through the high countries, heard say that Elimais in the country of Persia, was a city greatly renowned for riches, silver, and gold, and that there was in it a very rich temple, wherein were coverings of gold, and breastplates, and shields, which Alexander son of Philip the Macedonian king, who reigned first among the Grecians, had left there. Wherefore, he came and sought to take the city, and to spoil it, but he was not able, because they of the city having had warning thereof, rose up against him in battle: so he fled and departed thence with great heaviness, and returned to Babylon. Moreover, there came one, who brought in tidings into Persia, that the armies which went against the land of Judea, were put to flight: and that Lisius . . . was driven away of the Jews . . . also that *they had pulled down the abomination which he had set up upon the altar in Jerusalem . . . .* [This occurred on December 25, 165 B.C.] Now when the king had heard these words, he was astonished, and sore moved, whereupon he laid him down upon his bed, and fell sick for grief. . . . So King *Antiochus died there in the one hundred and forty-ninth year* [164 B.C.].

Antiochus died approximately four years after December 25, 168 B.C., which was when he sacrificed upon the idol altar which was upon the altar of God. I Maccabees 1:54 says, "Now the fifteenth day of the month Casleu, in the one hundred and forty-fifth year, they set up the abomination of desolation upon the altar. . . ." If Antiochus had lived to December 25, 164 B.C., he would have lived only four years after his desolating of the temple by offering the swine on the idol altar and by sprinkling its blood in the temple. Four (years) times 365 days equals 1,460 days, and if we add one day for leap year, the total is 1,461 days. *The 1,461 days is not equivalent to the 2,300 days of Daniel 8:14.* We must keep in mind, however, that *the cleansing of the temple by the Maccabees occurred approximately a year before Antiochus died; the second temple was cleansed by the Maccabees on December 25, 165 B.C.*

Second, consider the evidence from the *Babylonian Talmud,* which says:

On the 25th of Casleu, the ninth month of the Jewish year, [corresponding to December] *commence the days of Hanukkah* . . . for when the Greeks entered the temple, they defiled all the oils therein, and when the Hasmonean Dynasty prevailed against and defeated them, they made search and found only one cruse of oil which lay with the seal of the High Priest, but which contains efficient for one day's riding only; yet, a miracle was wrought therein and they lit therewith for eight days . . . *this lighting took place in 165 B.C.E.; exactly three years before, on the same day, Antiochus Epiphanes had a pagan altar erected in the temple, upon which sacrifices were offered* (I Maccabees 1:46-64).[7]

Third, ponder the evidence from Rufus Learsi, who writes:

Antiochus followed up his victory with a decree commanding that all should be one people, and everyone should leave his laws, an edict aimed at the Jews alone, thence the others had no scruples about accepting the cultures of the Greeks or worshipping their gods. *On the fifteenth day of the month Kislev, 168 B.C.E., a statue of Zeus was erected in the sanctuary and the king ordered a swine,* an animal held in special abhorrence by the Jews, *to be sacrificed on the altar* . . . . In the court of the temple, beside the altar, stood 'the abomination of desolation,' . . . the statue of Zeus . . . it was the year 165 B.C.E.- Judas won another great victory . . . *Judas, in the late fall of the same year,* entered Jerusalem and *cleansed the temple of its pagan pollutions.* He removed the idols and replaced the solid altar and its vessels. *On twenty-fifth of Kislev,* and for the seven days that followed, the dedication, or Hanukkah, of the purified sanctuary was solemnized with praise and sacrifice . . . .[8]

Fourth, contemplate the evidence from Solomon Grayzel, who writes:

In the temple above the altar was placed a statue of Jupiter bearing an obvious resemblance to Antiochus . . . . To that statue were brought as sacrifices the animal most detested by the Jews, the pig. An abominable act had been perpetrated *on the twenty-fifth day of Kislev in the year 168 B.C.E.,* and to use the de-

---

[7] Epstein Isidore, *The Babylonian Talmud* (London: Soncino Press 1935-1960), Shabbath, 21B.

[8] Rufus Learsi [Israel Goldberg], *A History of the Jewish People* (Cleveland, Ohio: World Publishing Co., 1949), pp. 131, 133, 134.

scriptive expression in the book of Maccabees, it left the Jewish people desolate.[9]

Grayzel continues:

The Maccabean army approached the sacred city which had been in the hands of the enemy for almost three years . . . only a small Syrian force remained, protected by the walls of Acra, a fortress they had built near the temple. But the Maccabean soldiers did not advance against Acra. Around that fort they stationed enough men to keep the garrison from interfering in other work they were planning. The simple peasants . . . now drop the sword in order to do what they had really been fighting for: cleanse the temple and re-establish its worship. They removed every sign of paganism. They took apart the altar which had been defiled by pagan sacrifices and put aside its stones. They erected a new altar in its place. *Exactly three years after the 'desolating abomination' had been introduced into the temple*, they ground the statue of Zeus--Antiochus, into dust, and rededicated the temple to the worship of God. *Beginning with the twenty-fifth of Kislev (165 B.C.E.), they celebrated the dedication--feast* (Hanukkah) for eight days.[10]

Fifth, weigh the evidence from *Israel My Glory*. It says:

Antiochus had launched a successful military campaign against Egypt. *In the year 168 B.C.* he returned a second time. The purpose of this expedition was to consolidate his early victory and bring Egypt under Syrian domination. History records that on this occasion he was met by a courier empowered by the senate in Rome who, for political reasons, opposed Syria's conquest of Egypt.

---

[9] Solomon Grayzel, *A History of the Jews* (Philadelphia, Pa.: Jewish Publication Society of America, 1947), p. 56.
[10] Ibid., p. 61.

The choice he was offered was clear: he must break off his attack against Egypt or face war with Rome. Frustrated in his attempt to expand his kingdom at the very moment of apparent success, he started home. On the way *Antiochus stopped in Jerusalem. He had a pig killed on the brazen altar* at the Temple. And then Antiochus committed, to the religious Jew, the ultimate offence--he had his soldiers carry a statue of Zeus Olympius, the chief Syrian deity, into the holy of holies . . . . *After a three-year struggle, the Jews drove the Syrian army out of the Promised Land.* For the triumphant Jews, the first order of business was the Temple of Jehovah at Jerusalem. Both the altar and the holy of holies had been desecrated. A pig had been slain on the altar, and the image of a heathen deity had been carried into the Temple. *This desecration had occurred on the twenty-fifth day of the Hebrew month Kislev (corresponding to December 25), and exactly three years later, to the day, the altar and temple were cleansed.*[11]

Sixth, reflect upon the evidence from James Hastings, who writes:

Upon the altar of burnt-offering a smaller altar was built, and *on the twenty-fifth of Kislev (December 168) sacrifice was offered upon it to the olympic Zeus* . . . . *In B.C. 165 Lysias* in person led a still larger army against Judas, but *was completely defeated* at Bethzur . . . Judas regained possession of the entire country except the citadel in Jerus., *and on the twenty-fifth of Kislev the daily sacrifices were restored* . . . . [12]

Seventh, esteem the evidence of Biederwolf, who writes:

---

[11] Marvin Rosenthal, "Why Do We Celebrate Christmas on December 25th?" *Israel My Glory*, December/January 1986-87, p. 3.

[12] James Hastings, *A Dictionary of the Bible, Volume I* (Edinburgh: T & T Clark, 1898), p. 106.

Antiochus Epiphanes took Jerusalem in B.C. 170. Three years later, B.C. 167, in June he sent Appolonius against the city who at that time caused all sacrifices to cease. On December of the same year Appolonius set up the heathen altar in the temple and *on December 25 the heathen sacrifices began. Three years later on this same date, December 25, B.C. 164, Judas Maccabeus restored the true sacrifice . . . .*[13]

Eighth, ponder the evidence of Alfred Edersheim, who writes:

The date of the final profanation of the temple was the twenty-fifth Chislev (corresponding to our December)--the same on which, after its purification by Judas Maccabee, *its services were restored . . .* Mattathias died before it came to any actual engagement with the Syrians, but victory after victory attended the arms of his son Judas the Maccabee, till at last the temple could be purified and its services restored, *exactly three years after its desecration (25 Chislev, 165 B.C.).*[14]

The dates given by Jewish authorities are December 25, 168 B.C., and December 25, 165 B.C. The dates given by some Christian authorities are December 25, 167 B.C., and December 25, 164 B.C. The crucial fact is that *the time between the offering of the pagan sacrifice* in the second temple on December 25 *and the cleansing of the temple* on a later December 25 *was exactly three years.* Three solar years equals 1,095 and three-quarter days. Knowledge of this fact is vital if we are to get off the rabbit trail and get back on the 'possum trail.

---

[13] Biederwolf, p. 215.

[14] Alfred Edersheim, *The Life and Times of Jesus the Messiah, Volume Two* (Grand Rapids, Mich.: Wm. B. Eerdmans Publishing Co., n.d.), pp. 670, 671.

The preceding historical information is extremely important, *because* it proves that *the little horn of Daniel 8:9-14 could not have been Antiochus Epiphanes.* The reason is simple. Antiochus Epiphanes defiled the second temple for exactly three years. Three years is 1,095 and three-quarter days. The Bible says that the little horn of Daniel 8:9-14 will desolate the sanctuary for 2,300 days. If you take the Bible literally, 2,300 days is not equivalent to 1,095 and three-quarter days. Accordingly, *the little horn of Daniel 8:9-14 cannot be Antiochus Epiphanes.*

Therefore, *the little horn of Daniel 8:9 must refer to the coming Antichrist* at the "time of the end." Antiochus Epiphanes did not desecrate the second temple for 2,300 days. He desecrated the second temple for 1,095 and three-quarter days or exactly three solar years. For those who truly interpret the Bible literally, Antiochus Epiphanes could not have been the little horn of Daniel 8:9-14, because the number of days that he defiled the second sanctuary does not match the number of days that the little horn will defile the third sanctuary.

Not only do we have historical evidence concerning Antiochus Epiphanes, but we also have additional evidence found in Daniel eight. The inspired words describing the career of the little horn further confirm that the little horn of Daniel 8:9-14 must refer to the Antichrist of "the time of the end."

For instance, Daniel 8:10 says, "And it [the little horn] waxed great, even to the host of heaven; and *it cast down some* of the host and *of the stars to the ground,* and stamped upon them." Antiochus never had this kind of power, and he never cast stars to the ground. Antichrist, on the other hand, will be empowered by Satan, who will cast angels to the earth. In the book of Revelation, John writes:

> And I . . . saw a beast rise up out of the sea . . . and *the dragon gave him his power*, and his seat, and great authority . . . . And they worshipped the dragon which gave power unto the beast: and they worshipped the beast . . . and power was given unto him to continue forty and two months. And he opened his mouth in blasphemy against God, to blaspheme his name . . . . And it was given unto him to make war with the saints, and to overcome them . . . .[15]

In Revelation chapter twelve, we read about the dragon who gives the beast his power and his seat and great authority. John writes:

> And there appeared another wonder in heaven; and behold *a great red dragon . . . and his tail drew the third part of the stars of heaven, and did cast them to the earth* [These stars are angel stars, like the stars in Job 38:7, Revelation 1:20, and Revelation 9:1. The stars in Job 38:7 and Revelation 1:20 are good angels, and the stars in Revelation 12:4 and 9 are evil angels].[16]

Moreover, in Revelation chapter twelve, John said, "And the great dragon was cast out, that old serpent, called the Devil, and Satan, which deceiveth the whole world: he was cast out into the earth, and *his angels were cast out with him.*"[17] Here we see that the *stars* of Revelation 12:4 are said to be *angels* in Revelation 12:9.

Getting back to Daniel, we must emphasize that Antiochus Epiphanes never had the power "to cast down some of the host and of the stars to the ground." Further-

---

[15] Revelation 13:1, 2, 4-7.

[16] Revelation 12:3, 4, 9.

[17] Revelation 12:9.

more, there is nothing in the Bible to indicate that stars were cast down in 168 B.C.

Daniel 8:11 says, "Yea, he [the little horn] magnified himself even to the prince of the host [Larkin said, "the Lord Himself"], and by him the daily sacrifice was taken away." The Antichrist will cause the sacrifice and the oblation to cease in the midst of Daniel's Seventieth Week, when the abomination of desolation stands in the holy place.[18]

Daniel 8:15-17 says:

> And it came to pass, when I, even I Daniel, had seen the vision, and sought for the meaning, then, behold, there stood before me as the appearance of a man. And I heard a man's voice between the banks of Ulai, which called, and said, *Gabriel, make this man to understand the vision.* So he came near where I stood: and when he came, I was afraid, and fell upon my face: but he said unto me, Understand, O son of man: for *at the time of the end shall be the vision.*

Here, Gabriel explains to Daniel that the vision will be *at the time of the end.* Antiochus Epiphanes did *not* live at the time of the end; he did *not* even live at the time of the end of the Seleucid empire, for he was the eighth of 26 kings in the Seleucid line. Certainly, Antiochus Epiphanes, who died in 164 B.C., will not be around "at the time of the end," which will occur at the end of the Great Tribulation period.[19]

It must be stressed emphatically that Antiochus Epiphanes simply does not qualify as the little horn of Daniel 8:9. The only one who does qualify is the Antichrist of "the time of the end."

---

[18] Daniel 9:27, Matthew 24:15.
[19] Matthew 24:13, 14.

In Daniel eight, Gabriel continues, "Behold, I will make thee know what shall be *in the last end of the indignation*: for at the time appointed *the end* shall be."[20] Then Daniel 8:24 says, "And his power shall be mighty, but not by his own power: and he shall destroy wonderfully . . . and shall destroy the mighty and the holy people." Daniel 8:25b continues, *"He shall also stand up against the Prince of princes . . . ."* Bear in mind that Antiochus Epiphanes never stood up against the Prince of princes.

However, the Antichrist will literally stand up against the Prince of princes, for in Revelation, John writes, *"And I saw the beast, and the kings of the earth, and their armies, gathered together to make war against him that sat on the horse, and against his army."*[21]

Daniel 8:25b says, "But he shall *be broken* without hand." I Maccabees 6:4, 16 inform us that *Antiochus Epiphanes died a natural death* in Babylon. On the other hand, Scripture reveals that the Antichrist will be destroyed by the Lord Himself. Paul said, "And then shall that Wicked be revealed, whom the Lord shall *consume* with the spirit of his mouth, and shall *destroy* with the brightness of his coming."[22]

The determinative interpretation given by Gabriel to Daniel proves clearly that the little horn could not have been Antiochus Epiphanes. Rather, the interpretation given by Gabriel to Daniel clearly shows that the little horn of Daniel eight is none other than the Antichrist of "the time of the end."

---

[20] Daniel 8:19.

[21] Revelation 19:19.

[22] II Thessalonians 2:8.

Clarence Larkin, who saw this truth, writes:

> Now notice, and this is the *'key'* to the Vision, that the Vision
> has to do with the *'time of the end.'* The *'time of the end'* is a
> definite statement of Scripture, and has reference to the *'end'* of
> the 'Times of the Gentiles.' The Vision then had no bearing
> upon the times in which he lived, and so, after it had been
> explained to him, he was told 'to shut it up,' for it would not be
> fulfilled for *'many days,'* (verse 26), that is, until the *'time of the
> end.'* So the *'end time'* of this Vision is the same *'end time'* of
> all the 'Dreams' and 'Visions' in the Book.[23]

In short, the "little horn" of Daniel 8:9 was not fulfilled in and by the historical personage of Antiochus
Epiphanes. Therefore, the little horn of Daniel 8:9 can be
none other than the Antichrist of "the time of the end."
Understanding that the little horn of Daniel 8:9 refers to
the Antichrist is *the key* to comprehending the revelation
of "the transgression of desolation," which the Bible says
will last for exactly 2,300 days.

What will occur during the 2,300 days of the transgression of desolation? The answer is given in the next
chapter.

---

[23] Larkin, p. 159.

ANTIOCHUS EPIPHANES' DESECRATION OF 2ND TEMPLE

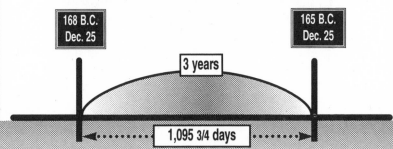

Antiochus IV, Epiphanes reigned 175 – 164
Source: Webster's 9th New Collegiate Dictionary

Antiochus IV, Epiphanes reigned 176 – 164 B.C.
Source: Encyclopaedia Britannica – 11th edition

The Jews were ordered under pain of death to substitute for their own observances the pagan rites prescribed for the empire generally. In December 168, sacrifice was offered to Zeus upon an idol altar....
Source: Encyclopaedia Britannica – 11th edition

Antiochus IV, or Antiochus Epiphanes (d. 164 B.C.)
Source: The Encyclopaedia Americana

Jerusalem was overrun, pagan rites were ordered to be substituted for Jewish, and a sacrifice to Zeus was offered (168) on the Temple altar. In 165, he [Judas Maccabaeus] reconsecrated the Temple amid the exultation of the people – the festival of Hanukkah, in memory of this restoration, is still observed by the Jews....
Source: Encyclopaedia Britannica – 11th edition

CHART 7

The "little horn" of Daniel 8:13, 14 cannot be Antiochus Epiphanes, for he did not defile the second temple for 2,300 days. The little horn of Daniel 8 is the future Antichrist.

EIGHT

THE TRANSGRESSION OF DESOLATION

". . . How long shall be the vision concerning the daily sacrifice, and the transgression of desolation, to give both the sanctuary and the host to be trodden under foot?"

— *Daniel 8:13b*

In the third year of the reign of king Belshazzar, a vision of overriding importance was given to Daniel. The vision deals with the little horn and *the transgression of desolation.* The crucial passage which records the vision says:

And out of one of them came forth a little horn, which waxed exceeding great, toward the south, and toward the east, and toward the pleasant land. And it waxed great, even to the host of heaven; and it cast down some of the host and of the stars to the ground, and stamped upon them. Yea, he magnified himself even to the prince of the host, and by him the daily sacrifice was taken away, and the place of his sanctuary was cast down. And an host was given him against the daily sacrifice by reason of transgression, and it cast down the truth to the ground; and it practised, and prospered. Then I heard one saint speaking, and another saint said unto that certain saint which spake, *How long shall be* the vision concerning the daily sacrifice, and *the transgression of desolation, to give both the sanctuary and the host to be trodden under foot?* And he said unto me, *Unto two thousand and three hundred days; then shall the sanctuary be cleansed.*[1]

After receiving the vision, Daniel said, "When I, even I Daniel, had seen the vision, and sought for the meaning, then . . . I heard a man's voice . . . which called and said, Gabriel, make this man to understand the vision."[2] Then Gabriel said to Daniel:

> *Understand*, O son of man: for *at the time of the end* shall be the vision . . . Behold, I will make thee know what shall be in *the last end of the indignation*: for at the time appointed *the end* shall be.[3]

In these vital verses, Gabriel revealed that the vision concerning *the transgression of desolation will occur at the time of the end.* Now, let us zoom in on what the Bible calls the transgression of desolation.

WHAT WILL OCCUR DURING THE TRANSGRESSION OF DESOLATION?

Daniel 8:9-14 reveals that the little horn will do the following things:

1.   He will wax great, even to the host of heaven.

2.   He will cast down some of the host and of the stars to the ground.

3.   He will magnify himself even to the prince of the

---

[1] Daniel 8:9-14.
[2] Daniel 8:15, 16.
[3] Daniel 8:17-19.

host. Larkin says that the prince of the host is the Lord Jesus Christ.[4] Lange likewise said, "The 'prince of the host' is . . . the Most High God Himself . . . ."[5]

4. He will take away the daily sacrifice.

5. He will cast down the place of the sanctuary. Larkin says that "cast down" means "desolate." According to Webster's 1828 Dictionary, desolate means, "To lay waste; to ruin; to ravage; to destroy . . . ."[6]

6. A host will be given him against the daily sacrifice. Regarding this passage, Lange said,

. . . war raised against the daily sacrifice . . . [the] idea is that compulsion is employed for the purpose of introducing idolatrous worship in place of the service of the true God, and particularly, compulsion to service in the host, so that 'host stands opposed to host, serfdom to the true service (of God), coercion to freedom.'[7]

7. He will cast down truth to the ground. Concerning this statement, Lange says, "The 'truth' to be cast down by this 'horn' is the true reli-

[4] Larkin, p. 157.

[5] John Peter Lange, *Lange's Commentary on the Holy Scriptures, Volume 7* (Grand Rapids, Mich.: Zondervan Publishing House, 1960), p. 176.

[6] Noah Webster, *American Dictionary of the English Language, 1828 Edition* (San Francisco, Calif.: Foundation for American Christian Education, 1967).

[7] Lange, p. 176.

gion, the objective truth of God, which is revealed in the law and the prophets . . . ."[8]

8. He will practice and prosper. Regarding this
statement, Lange says, ". . . it accomplishes this,
and prospers, namely, because of the Divine permission."[9]

These wicked deeds of the little horn of Daniel eight
include specific deeds that will constitute the transgression of desolation.

WHO IS THE DESOLATER?

In Daniel 8:9-14, *the desolater of the sanctuary is the
little horn.* In the previous chapter, it was demonstrated
that the little horn of Daniel eight was not fulfilled in and
by Antiochus Epiphanes. Furthermore, it was established
that the little horn of Daniel eight is none other than the
Antichrist of the end time. That *the little horn, namely,
the Antichrist, will be the desolater of the third temple* is
confirmed by Daniel 9:27, which says:

And he shall confirm the covenant with many for one week: and
in the midst of the week he shall cause the sacrifice and the
oblation to cease, and for the overspreading of abominations *he
shall make it desolate*, even until the consummation, and that
determined shall be poured upon the desolate.

This verse states clearly that he (Antichrist) will make
it (the third sanctuary) desolate. Moreover, in Matthew
24:15 Jesus says, "When ye therefore shall see the abomi-

---

[8] Ibid., p. 177.
[9] Ibid.

nation of desolation, *spoken of by Daniel the prophet*,
stand in the holy place, (whoso readeth, let him understand:) . . . for then shall be great tribulation . . . ." The
Antichrist will be involved with the placing of the abomination of desolation in the holy place of the third sanctuary.

Once again, while writing about the Antichrist, Paul
said, "Who opposeth and exalteth himself above all that is
called God, or that is worshipped; so that *he as God
sitteth in the temple of God,* shewing himself that he is
God."[10] This blasphemous act will desolate the sanctuary
or temple. The Bible is perfectly clear in its teaching that
the Antichrist will desolate the third sanctuary. Larkin
writes, "When Christ shall return . . . *the 'desolater'
(Antichrist)* shall be destroyed by 'the brightness of his
coming.'"[11] Regarding the identity of the desolater, that
is, the little horn in Daniel chapter eight, Arthur Pink
writes:

> In Dan. 8 *the little horn* is before us again, and that it *is the
> same dread personage as in chapter 7* appears from what is
> predicted of him. First, he is referred to as 'a king of fierce
> countenance' (8:23), which agrees with 'whose look was more
> stout than his fellows' (7:20). Second, it is said of him that he
> 'waxed exceeding great (first) towards the south, and (second)
> towards the east, and (third) toward the pleasant land' (8:9),
> which agrees with 'there came up among them another little
> horn, before whom there were three of the first horns plucked
> up' (7:8). Third, it should be said that he 'shall destroy the
> mighty and the holy people' (8:24), which agrees with 'and the
> same horn made war against the saints and prevailed against
> them' (7:21). There should, then, be no doubt whatever that the

[10] II Thessalonians 2:4.
[11] Larkin, p. 214.

'little horn' of Daniel 7 and the 'little horn' of Daniel 8 refer to one and the same person. Their moral features coincide: both persecute the people of God: both are stricken down by direct interposition of God. We may add that Messrs. B.W. Newton, James Inglis, G.H. Pember, Sir Robert Anderson, Drs. Tregelles, J.H. Brookes, Haldeman, and a host of other devout scholars and students, take the same view, namely, that the 'little horn' of Daniel 7 and 8 and the Man of Sin are one and the same person.[12]

Clarence Larkin was dogmatic in identifying the little horn of Daniel seven and eight as the Antichrist. He writes:

Neither will it do to say that by the 'Little Horn' Antiochus Epiphanes is meant. Antiochus did not live in the 'Latter Time' of those Kingdoms [Greece, Egypt, Thrace, Syria]. He was the eighth of twenty-six kings that ruled over Syria, and died in B.C. 164, or 134 years before the last of the 'Four Kingdoms' disappeared. As Antiochus was one of the twenty-six kings who constituted the 'Syrian Horn,' he could not be that 'Horn' and also the 'Little Horn' that sprang out of it. The 'Little Horn' waxed exceedingly great, but Antiochus never did. It is true that he desecrated the temple at Jerusalem, but the Maccabees rebelled, and in B.C. 165 restored its worship. When Jesus spoke of the 'abomination of desolation' spoken of by Daniel the prophet (Matthew 24:15), He did not refer to it as a thing of the past, but as something still future, therefore, it was not something connected with the career of Antiochus, for he had been dead nearly 200 years. Antiochus never stood up against the 'Prince of Princes' (Christ), for he died 160 years before Christ was born. Neither was he 'broken without hand,' for he died a natural death at Tabae (Persia) in B.C. 164. It will not do to say that verses 9-12 refer to Antiochus, and verses 23-25 to Antichrist, for verses 23-25 refer to some future person. *Verses*

[12] Arthur W. Pink, *The Antichrist* (Grand Rapids, Mich.: Kregel Publications, 1988), pp. 151, 152.

23-25 are the interpretation of verses 9-12, and therefore, the same person [Antichrist] *must be meant.* Therefore, if verses 23-25 refer to some future person, verses 9-12 cannot refer to Antiochus. [13]

WHAT WILL BE DESOLATED?

In Daniel 8:9-14, it is apparent that the sanctuary will be cast down (desolated) and trodden under foot. This truth is confirmed by Daniel 9:27, which says:

> And he shall confirm the covenant with many for one week: and *in the midst of the week* he shall cause the sacrifice and the oblation to cease, and for the overspreading of abominations *he* [Antichrist] *shall make it* [the sanctuary] *desolate*, even until the consummation, and that determined shall be poured upon the desolate.

The desolation of the sanctuary and its service is further confirmed by Daniel 12:11, which says, "And from the time that the daily sacrifice shall be taken away, and the abomination that maketh desolate set up, there shall be a thousand two hundred and ninety days." In His Olivet Discourse, Jesus referred to these statements in the book of Daniel, when He said, "When ye therefore shall see *the abomination of desolation, spoken of by Daniel the prophet*, stand in the holy place, (whoso readeth, let him understand:) . . . ."[14] The abomination of desolation, which will stand in the holy place of the third sanctuary, will desolate that sanctuary. Therefore, the Bible teaches plainly that the third sanctuary will be desolated.

---

[13] Larkin, pp. 164, 165.
[14] Matthew 24:15.

WHAT EVENTS WILL DESOLATE THE SANCTUARY?

One event that will desolate the tribulation sanctuary will be the standing of the abomination of desolation in the holy place. The abomination to which Jesus referred in His Olivet Discourse (in the phrase "the abomination of desolation") is not a person; it is a thing. The Greek words for "the abomination" are <u>to</u> <u>bdelugma</u>. These words are neuter. Therefore, the abomination is a thing, not a person. This is confirmed in the Authorized Version, for Mark 13:14 says, "But when ye shall see the abomination of desolation, spoken of by Daniel the prophet, standing where *it* ought not . . . ." Larkin writes:

> . . . in the 'Midst of the seventieth week,' the Antichrist will break the Covenant . . . and cause the 'Sacrifice and oblation' to cease, and the 'Abomination of Desolation' to stand in the Holy Place of the rebuilt temple (Matthew 24:15), which 'Abomination of Desolation' will be an *'Image of the Beast*,' that the 'False Prophet' will cause the followers of Antichrist to erect and worship under penalty of death . . . This 'Image' will be the Anti-type of the 'Golden Image' that Nebuchadnezzar commanded to be made in the 'Plain of Dura' in the Province of Babylon (Daniel 3:1-30), before which, at the sounding of musical instruments, the people were commanded to bow down and worship under penalty, for those who disobeyed, of being cast into a *"Burning Fiery Furnace."* Doubtless there will be many in the 'Day of Antichrist' who will refuse to bow down and worship the 'Image of the Beast' and who will not escape as did the 'Three Hebrew Children,' unless miraculously delivered by God, *but will die by the 'Guillotine.'* Rev. 20:4.[15]

---

[15] Larkin, pp. 213, 214.

Another event that will desolate the tribulation sanctuary will be the Antichrist himself sitting in the tribulation sanctuary, showing himself that he is God. Concerning the man of sin, Paul writes: "Who opposeth and exalteth himself above all that is called God, or that is worshipped; so that *he as God sitteth in the temple of God,* shewing himself that he is God."[16]

Yet another event that will desolate the third sanctuary will be its cleansing by destruction. This writer, along with others, believes that the third sanctuary will be destroyed at the end of the 2,300 days.

The first temple was desolated by Jewish idolatry (Ezekiel 8), and it was destroyed by the Babylonians in 586 B.C. The second temple was desolated by the Jews who rejected Jesus Christ and continued to offer animal sacrifices, which were, in effect, a blasphemous repudiation of the finished work of Christ. Hence, the second temple was destroyed by the Romans in A.D. 70. In their book *The Coming Temple*, Chuck Missler and Don Stewart write:

> With four Legions, Titus the Roman began a siege of Jerusalem in April, A.D. 70. He posted his 10th legion on the Mount of Olives, directly east of and overlooking the Temple Mount. The 12th and 15th legions were stationed on Mount Scopus, further to the east and commanding all ways to Jerusalem from east to north. The 5th legion was held in reserve . . . 'The principal [sic] officers were of the opinion that nothing less than the utter destruction of the Temple would secure a lasting peace' . . . . On the 10th of August, in A.D. 70, . . . the very day when Nebuchad-

---

[16] II Thessalonians 2:4.

nezzar burned the Temple in 586 B.C., the Temple was burned again. Titus took the city and put it to the torch.[17]

Moreover, when Hezekiah became king of Judah, the land had been desolated by idolatry and abominations of all kinds. Hezekiah cleansed the land *by destroying the unclean things.* Regarding the cleansing of the land by Hezekiah, the Bible says:

> Now it came to pass in the third year of Hoshea son of Elah king of Israel, that Hezekiah the son of Ahaz king of Judah began to reign . . . And he did that which was right in the sight of the LORD, according to all that David his father did. *He removed the high places, and brake the images, and cut down the groves, and brake in pieces the brasen serpent* that Moses had made: for unto those days the children of Israel did burn incense to it . . . .[18]

Another important fact to consider, while pondering the cleansing of the third sanctuary, is that the Lord Himself will build the millennial temple. Therefore, there will be no need for the continuing existence of the tribulation sanctuary. Zechariah 6:11, 13 say,

> . . . Thus speaketh the LORD of hosts, saying, Behold the man whose name is The BRANCH; and he shall grow up out of his place, and *he [namely, Christ] shall build the temple* of the Lord: *even he shall build the temple of the Lord; and he shall bear the glory, and shall sit and rule upon his throne:* and he shall be a priest upon his throne: and the counsel of peace shall be between them both.

---

[17] Chuck Missler and Don Stewart, *The Coming Temple* (Orange, Calif.: Dart Press, 1991), pp. 52, 53.

[18] II Kings 18:1-4.

Missler and Stewart write: "What will become of the Tribulation Temple? It will probably be destroyed . . . ."[19]

WHEN WILL THE TRANSGRESSION OF DESOLATION BEGIN?

Daniel 8:11 says, ". . . *by him* [the little horn, namely, the Antichrist] *the daily sacrifice was taken away, and the place of his sanctuary was cast down.*" In Daniel 9:27, the Scripture says, "And he shall confirm the covenant with many for one week: and *in the midst of the week he shall cause the sacrifice and the oblation to cease, and for the overspreading of abominations he shall make it desolate . . . .*" These two verses taken together show that the little horn, namely, the Antichrist, will cause the sacrifice and oblation to cease and will cast down (desolate) the sanctuary in the midst of the Seventieth Week. Since the Seventieth Week is seven years long, the desolation of the sanctuary will start precisely three and one-half years before the end of the Seventieth Week. Again, in Matthew 24:15, 21 Jesus says:

> *When ye therefore shall see the abomination of desolation, spoken of by Daniel the prophet, stand in the holy place,* (whoso readeth, let him understand:) . . . *For then shall be great tribulation,* such as was not since the beginning of the world to this time, no, nor ever shall be.

Inasmuch as the placing of the abomination of desolation in the holy place will start the Great Tribulation, and because the Great Tribulation will run for the last three and one-half years of Daniel's Seventieth Week, the

---

[19] Missler and Stewart, p. 198.

Great Tribulation will, accordingly, begin in the midst of the Seventieth Week. Furthermore, since the Great Tribulation and the transgression of desolation will start at the same time, the transgression of desolation will, therefore, begin in the midst of the Seventieth Week, or three and one-half years before the end of the Great Tribulation.

Speaking of the little horn of Daniel eight, whom he identifies as the Antichrist, Pink writes:

> 'In the midst of the week he shall cause the sacrifice and oblation to cease.' The returned Jews will rebuild their temple and there offer sacrifices. But these, so far from being acceptable to God, will be an offense . . . But three and a half years before the end, the Prince will issue a decree demanding that the sacrifices must cease, and the worship of Jehovah be transferred to himself, for it is at this point that he shall 'exalt himself above all that is called God, or that is worshipped' (II Thess. 2:4). The fact that we are here told that *he* causes the sacrifices and the oblation to cease, at once identifies this Prince . . . as the Antichrist -- cf. 8:11.[20]

In his commentary on Daniel, Larkin writes:

> The question . . . was, 'How long shall be the vision concerning the "Daily Sacrifice," and the "Transgression of Desolation," to give both the Sanctuary and the host to be trodden under foot?' This question was prompted by the previous statement, that the 'Little Horn' would take away the 'Daily Sacrifice' and the 'Place of His Sanctuary' (the temple) would be cast down, or desolated. The answer to the question was--'Unto two thousand and three hundred days.' *Now as these days are literal days, and date from the time when the Daily Sacrifice' shall be taken away by the 'Little Horn'* (the Antichrist), *which is in the 'Middle' of*

---

[20] Pink, pp. 157, 158.

Daniel's 'Seventieth week' (Daniel 9:27), then these 2,300 days begin in the 'Middle of the seventieth week,' . . . .[21]

The Bible teaches plainly that the transgression of desolation will begin when the Great Tribulation begins in the midst of Daniel's Seventieth Week. This will be three and one-half years before the end of the Great Tribulation and Daniel's Seventieth Week.

HOW LONG WILL THE TRANSGRESSION OF DESOLATION LAST?

The question posed in the above heading was asked by one saint and answered by another. Daniel wrote:

> Then I heard one saint speaking, and another saint said unto that certain saint which spake, *How long shall be* the vision concerning the daily sacrifice, and *the transgression of desolation, to give both the sanctuary and the host to be trodden under foot?* And he said unto me, *Unto two thousand and three hundred days*; then shall the sanctuary be cleansed.[22]

The question was, *"How long shall be* the vision concerning the daily sacrifice and *the transgression of desolation, to give both the sanctuary and the host to be trodden under foot . . . ?"*

The answer was clear, plain, explicit, unclouded, open, and unambiguous. The saint said, *"Unto two thousand three hundred days*; then shall the sanctuary be cleansed."

Pink wrote, "This two thousand three hundred days is the whole period during which the false messiah will

---

[21] Larkin, p. 158.
[22] Daniel 8:13, 14.

practice *in Jerusalem and have power over the 'sanctuary'....*"[23]

Larkin wrote,

> *Now these days are literal days*, and date from the time when the 'Daily Sacrifice' shall be taken away by the 'Little Horn' (the Antichrist), which is in the 'Middle' of Daniel's 'Seventieth Week' (Daniel 9:27) ....[24]

An 1830 article entitled "Review of Maitland on the 1260 Days" makes the viewpoint of early nineteenth-century Bible scholars quite clear. MacPherson writes:

> With reference to Daniel 8:14's 2300 days ... ending in the sanctuary cleansing, an anonymous writer in the same Irvingite journal (June 1830) declared: *'The number two thousand three hundred... must also of very necessity reach down to the cleansing of the sanctuary... which, by the confession of all, is still future* ....[25]

Did you get that? *"The confession of all,"* in 1830, was that the cleansing of the sanctuary was still future!

WILL THE 2,300 DAYS OVERRUN THE GREAT TRIBULATION?

In our chapter on "The Tribulation," it was shown that the Great Tribulation will last exactly three and one-half years or forty-two months or 1,260 days. *The transgression of desolation*, which begins in the midst of the Seventieth Week, as does the Great Tribulation, *will run*

---

[23] Pink, p. 102.

[24] Larkin, p. 158.

[25] Dave MacPherson, *The Rapture Plot* (Simpsonville, S.C.: Millennium III Publishers, 1994), p. 105.

for 2,300 days. Therefore, *the transgression of desolation will overrun the Great Tribulation by 1,040 days. Accordingly, this overrun means that the transgression of desolation will continue 1,040 days beyond the end of the Great Tribulation into the millennial kingdom.* A literal interpretation of the Bible makes this view mandatory.

Larkin writes:

> Now as these days are literal days, and date from the time when the 'Daily Sacrifice' shall be taken away by the 'Little Horn' (the Antichrist), which is in the 'Middle' of Daniel's 'Seventieth Week' (Daniel 9:27), then these 2,300 days begin in the 'Middle of the Seventieth Week,' and as the 'Week' is seven years long, half the 'Week' would be three and one-half years, or forty-two months of thirty days each, or 1,260 days. *This would make the 2,300 days overrun the last half of the Seventieth Week 1,040 days, or two years, ten months, and twenty days.*[26]

Notice carefully what Larkin saw. He saw that since the duration of the transgression of desolation will be 2,300 days, the transgression of desolation will, therefore, overrun the Great Tribulation 1,040 days. While reading Daniel eight, the writer saw the same truth, independently of Larkin. The writer simply subtracted 1,260 days from 2,300 days. The remainder was 1,040 days. The writer then understood that the transgression of desolation must overrun the Great Tribulation 1,040 days into the millennium. Later, when reading Larkin, the writer learned that Larkin had previously seen the same truth.

---

[26] Larkin, p. 158.

WILL ANTICHRIST'S REIGN CONTINUE THROUGH THE 2,300 DAYS?

Immediately *after* the Great Tribulation, when the sixth seal is opened, the Antichrist and his kingdom will come under fierce onslaught.

1.   His kingdom and dominion will come under assault by the infinitely more powerful Kingdom of Christ.

2.   When the saints who survive the Great Tribulation are delivered from his hand by the post-tribulational rapture, his war to kill all the saints will end without his goal having been achieved.

The downfall of Antichrist's kingdom and dominion is described in Daniel seven, which says:

And he shall speak great words against the most High, and shall wear out the saints of the most High . . . and they shall be given into his hand until a time and times and the dividing of time. But the judgment shall sit, and they shall take away his dominion, to consume and to destroy it unto the end. And the kingdom and dominion, and the greatness of the kingdom under the whole heaven, shall be given to the people of the saints of the most High, whose kingdom is an everlasting kingdom, and all dominions shall serve and obey him.[27]

In II Kings chapter three, we have a biblical example of what will happen during the 1,040 days, when the Day of the Lord begins *after* the Great Tribulation. This chapter tells of Jehoram, king of Israel, crushing the rebellion

---

[27] Daniel 7:25-28.

of the king of Moab. Jehoram, whose reign continued during and after the rebellion, formed a coalition with Jehoshaphat (the king of Judah) and the king of Edom. During the time that the coalition was being formed and the armies were being trained to put down the rebellion in a great battle, Jehoram reigned as the king of Israel. Mesha, although he was a king, was not the supreme king of the region; he was a mere rebel king. The putting down of the rebellion required some time, but throughout the duration of the rebellion, Jehoram was reigning as the king of Israel, and *he was the supreme king of the region.*

Even so, when the Day of the Lord (namely, the millennial kingdom) begins just after the sun and moon are darkened and the stars fall from heaven to the earth, Jesus Christ will begin His reign over the kingdoms of this world. At the time Christ begins His reign, there will still be rebellion on the earth. That rebellion, still led by the Antichrist, will be crushed during the 1,040 days by means of the seven trumpet judgments, the seven vial judgments, and the Battle of Armageddon.

The kingdom of our God and the power of His Christ will begin just after the sun and moon are darkened immediately after the Great Tribulation, *when the stars will fall from heaven to the earth.* These stars are fallen angels, as we have seen, and when these stars are cast from heaven to the earth, the millennial kingdom will begin. John writes:

> *And the great dragon was cast out*, that old serpent, called the Devil, and Satan, which deceiveth the whole world: *he was cast out into the earth, and his angels were cast out with him.* And I heard a loud voice saying in heaven, *now is come . . . the kingdom of our God, and the power of his Christ: for the*

accuser of our brethren is cast down, which accused them before our God day and night.[28]

The writer's view that the rebellion will continue on the earth during the first 1,040 days of Christ's reign is confirmed by Paul, who writes, *"For he must reign, till he hath put all enemies under his feet."*[29] The Lord Jesus Christ, the King of kings and the Lord of lords, will put the Antichrist, the kings of the earth, and their armies under His feet during the 1,040 days. Later, the final putting of His enemies under His feet will occur with the putting down of the final revolt (Revelation 20:7-9).

WHAT WILL HAPPEN AT THE END OF THE 2,300 DAYS?

Daniel 8:13 says, ". . . How long shall be the vision concerning the daily sacrifice, and the transgression of desolation, to give both the sanctuary and the host to be trodden under foot?" The answer to both the question in verse thirteen and the question in this chapter subheading is given in Daniel 8:14, which says: "And he said unto me, Unto two thousand and three hundred days; *then shall the sanctuary be cleansed.*" The answer to the question (What will happen at the end of the 2,300 days?) is as plain as day. At the end of the 2,300 days, the sanctuary, which will have been trodden under foot for 2,300 days, will be cleansed.

Another event that will occur after the 2,300 days will be the casting of the little horn, namely, the Antichrist, into the lake of fire. After the Antichrist has trodden

---

[28] Revelation 12:9, 10.
[29] Corinthians 15:25.

under foot the sanctuary for 2,300 days, he will meet his Waterloo. John writes:

> And I saw the beast, and the kings of the earth, and their armies, gathered together to make war against him that sat on the horse, and against his army. And the beast was taken, and with him the false prophet that wrought miracles before him, with which he deceived them that had received the mark of the beast, and them that worshipped his image. These both were cast alive into a lake of fire burning with brimstone.[30]

We can now draw several conclusions regarding the transgression of desolation:

1. The Antichrist will cause the sacrifice and oblation to cease in the midst of the Seventieth Week.

2. The Antichrist will tread under foot and desolate the sanctuary, namely, the third temple, for 2,300 days.

3. The Antichrist's desolation of the sanctuary will render it unclean.

4. At the end of the 2,300 days, the sanctuary will be cleansed.

5. The Antichrist, that is, the desolater of the sanctuary, will be cast into the lake of fire at the conclusion of the Battle of Armageddon (Revelation 19:19, 20).

---

[30] Revelation 19:19, 20.

6.   Since the Antichrist will desolate and tread under foot the sanctuary for 2,300 days, and since the Antichrist will be cast into the lake of fire at the conclusion of the Battle of Armageddon, the Battle of Armageddon cannot occur until the 2,300 days have ended.

7.   Since Christ will come in the clouds with power and great glory immediately after the 1,260 days of Great Tribulation, and since the coming of Christ on the white horse for the Battle of Armageddon cannot occur until the 2,300 days have ended, there must, therefore, be a period of 1,040 days between the coming of Christ in the clouds and the coming of Christ on the white horse.

8.   By the pouring out of God's wrath, the Antichrist's kingdom, power, and rebellion will be destroyed during the 1,040 days.

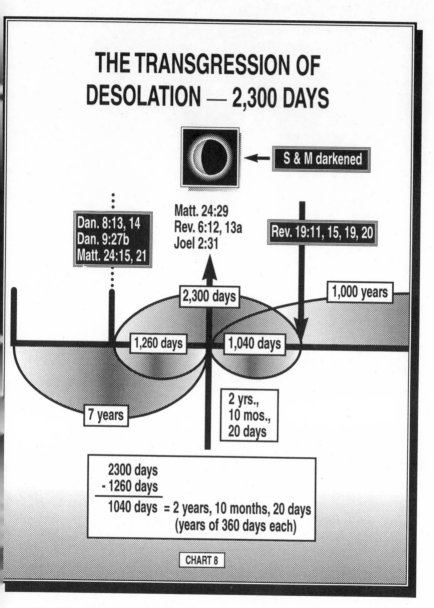

The Trangression of Desolation refers to the future defilement of the third temple by Antichrist. This 2,300-day period begins in the midst of the Seventieth Week and overruns it by 1,040 days into the millennium.

NINE

THE GREAT DAY OF HIS WRATH

"For the great day of his wrath is come; and who shall be able to stand?"

— *Revelation 6:17*

A t the opening of the sixth seal, the sun will be darkened, and the moon will become as blood. This alarming portent will occur immediately after the Great Tribulation. Then, the kings of the earth, every bondman, and every free man will cry to the mountains and rocks, "Fall on us, and hide us from . . . the wrath of the Lamb: *For the great day of his wrath is come*; and who shall be able to stand?" This cry of terrified men is recorded in Revelation six, where John wrote:

And I beheld *when he had opened the sixth seal*, and, lo, there was a great earthquake; and *the sun became black as sackcloth of hair, and the moon became as blood*; And the stars of heaven fell unto the earth, even as a fig tree casteth her untimely figs, when she is shaken of a mighty wind. And the heaven departed as a scroll when it is rolled together; and every mountain and island were moved out of their places. *And the kings of the earth*, and the great men, and the rich men, and the chief captains, and the mighty men, and every bondman, and *every free man, hid themselves in the dens and in the rocks of the mountains; and said* to the mountains and rocks, *Fall on us, and hide us* from the face of him that sitteth on the throne, and *from the wrath of the Lamb: for the great day of his wrath is come;* and who shall be able to stand?[1]

WHAT IS THE GREAT DAY OF HIS WRATH?

"The great day of His wrath" is the period of time during which "the wrath of the Lamb" will be poured out upon a world that has rejected Christ and worshiped Antichrist. It will be coincident with the first 1,040 days of the Day of the Lord just *after* the Great Tribulation. In this chapter, it will be demonstrated that the wrath of the Lamb will be poured out *in* the Day of the Lord *after* Daniel's Seventieth Week (the last half of which is the Great Tribulation).

Walvoord writes, ". . . pretribulationists have identified the day of the Lord as *the millennial kingdom including the judgments that introduce the kingdom.*"[2] The wrath of the Lamb will constitute those judgments that introduce the millennial kingdom, and those judgments will be poured out *in* the great day of His wrath, *in* the early part of the Day of the Lord *after* the Great Tribulation.

WHAT EVENTS WILL OCCUR IN THE GREAT DAY OF HIS WRATH?

Revelation 6:14 through Revelation 19:21 describes the dreadful events of the great day of His wrath. These horrifying happenings will occur *in* the Day of the Lord.

---

[1] Revelation 6:12-17.
[2] Walvoord, *Rapture Question: Revised*, p. 213.

After the sealing of the 144,000 and the opening of the seventh seal (Revelation 7:1-8; 8:1, 7), the seven trumpet judgments will be poured out. Therefore, these horrendous events, which will be an outpouring of the wrath of the Lamb and which will constitute the judgments that introduce the millennial kingdom, will *not* occur during the Seventieth Week of Daniel. Rather, they will occur *in* the Day of the Lord *after* the commencement of the millennial kingdom. This terrifying time, which is called *the great day of His wrath*, will include the following judgments or outpourings of the wrath of the Lamb:

First Trumpet — The third part of trees will be burned up, and all green grass will be burned up.

Second Trumpet — The third part of the sea will become blood; the third part of creatures which are in the sea will die; and the third part of ships will be destroyed.

Third Trumpet — The third part of the rivers and the fountains of waters will become wormwood; and many men will die of the waters, because they will be made bitter.

Fourth Trumpet — The third part of the sun and moon will be smitten, so the third part of them will be darkened.

Fifth Trumpet — The bottomless pit will be opened, and smoke will arise out of the pit. Locusts will arise out of smoke, and the locusts will torment men for five months.

Sixth Trumpet — The third part of men will be killed.

Seventh Trumpet — There will be lightnings, and voices, and thunderings, and an earthquake, and great hail.

After the seven trumpet judgments, the seven vials of God's wrath will be poured out. They will be as follows:

First Vial — Noisome and grievous sores will fall upon the men which will have received the mark of the beast.

Second Vial — The sea will become as blood, and every living soul in the sea will die.

Third Vial — The rivers and fountains of waters will become blood, and those who will have shed the blood of saints will be given blood to drink.

Fourth Vial — Power will be given unto the sun to scorch men with fire and great heat.

Fifth Vial   - Darkness and pain and sores will
                    afflict the kingdom of the beast and
                    the wicked.

Sixth Vial   - The Euphrates River will be dried up
                    that the way of the kings of the east
                    might be prepared; three unclean
                    spirits will gather the kings of the
                    earth to the battle of that great day of
                    God Almighty.

Seventh Vial   - There will be voices, and thunders,
                    and lightnings, and a great earth-
                    quake, and the great city will be
                    divided into three parts, and the cities
                    of nations will fall, and great Babylon
                    will come into remembrance before
                    God, to give unto her the cup of his
                    wrath, and there will fall upon men a
                    great hail, every stone about the
                    weight of a talent.

After the pouring out of the vials of God's wrath, the great whore, Mystery, Babylon the Great, Mother of Harlots and Abominations of the Earth, will be judged.

Then, Christ will come on a white horse to unleash more wrath at Armageddon. John writes:

And I saw heaven opened, and behold a white horse; and he that sat upon him was called Faithful and True, and in righteousness he doth judge and make war. His eyes were as a flame of fire, and on his head were many crowns; and he had a name written, that no man knew, but he himself. And he was clothed with a vesture dipped in blood: and his name is called The Word of

God. And the armies which were in heaven followed him upon white horses, clothed in fine linen, white and clean. *And out of his mouth goeth a sharp sword, that with it he should smite the nations:* and he shall rule them with a rod of iron: *and he treadeth the winepress of the fierceness and wrath of Almighty God. And he hath on his vesture and on his thigh a name written, King of Kings, and Lord of Lords.* And I saw an angel standing in the sun; and he cried with a loud voice, saying to all the fowls that fly in the midst of heaven, Come and gather yourselves together unto the supper of the great God; that ye may eat the flesh of captains, and the flesh of mighty men, and the flesh of horses, and of them that sit on them, and the flesh of all men, both free and bond, both small and great. *And I saw the beast, and the kings of the earth, and their armies, gathered together to make war against him that sat on the horse, and against his army. And the beast was taken, and with him the false prophet* that wrought miracles before him, with which he deceived them that had received the mark of the beast, and them that worshipped his image. *These both were cast alive into a lake of fire burning with brimstone.*[3]

WHEN WILL THE GREAT DAY OF HIS WRATH BEGIN?

First, the opening of the sixth seal will occur *before* the great day of his wrath begins. Revelation 6:12-17 says:

And I beheld *when he had opened the sixth seal,* and, lo, there was a great earthquake; and *the sun became black as sackcloth of hair, and the moon became as blood* . . . And the kings of the earth, and the great men, and the rich men, and the chief captains, and the mighty men, and every bondman, and every free man . . . *said to the mountains and the rocks, Fall on us, and hide us from . . . the wrath of the Lamb: for the great day of his wrath is come; and who shall be able to stand?*

---

[3] Revelation 19:11-20.

Observe carefully that the declaration ("the great day of his wrath is come") is not made until *after* the sixth seal is opened. In the Greek, there is a very important word in Revelation 6:17. That word is <u>elthen</u> ("is come"), and <u>elthen</u> is a second aorist indicative. Regarding the use of the aorist indicative in this verse, Fruchtenbaum said:

> Rosenthal, grammatically speaking, has no more basis to take it [is come] as a future event than Pretribs have to take it as a past event . . . . It is best to go with the context, especially the imme-diate context and see if it indicates how best to take the aorist. In passing, it should be noted that the future use of the aorist is rare, and normally it does refer to a past action. There is no grammatical or contextual reason to make [the] usage of Reve-lation 6:17 future; it is only a theological necessity for Rosenthal. The context does not favor a future meaning . . . . Those speak-ing . . . [in the] text 6:17 are in context responding to the cosmic convulsions . . . [Rev. 6:12-14]; for it is the events of the sixth seal that cause the unbelieving world to flee to the moun-tains and cry 'the [great day of His] wrath . . . has come.' And so, the context favors a past not a future reference. While the wrath of 6:17 may not refer to all the preceding seals, though it may [says who?], *it at least refers to the events of the sixth seal* . . . . It is correct that *there is no grammatical reason to make the aorist tense of the sixth seal retroactive*, but neither is there a grammatical reason to make it future. But there is another grammatical reason to make it past. In the Greek text, the word for 'is come' is not only an aorist, but it is also in the indicative mood. According to Greek grammarians such as Dana and Mantey, this always refers to a past and not a future event.[4]

The aorist indicative in Revelation 6:17 denotes that the action of entrance into the condition of the great day of his wrath occurred in past time with reference to the

---

[4] Fruchtenbaum, "Problems with the Pre-Wrath Rapture," Tape on file at Post-Trib Research Center.

declaration ("the great day of His wrath is come"). Furthermore, the action of entrance into the condition of the great day of his wrath will occur *after* the sixth seal is opened. Fruchtenbaum admitted, "... *there is no grammatical reason to make the aorist tense of the sixth seal retroactive*," that is, to go back to include the events of the first five seals. Not only is there no grammatical reason to make the aorist tense of the sixth seal retroactive, but also, there is a scriptural reason for not doing so. Revelation 6:9-11 shows that entrance into the great day of His wrath has not yet occurred when the fifth seal is opened. This truth will be explained later in this chapter.

Second, the Seventieth Week of Daniel will be completed *before* the great day of His wrath begins. This truth is established clearly by the Scriptures. Jesus said, "Immediately *after* the tribulation of those days shall the sun be darkened, and the moon shall not give her light, and the stars shall fall from heaven, and the powers of the heavens shall be shaken."[5] Here Jesus taught plainly that the sun and moon will be darkened immediately *after* the Great Tribulation. John wrote, "And I beheld when he had opened the sixth seal ... the sun became black as sackcloth of hair, and the moon became as blood: and the stars of heaven fell unto the earth ...."[6] Here, John taught clearly that the sun and the moon will be darkened *when* the sixth seal is opened. Accordingly, the opening of the sixth seal and the end of the Great Tribulation will occur at the same time. It has been shown that the action of entrance into the condition of the great day of His wrath will occur after the sixth seal is opened at the end

---

[5] Matthew 24:29.
[6] Revelation 6:12.

of the Great Tribulation. Since the Great Tribulation is the last half of Daniel's Seventieth Week, the great day of His wrath will begin *after* Daniel's Seventieth Week. Remember, Fruchtenbaum admitted, "... there is no grammatical reason to make the aorist tense of the sixth seal retroactive."[7] Fruchtenbaum's admission will be confirmed later in this chapter when the events that follow the opening of the fifth seal are discussed.

Third, the millennial kingdom will begin before the wrath of the Lamb is poured out during the seven trumpets, the seven vials, and Armageddon. It has been shown that the millennial kingdom will begin when Satan and his angels are cast from heaven to the earth (Revelation 12:4, 9, 10). Furthermore, it has been demonstrated that Satan and his angels will be cast to the earth immediately after the Great Tribulation at the opening of the sixth seal (Matthew 24:29; Revelation 6:12, 13). Consequently, the millennial kingdom, which will commence at the opening of the sixth seal, will begin before the wrath of the Lamb is poured out during the seven trumpets, the seven vials, and Armageddon, for the unparalleled wrath of the trumpets, the vials, and Armageddon will not be poured out until after the seventh seal is opened (Revelation 8:1-7).

This truth is confirmed by the aorist indicative <u>egenonto</u> ("are become") in Revelation 11:15, which says, "And the seventh angel sounded; and there were great voices in heaven, saying, The kingdoms of this world *are become* the kingdoms of our Lord, and of his Christ; and he shall reign for ever and ever." <u>Egenonto</u> ("are become") is a second aorist *indicative*. Regarding the aorist

---

[7] Fruchtenbaum, "Problems with the Pre-Wrath Rapture, Tape on file at Post-Trib Research Center.

tense, Dana and Mantey wrote, *"Its time relations being found . . . in the indicative, where it is used as past and hence augmented."*[8] Therefore, the aorist indicative in Revelation 11:15 proves that *the action of entrance* into the condition of the kingdom *will occur prior to the declaration* ("the kingdoms of this world *are become* the kingdoms of our Lord") at the sounding of the seventh trumpet.[9] This truth is confirmed by Dr. A.T. Robertson, America's greatest Greek scholar, who said that here the aorist indicative signifies *"did become . . . already a fact."*[10] The writer is aware that Robertson's comments pertained to the word in the singular, for Robertson used the Alexandrian Text, where the word is <u>egeneto</u> ("is become"). However, the singular makes no difference, for the singular word is still a second aorist *indicative*.

This writer believes that the King James Version is without error; hence, he believes <u>egenonto</u> is the correct word. However, translators of other English versions have understood the meaning of <u>egeneto</u> in Revelation 11:15, and they have rendered its action as having occurred in past time with reference to the declaration itself. Following are three examples:

The New International Version says, "The seventh angel sounded his trumpet, and there were loud voices in heaven, which said: 'The kingdom of the world *has become* the kingdom of our Lord and of his Christ . . . .'"

---

[8] H.E. Dana and Julius R. Mantey, *A Manual Grammar of the Greek New Testament* (New York: MacMillian Publishing Co., 1927), p. 193.

[9] See Appendix B.

[10] Robertson, *Word Pictures in the New Testament*, p. 384.

The New American Standard Bible says, "And the seventh angel sounded; and there arose loud voices in heaven, saying, 'The kingdom of the world *has become* the kingdom of our Lord, and of His Christ; and He will reign forever and ever.'"

The New King James Version says, "Then the seventh angel sounded: And there were loud voices in heaven, saying, 'The kingdoms of this world *have become* the kingdoms of our Lord and of His Christ, and He shall reign forever and ever!'"

Therefore, the millennial kingdom will begin *before* the wrath of the Lamb is poured out during the seven trumpets, the seven vials, and Armageddon. It will be shown later in this chapter that the wrath of the first six trumpet judgments will also be poured out *after* the kingdom begins, and that the wrath of those judgments will constitute part of the wrath of the Lamb. When the seventh trumpet sounds, there will be lightnings, thunderings, an earthquake, and great hail. These events will constitute the wrath of the seventh trumpet judgment.

Fourth, the millennial reign of Christ will begin before the wrath of the Lamb is poured out during the seven trumpets, the seven vials, and Armageddon. It has been shown that the millennial reign of Christ will begin when Satan and his angels are cast to the earth (Revelation 12:4, 9, 10). These scriptures say:

> And his [namely, the great red dragon's] tail drew the third part of the stars of heaven, and did cast them to the earth . . . . And the great dragon was cast out, that old serpent, called the Devil, and Satan . . . he was cast out into the earth, and his angels were cast out with him. And I heard a loud voice saying in heaven, Now is come . . . the kingdom of our God, and the power of his Christ: for the accuser of our brethren is cast down . . . .

These scriptures teach plainly that the millennial kingdom and the reign of Christ will begin when Satan and his angels are cast down to the earth. The Bible teaches clearly that Satan and his angels will be cast to the earth immediately after the Great Tribulation at the opening of the sixth seal (Matthew 24:29; Revelation 6:12, 13). This truth was explained in greater detail in chapter six of this book. The wrath of the Lamb will be poured out sequentially during the seven trumpets, the seven vials, and Armageddon, after the seventh seal is opened (Revelation 8:1-7).

This truth is confirmed by the aorist indicative ebasileusas ("thou hast reigned") in Revelation 11:17, which says, ". . . We give thee thanks, O Lord God Almighty, which art, and wast, and art to come; because thou hast taken to thee thy great power, and hast reigned." The aorist indicative ebasileusas ("thou hast reigned") signifies that the action of Christ's entrance into the condition of His reign occurred in past time, that is, prior to the declaration ("thou . . . hast reigned"), which will be made at the sounding of the seventh trumpet. Consequently, the wrath of the seventh trumpet (and of the first six trumpets also, as will be shown later in this chapter), the seven vials, and Armageddon will be poured out after the millennial reign of Christ has begun. In short, the millennial reign of Christ will begin *before* the wrath of the Lamb is poured out in the great day of His wrath through the seven trumpet judgments, the seven vial judgments, and Armageddon.

Fifth, the early part of the Day of the Lord (that is, the first 1,040 days) and the great day of His wrath are coincident and equivalent. The Bible teaches plainly that the Day of the Lord will begin *after* the Great Tribulation at the opening of the sixth seal (Matthew 24:29; Revelation 6:12, 13; Joel 2:31). Further, it has been shown that the great day of His wrath will begin after the Great Tribulation at the opening of the sixth seal (Matthew 24:29; Revelation 6:12-17). Accordingly, the Day of the Lord and the great day of His wrath is the time during which the wrath of the Lamb will be poured out during the seven trumpets, the seven vials, and Armageddon. The early part of the Day of the Lord (the first 1,040 days) is "the great and terrible" aspect of the Day of the Lord, during which God's wrath will be poured out through the seven trumpets, the seven vials, and Armageddon. This truth is confirmed by Zephaniah 1:14, 15 which says,

> The great day of the LORD is near, it is near, and hasteth greatly, even the voice of the day of the LORD: the mighty man shall cry there bitterly. *That day is a day of wrath*, a day of trouble and distress, a day of wasteness and desolation, a day of darkness and gloominess, a day of clouds and thick darkness . . . .

In short, the early part of the Day of the Lord and the great day of His wrath will be concurrent and equivalent.

WHEN WILL THE WRATH OF THE LAMB ITSELF BEGIN?

When will the unparalleled wrath of the Lamb commence? The answer to this question is found in the book of Revelation. Pretribulationism claims that this unparalleled wrath will be poured out in the Seventieth Week of Daniel. This view is not based on sound biblical exegesis, but it is the result of theological necessity. Pretribulationists need to place the wrath of the Lamb in the Seventieth Week, so a pretribulational rapture is necessary to deliver the church from that wrath. This deadly error in interpretation has been thoroughly exposed throughout this book. Understanding that the opening of the sixth seal marks both the end of Daniel's Seventieth Week and the beginning of the Day of the Lord supplies us with the needed truth to determine the beginning point of the wrath of the Lamb itself.

The opening of the fifth seal takes place prior to the opening of the sixth seal. This fact places the opening of the fifth seal and its events in the Seventieth Week of Daniel. Revelation 6:9-11 says:

> And when he had opened the fifth seal, *I saw under the altar the souls of them that were slain for the word of God, and for the testimony which they held: and they cried with a loud voice, saying, how long, O Lord, holy and true, dost thou not judge and avenge our blood on them that dwell on the earth?* And white robes were given unto every one of them; and *it was said unto them, that they should rest yet for a little season, until their fellowservants also and their brethren, that should be killed as they were, should be fulfilled.*

To understand the full impact of Revelation 6:9-11, we must first answer two questions:

1. Who are the souls under the altar who are given white robes?

2. What are they crying in a loud voice to the Lord?

The answer to the first question is given by one of the twenty-four elders, who said,

And one of the elders answered, saying unto me, What are these which are arrayed in white robes? and whence came they? And I said unto him, Sir, thou knowest. And he said to me, *These are they which came out of great tribulation*, and have washed their robes, and made them white in the blood of the Lamb.[11]

We are told plainly that these are "tribulation" saints. A comparison of Revelation 6:9-11 with Revelation 7:13, 14 can lead only to the following conclusion: these are martyrs who will be slain in the Great Tribulation, namely, the last half of the Seventieth Week. What is it that these martyrs are crying loudly to the Lord? The Bible says, "And they cried with a loud voice, saying, *How long*, O Lord, holy and true, *dost thou not judge and avenge our blood on them that dwell on the earth?*"[12] There can be no mistaking their plea to God; their plea is for judgment upon "them that dwell [present participle] on the earth." They are crying for judgment upon "the ones dwelling" on the earth at the very time the fifth seal is opened.

A literal interpreter of the Bible can only conclude that the wrath of the Lamb has not yet fallen upon those that *are dwelling* on the earth at the time the fifth seal is opened. This fact is of the utmost importance, because it proves that the wrath of God, namely, the unparalleled wrath of the Lamb (which will be poured out in the great day of His wrath), has not yet been unleashed upon the world when the fifth seal is opened. This is easily verified by the following facts:

1. These souls are the spirits of just men made perfect (Hebrews 12:23), and they are dwelling in heaven.

---

[11] Revelation 7:13, 14.
[12] Revelation 6:10.

Consequently, they are keenly aware that the awaited divine judgment has not yet fallen.

2. These martyred souls are not corrected by being told that *judgment is presently falling* or that *judgment has come already in the events of the first four seals.* Rather, they are told ". . . rest yet for a little season . . ." because the martyrdom of their fellowservants and brethren must be fulfilled before the appointed judgment and vengeance will fall.

3. These souls are crying specifically for the wrath of the Lamb to fall, for they say, "How long, O Lord, holy and true, dost thou not judge and avenge our blood on them that dwell on the earth?"

This truth is confirmed by Jeremiah 46:10 and Zephaniah 2:3, which equate the words "judge" and "avenge" with the judgments in the Day of the Lord. Jeremiah 46:10 says,

> For this is *the day of the Lord* God of hosts, A *day of vengeance*, that he may *avenge* him of his adversaries: and the sword shall devour, and it shall be satiate and made drunk with their blood . . . .

Zephaniah 2:3 says, "Seek ye the Lord, all ye meek of the earth, which have wrought *his judgment*; seek righteousness, seek meekness: it may be ye shall be hid *in the day of the Lord's anger.*"

The events of the fifth seal are devastating to the pre-tribulational view, which teaches that the trumpet judgments and the vial judgments (clearly associated with the unparalleled wrath of God) occur in the Seventieth Week

of Daniel. When the fifth seal is opened, the souls of martyred Great Tribulation saints are testifying that *the wrath
of the Lamb has not yet come at the opening of the fifth
seal*. A literal interpreter of the Bible can only conclude
that the wrath of the Lamb has not yet been poured out
up to the time of the opening of the fifth seal during the
Great Tribulation. Moreover, Revelation 6:11 proclaims
with divine authority that this wrath *cannot come* "for a
little season," that is, *until the martyrdom of other saints
is fulfilled.*

Therefore, *the events of the fifth seal demonstrate
plainly that the wrath of the Lamb will not fall prior to
the opening of the fifth seal,* and strongly suggest that this
unparalleled wrath will not be poured out until after the
Great Tribulation is over. *These events also rule out any
claims that the wrath of the Lamb is retroactive through
the first four seals or is equivalent to their events.*

This brings us to the sixth seal in Revelation 6:12. It
has already been established that the wrath of the Lamb
will not be poured out until *after* the sixth seal is opened,
for the Day of the Lord cannot begin until *after* the darkening of the sun and moon at the opening of the sixth seal.
Our Lord Jesus Himself established the fact that this darkening will occur immediately *after* the Great Tribulation.[13]
Joel teaches that the Day of the Lord will begin *after*
these alarming cosmic events, for he says, "The sun shall
be turned into darkness, and the moon into blood, before
the great and the terrible day of the Lord come."[14]

To build upon the events of the fifth seal, it is important to emphasize that the Day of the Lord, in which the

---

[13] Matthew 24:29.
[14] Joel 2:31.

wrath of the Lamb falls, consecutively follows the Great Tribulation. The events of the fifth seal show that the wrath of the Lamb will not be poured out prior to the opening of the fifth seal in the Seventieth Week of Daniel. Matthew 24:29, Revelation 6:12, and Joel 2:31 prove that the wrath of the Lamb will not be poured out until after the end of the Seventieth Week; this is an indisputable Bible doctrine.

We see then, that the Day of the Lord (which opens with the great day of His wrath) begins after the sixth seal is opened. It will be early in the Day of the Lord that the great day of His wrath occurs. Joel 2:31 declares that the sun and moon will be darkened before "the great and the terrible day of the Lord come." Joel, in doing so, indicates clearly that the condition of God's wrath will be entered *after* the cosmic events that mark the end of the Great Tribulation. This is further verified in Revelation 6:15-17, which says,

> *And the kings of the earth* . . . and every free man . . . *said* to the mountains and rocks, Fall on us, and *hide us* from the face of him that sitteth on the throne, and *from the wrath of the Lamb*: *For the great day of his wrath is come*; and who shall be able to stand?

As it has been shown, the aorist *indicative* elthen ("is come") denotes that the action of entrance into the state of the great day of His wrath occurs in past time with reference to the declaration ("the great day of his wrath is come"). That condition is entered into at the opening of the sixth seal, but not any earlier due to the events of the fifth seal. It should be observed that there is a distinction between the time of the entrance into the condition of the great day of His wrath and the time of entrance into the unparalleled wrath itself. Revelation 11:15-18 says:

> And the seventh angel sounded; and there were great voices in heaven, saying, The kingdoms of this world are become the kingdoms of our Lord, and of his Christ; and he shall reign for ever and ever. And the four and twenty elders, which sat before God on their seats, fell upon their faces, and worshipped God, saying, we give thee thanks, O Lord God Almighty, which art, and wast, and art to come; because thou hast taken to thee thy great power, and hast reigned. And the nations were angry, and *thy wrath is come*, and the time of the dead, that thou shouldest give reward unto thy servants the prophets, and to the saints, and them that fear thy name, small and great; and shouldest destroy them which destroy the earth.

When comparing the declaration in Revelation 11:18 ("thy wrath is come") to the declaration in Revelation 6:17 ("for the great day of his wrath is come"), the distinction between the entrance into the condition of the great day of His wrath and the entrance into the wrath itself becomes apparent. At the sounding of the seventh trumpet, great voices in heaven say, ". . . *thy wrath is come*" (Revelation 11:18). This declaration unmistakably speaks of the unparalleled wrath of the Lamb. The aorist *indicative* elthen ("is come") denotes that the unparalleled wrath itself will have begun before the declaration ("thy wrath is come") at the sounding of the seventh trumpet.

There can be no question that the seventh trumpet judgment is unparalleled wrath. However, even though the aorist indicative elthen ("is come") denotes action that occurred in past time, there is no grammatical reason to make this wrath retroactive beyond the seventh trumpet. This is consistent with the grammatical interpretation of elthen in Revelation 6:17, which has been previously discussed in this chapter. Accordingly, based upon Greek grammar alone, one cannot make this unparalleled wrath retroactive to include the other six trumpets.

Can it be demonstrated by other scriptures that this unparalleled wrath will be poured out in all of the trumpet judgments? Since the seventh trumpet judgment is defined plainly as wrath, by association it is reasonable to conclude that all of the other trumpet judgments are wrath as well. Remember that the 144,000 Israelites are sealed for the express purpose of protecting them from the unparalleled wrath of God. The time of their sealing is solid evidence that all of the trumpet judgments are indeed unparalleled wrath. The time of the sealing of the 144,000 is made clear by the following:

1. The sealing is after the Great Tribulation is over (Matthew 24:29; Revelation 6:12, 13; 7:1-3).

2. The sealing is after the sixth seal is opened (Revelation 6:12, 13; 7:1-3).

3. The sealing is after the sun and moon are darkened (Matthew 24:29; Revelation 6:12, 13; 7:1-3).

4. The sealing is after the posttribulational rapture (Mark 13:24-27; Revelation 6:12, 13, 7:1-3).

5. The sealing is in the early moments of the millennial kingdom (Matthew 24:29; Revelation 6:12, 13; 7:1-3; 12:4, 9, 10).

6. The sealing is in the early moments of the Day of the Lord (Matthew 24:29; Joel 2:31).

7.   The sealing is in the early moments of the great day
     of His wrath, which opens the Day of the Lord
     (Revelation 6:17-7:3).

The time of their sealing is pinpointed by the fact that
John tells us they are called servants and sealed "after
these things" in Revelation 7:1. The definitive meaning of
<u>meta tauta</u> ("after these things") was discussed in detail in
chapter six. The time of the sealing is further pinpointed,
since it occurs before the following:

1.   The sealing is before the opening of the seventh
     seal (Revelation 8:1).

2.   The sealing is before the unparalleled wrath of the
     Lamb begins (Revelation 7:1-8; 8:1, 7).

3.   The sealing is before the first trumpet judgment
     (Revelation 7:3; 8:7).

With the knowledge of the exact time that the
144,000 are sealed, one has evidence that all of the trumpet judgments are unparalleled wrath. Further, Revelation
7:3 says, ". . . Hurt not the earth, neither the sea, nor the
trees, till we have sealed the servants of our God in their
foreheads." The command to hurt not the earth, neither
the sea, nor the trees obviously refers to the first trumpet
judgment found in Revelation 8:7, which says, "The first
angel sounded, and there followed hail and fire mingled
with blood, and they were cast upon the earth: and *the
third part of trees was burnt up, and all green grass was
burnt up.*" The command to hurt not the sea in Revelation 7:3 refers to the second trumpet judgment, found in

Revelation 8:8, which says, "And the second angel sounded, and as it were a great mountain burning with fire was cast into the sea: and *the third part of the sea became blood.*"

The Bible teaches explicitly that the 144,000 are sealed before the first trumpet judgment. It is crystal-clear that the sealing of these 144,000 servants of God is for the purpose of protecting them from divine wrath. The command to withhold all hurt from the earth, trees, and sea refers to the devastating first and second trumpet judgments.   Since the command, "Hurt not the earth, neither the sea, nor the trees," is enforced "till we have sealed the servants of our God in their foreheads," it can only be concluded that the first two trumpet judgments are unparalleled divine wrath.

Moreover, if the first, second, and seventh trumpet judgments are unquestionably divine wrath, then *all the trumpet judgments must be divine wrath.* The fact that the trumpet judgments are withheld until the sealing takes place demands this conclusion.

The unparalleled wrath of God will be poured out after the seventh seal is opened, and not before. Revelation 6:9-11 tells us that the wrath of the Lamb has not yet come at the opening of the fifth seal. *This truth proves that the first four seals are not equivalent to the unparalleled wrath of the Lamb.* Joel 2:31 indicates that the darkening of the sun and moon at the opening of the sixth seal precedes the Day of the Lord, which includes the judgments that introduce the kingdom.

The aorist indicative <u>elthen</u> ("is come") in Revelation 6:17 shows that the action of entering into the condition of the great day of His wrath occurs before the declaration ("the great day of His wrath is come"). According to Revelation 6:17, the wrath of the Lamb will come after the opening of the sixth seal; but it cannot come before because of the events of the fifth seal. Revelation 11:18 defines the seventh trumpet judgment as wrath.

The time of the protective sealing of the 144,000 Israelites is before the first and second trumpet judgments. This is seen in Revelation 7:3, which clearly alludes to the first and second trumpet judgments. Since the first, second, and seventh trumpet judgments are wrath, all of the trumpet judgments must be part of the wrath of the Lamb. The wrath of the Lamb will be unleashed after the opening of the seventh seal in Revelation 8:1. Revelation 8:1-6 says:

> And when he had opened the seventh seal, there was silence in heaven about the space of half an hour. And I saw the seven angels which stood before God; and to them were given seven trumpets. And another angel came and stood at the altar, having a golden censer; and there was given unto him much incense, that he should offer it with the prayers of all saints upon the golden altar which was before the throne. And the smoke of the incense, which came with the prayers of the saints, ascended up before God out of the angel's hand. And the angel took the censer, and filled it with fire of the altar, and cast it into the earth: and there were voices, and thunderings, and lightnings, and an earthquake. And the seven angels which had the seven trumpets prepared themselves to sound.

There will be silence in heaven for about the space of half an hour after the opening of the seventh seal. The wrath of the Lamb will begin after this period of silence is past. It can be said dogmatically that the events of the seventh seal introduce the unparalleled wrath of the Lamb executed during the trumpets, the vials, and the Battle of Armageddon. There can be no denying that with the sound of the first trumpet comes the pure, undiluted wrath of the Lamb.

ARE THE EVENTS OF THE FIRST FOUR SEALS EQUIVALENT TO THE EVENTS OF THE GREAT DAY OF HIS WRATH?

Pretribulationists have a theological necessity to place the wrath of the Lamb in the Seventieth Week of Daniel, so they stick the unparalleled wrath of God in the Seventieth Week in order to create a need for a pretribulational rapture of the church, which is not appointed to wrath. Following are several reasons why the events of the first four seals cannot be equivalent to the events of the great day of His wrath.

First, the events of the first four seals occur *before* the sixth seal is opened, but the events of the great day of His wrath occur *after* the sixth seal is opened (Revelation 6:12-17). Keep in mind that Fruchtenbaum admitted, ". . . there is no grammatical reason to make the aorist tense of the sixth seal retroactive . . . ."[15] Moreover, as it has been shown, the events of the fifth seal prove that the wrath of the Lamb has not yet been poured out when that seal is opened. Therefore, the events of the first four seals, which occur *before* the opening of the fifth seal, cannot be equivalent to the events of the great day of His wrath, which occur after the sixth seal is opened.

Second, it has been established from the Scriptures that the great day of His wrath will begin *after* Daniel's Seventieth Week. The events of the first four seals occur

---

[15] Fruchtenbaum, "Problems with the Pre-Wrath Rapture," Tape on file at the Post-Trib Research Center.

during the Seventieth Week, but the events of the great day of His wrath occur *after* the Seventieth Week. Hence, the events of the first four seals cannot be equivalent to the events of the great day of His wrath.

Third, it has been shown that the great day of His wrath, that is, the first 1,040 days of the Day of the Lord, begins after the Great Tribulation (Matthew 24:29; Revelation 6:12-17). The events of the first four seals occur *before* the Great Tribulation is past, but the events of the great day of His wrath occur *after* the Great Tribulation is past. Consequently, the events of the first four seals cannot be equivalent to the events of the great day of His wrath.

Fourth, it has been demonstrated that the millennial kingdom begins before the wrath of the Lamb is poured out during the seven trumpets, the seven vials, and Armageddon, but the events of the first four seals occur during the Seventieth Week *before* the kingdom begins. Accordingly, the events of the first four seals which occur *during* the Seventieth Week cannot be equivalent to the events of the great day of His wrath, which occur after the millennial kingdom begins.

Fifth, the millennial reign of Christ begins before the wrath of the Lamb is poured out during the seven trumpets, the seven vials, and Armageddon. Hence, the events of the first four seals which occur during the Seventieth Week cannot be equivalent to the events of the great day of His wrath, which occur *after* the millennial reign of Christ begins.

Sixth, Revelation 6:10 teaches plainly that the wrath of the Lamb has not been poured out at the opening of the fifth seal during the Great Tribulation. Furthermore, Revelation 6:11 teaches that additional martyrdoms must

242 ■ THE POST-TRIB, PRE-WRATH RAPTURE

still take place before the wrath of the Lamb can be poured out. Therefore, the events of the first four seals, which occur before the end of the Great Tribulation, cannot be equivalent to the unparalleled wrath of God, which will be poured out *after* the sixth and seventh seals are opened (Revelation 6:12-17; 8:1-7) after the Great Tribulation.

Seventh, the Bible teaches that the 144,000 Israelites are sealed *after* the opening of the sixth seal (Revelation 6:12; 7:1-8). The purpose for the sealing of the 144,000 is to protect them from the wrath of the Lamb, which is to be poured out during the seven trumpets, the seven vials, and Armageddon (Revelation 9:3, 4). Consequently, the events of the first four seals, which occur during the Seventieth Week before the opening of the sixth seal, cannot be equivalent to the wrath of the Lamb which is poured out through the trumpets, the vials, and Armageddon, *after* the opening of the sixth seal and the sealing of the 144,000 (Revelation 6:12; 7:1-8; 8:1-19:21).

Eighth, the Day of the Lord is a day of wrath. The Bible says:

> The great day of the LORD is near, it is near, and hasteth greatly, even the voice of the day of the LORD: the mighty man shall cry there bitterly. *That day is a day of wrath*, a day of trouble and distress, a day of wasteness and desolation, a day of darkness and gloominess, a day of clouds and thick darkness . . . . [16]

Furthermore, the wrath of the Day of the Lord is unparalleled. Joel says,

---

[16] Zephaniah 1:14, 15.

Blow ye the trumpet in Zion, and sound an alarm in my holy mountain: let all the inhabitants of the land tremble: for the day of the LORD cometh, for it is nigh at hand; A day of darkness and of gloominess, a day of clouds and of thick darkness, as the morning spread upon the mountains: a great people and a strong; *there hath not been ever the like, neither shall be any more after it*, even to the years of many generations.[17]

During the great day of his wrath, in which the wrath of the Lamb will be poured out, men will desire to die (Revelation 6:16, 17; 9:4-6), but during the Great Tribulation, although many will be martyred, the saints will *not* desire to die.[18]

Down through history, the saints have experienced tribulation, but there "shall be great tribulation, such as was not since the beginning of the world to this time, no, nor ever shall be."[19] Similarly, the wrath of God has been manifested against all ungodliness and unrighteousness of men since the fall of man in the Garden of Eden, but there will be a time during which the wrath of the Lamb will be poured out in an *unparalleled way* in the great day of His wrath. In short, the events of the first four seals, which occur *during* the Seventieth Week, cannot be equivalent to the events of the great day of His wrath which occur *in* the Day of the Lord, *after* the opening of the sixth seal, when the sun and moon are darkened *after* the Great Tribulation.[20]

---

[17] Joel 2:1, 2.

[18] Revelation 20:4.

[19] Matthew 24:21.

[20] Joel 2:1,2

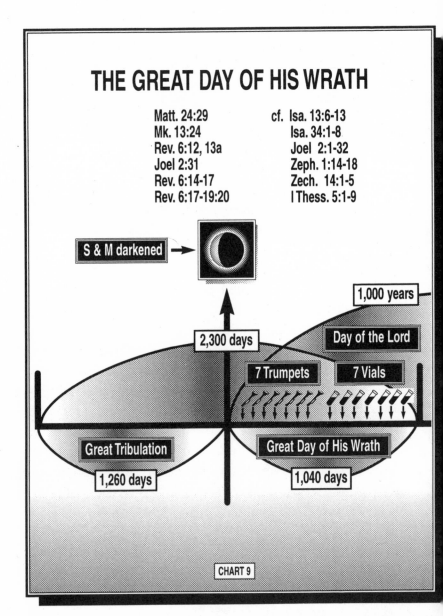

THE GREAT DAY OF HIS WRATH

Matt. 24:29	cf. Isa. 13:6-13
Mk. 13:24	Isa. 34:1-8
Rev. 6:12, 13a	Joel 2:1-32
Joel 2:31	Zeph. 1:14-18
Rev. 6:14-17	Zech. 14:1-5
Rev. 6:17-19:20	I Thess. 5:1-9

S & M darkened →

1,000 years

2,300 days

Day of the Lord

7 Trumpets   7 Vials

Great Tribulation   Great Day of His Wrath

1,260 days   1,040 days

CHART 9

The "great day of His wrath" is the period of time during the Day of the Lord, in which the unparalleled wrath of the Lamb is to be poured out. It begins at the opening of the sixth seal, and will last 1,040 days concluding with the Battle of Armageddon.

TEN

THE COMING OF CHRIST ON A WHITE HORSE

"And I saw heaven opened, and behold a white horse; and he that sat upon him was called Faithful and True, and in righteousness he doth judge and make war."

— Revelation 19:11

If you look, you can see the end of the age rapidly approaching and the stage being set for the emergence of the Antichrist. If you listen, you can hear the voices of those who are subverting our U.S. Constitutional system and promoting the New World Order. However, Christians know that in spite of the dark clouds looming on the horizon, *their King is coming on a white horse.*

The coming of Christ on a white horse is commonly called the second advent. This coming was described by the aged apostle John in the following Scripture:

And I saw heaven opened, and behold a white horse; and he that sat upon him was called Faithful and True, and in righteousness he doth judge and make war. His eyes were as a flame of fire, and on his head were many crowns; and he had a name written, that no man knew, but he himself. And he was clothed with a vesture dipped in blood: and his name is called The Word of God. And the armies which were in heaven followed him upon white horses, clothed in fine linen, white and clean. And out of his mouth goeth a sharp sword, that with it he should smite the nations: and he shall rule them with a rod of iron: and he treadeth the winepress of the fierceness and wrath of Almighty God. And he hath on his vesture and on his thigh a name written, *King of Kings, and Lord of Lords.* And I saw an angel standing in the sun; and he cried with a loud voice, saying to all the fowls that fly in the midst of heaven, Come and gather yourselves together unto the supper of the great God; that ye may eat the flesh of kings, and the flesh of captains, and the flesh of mighty men, and the flesh of horses, and of them that sit on them, and the flesh of all men, both free and bond, both small and great. And I saw the beast, and the kings of the earth, and their armies, gathered together to make war against him that sat on the horse, and against his army.   And the beast was taken, and with him the false prophet that wrought miracles before him, with which he deceived them that had received the mark of the beast, and them that worshipped his image. These both were cast alive into a lake of fire burning with brimstone. And the remnant were slain with the sword of him that sat upon the horse, which sword proceeded out of his mouth; and all the fowls were filled with their flesh.[1]

WHAT WILL HAPPEN WHEN CHRIST COMES ON A WHITE HORSE?

If we read carefully the above passage of Scripture, we shall notice the following:

1. Christ will return on a white horse.

2. In righteousness Christ will judge and make war.

3. His eyes will be as a flame of fire.

4. On His head will be many crowns.

---

[1] Revelation 19:11-21.

5. He will be clothed in a vesture dipped in blood.

6. The armies which were in heaven will follow Him upon white horses.

7. The armies will be clothed in fine linen, white and clean.

8. Out of His mouth will go a sharp sword with which He will smite the nations.

9. He will rule the nations with a rod of iron.

10. He will tread the winepress of the fierceness of the wrath of Almighty God.

11. He will have on His vesture a name written, King of kings, and Lord of lords.

12. An angel will cry with a loud voice, saying to all of the fowls that fly in the midst of heaven, Come and gather yourselves together unto the supper of the great God.

13. The beast, and the kings of the earth, and their armies will gather together to make war against Him that sat on the white horse.

14. The beast and the false prophet will be cast alive into the lake of fire burning with brimstone.

15. The remnant will be slain with the sword of Him that sat upon the horse.

16. The fowls will be filled with the flesh of those slain at the Battle of Armageddon.

It is perfectly clear that *when Christ returns on a white horse, the wrath of the Lamb will be poured out* upon the beast, the kings of the earth, and their armies, which will be gathered together to make war against Christ and His armies. The coming of Christ on a white horse will be a continuation of the outpouring of the wrath of the Lamb, which will begin after the opening of the seventh seal.

WHAT ARE THE DISTINCTIONS BETWEEN THE TWO PHASES OF CHRIST'S COMING?

There are several important distinctions between the coming of Christ in the clouds with power and great glory at the end of the Great Tribulation and the coming of Christ on a white horse at the end of the 1,040 days. These distinctions are real, and they cannot be glossed over or explained away. Therefore, the coming of Christ in the clouds with power and great glory must not be identified with the coming of Christ on a white horse for the Battle of Armageddon 1,040 days later. Let us observe carefully some of the distinctions between the two stages or phases of Christ's second coming.

Ruckman, in *Bible Believer's Bulletin*, March 1991, gives several distinctions which show that there must be two phases to the second advent:

1. The first phase is Christ's coming *to get His bride*. The second phase is Christ's returning *with His bride*.

2. In the first phase, *Christ comes down in the atmosphere in the air*. In the second phase, *Christ returns and lands on the earth*, at the Mount of Olives.

3. At the rapture, the believers are judged. At the advent, Israel and the Gentiles are judged.

4. The rapture affects believers only. At the advent, everyone is affected.

Walvoord, in *Rapture Question: Revised*, page 275, gives the following distinctions for the two phases of the second advent:

1. At the time of the rapture, the saints meet Christ in the air, while at the second coming Christ returns to the Mount of Olives to meet the saints on earth.

2. At the time of the rapture, the Mount of Olives is unchanged, while at the second coming it divides, and a valley is formed to the east of Jerusalem (Zechariah 14:4, 5).

3. At the rapture, living saints are translated, while no saints are translated in connection with the second coming of Christ to the earth.

4. At the rapture, saints go to heaven, while at the second coming to the earth, the saints remain on the earth without translation.

Pentecost, in *Things To Come*, page 207, gave the following distinctions for the two phases of the second advent:

1. The translation brings a message of comfort, while the second advent is accompanied by a message of judgment.

2. The translation is related to the program for the church, while the second advent is related to the program for Israel and the world.

3. At the translation, believers are judged, but at the second advent, the Gentiles and Israel are judged.

4. The translation is for believers only, but the second advent has its effect on all men.

It is apparent that there are several clear distinctions between the coming of Christ in the clouds and His coming on a white horse.

IS TIME NEEDED BETWEEN THE TWO STAGES OF CHRIST'S COMING?

With few exceptions, historic posttribulationism has not taught a two-stage or two-phase second coming. For example, posttribulationist Gundry writes:

> . . . the fact that the saints will meet the Lord in the air in no way implies that He will not continue His descent to the Mount of Olives . . . . There is no reason why Jesus cannot come *for* His

saints and continue to descend *with them.* The meeting in the air does not preclude a descent to the earth.[2]

The view set forth by Gundry has been called the "yo-yo" view or the "up-and-down" view. It is the judgment of this writer that historic posttribulationism has been vulnerable as a result of trying to crowd too many events into the day on which the Lord returns on a white horse. The one-stage or one-phase coming of historic posttribulationism requires that the opening of the seventh seal, the seven trumpet judgments, the seven vial judgments, the judgment of the great whore, and the Battle of Armageddon will all occur on the day of the one-stage coming of Christ. This problem is undoubtedly why many post-tribulationists teach that the seven vial judgments are merely a restatement of the seven trumpet judgments. However, a careful comparison of the seven vial judgments with the seven trumpet judgments will show that *they are not the same judgments* restated. The writer believes that the one-stage coming of Christ has been an Achilles' heel for historic posttribulationism. Moreover, if there is scriptural proof for an interval of time between Christ's coming in the clouds and Christ's coming on a white horse, then the one-stage or one-phase coming of historic posttribulationism must be rejected.

If one interprets the Bible literally and takes the book of Revelation chronologically, the need for a period of time to accommodate the pouring out of the wrath of the Lamb between the coming of Christ in the clouds and the coming of Christ on a white horse is perfectly obvious. On the one hand, the coming of Christ in the clouds will

---

[2] Gundry, p. 159.

occur at the time the sun and moon are darkened, immediately after the Great Tribulation at the opening of the
sixth seal. On the other hand, the coming of Christ on a
white horse cannot occur at the opening of the sixth seal,
for it will not occur until *after* the opening of the seventh
seal; and *after* the pouring out of the wrath of the Lamb
during the seven trumpet judgments; and *after* the pouring
out of the wrath of the Lamb during the seven vial
judgments; and *after* the destruction of the whore. These
events will occur *after* the opening of the sixth seal at
the end of the Great Tribulation, and *after* the coming of
Christ in the clouds. All of these events must occur before Christ can come on a white horse for the Battle of
Armageddon.

Furthermore, the pouring out of the wrath of the
Lamb during the seven trumpet judgments and the seven
vial judgments will require considerable time. For instance, the fifth trumpet judgment alone will last five
months. Concerning the fifth trumpet judgment, John
writes:

> And the fifth angel sounded, and I saw a star fall from heaven
> unto the earth: and to him was given the key of the bottomless
> pit. And he opened the bottomless pit; and there arose a smoke
> out of the pit, as the smoke of a great furnace; and the sun and
> the air were darkened by reason of the smoke of the pit. And
> there came out of the smoke locusts upon the earth: and unto
> them was given power, as the scorpions of the earth have power.
> And it was commanded them that they should not hurt the grass
> of the earth, neither any green thing, neither any tree; but only
> those men which have not the seal of God in their foreheads.
> And to them it was given that they should not kill them, but that

they should be tormented five months: and their torment was as the torment of a scorpion, when he striketh a man.[3]

The above passage reveals that, during the fifth trumpet judgment, five months are allotted to the locusts to torment those men who have not the seal of God in their foreheads. This outpouring of wrath associated with the sounding of the fifth trumpet will occur *after* the coming of Christ in the clouds at the opening of the sixth seal; and *after* 144,000 Israelites are sealed; and *after* the opening of the seventh seal; and *after* the pouring out of the wrath of the first four trumpet judgments. Hence, a time interval between the coming of Christ in the clouds and the coming of Christ on a white horse must be recognized by the literal interpreter of the Bible.

In addition to the five months needed for the fifth trumpet judgment, there is also a need for additional time for the pouring out of God's wrath during the other six trumpet judgments, and the pouring out of God's wrath during the seven vial judgments. The writer originally referred to this time period as the *five-months-plus* interval between the two stages of Christ's coming. The five months stood for the five months' duration of the locusts judgment, and the plus stood for the time necessary for the remaining six trumpet judgments, the seven vial judgments, and the destruction of the whore. It was not until December of 1989, while reading Daniel eight, that the writer saw that the five-months-plus time interval was precisely a time interval of 1,040 days. In chapter eight of this book, it was demonstrated that the 2,300-day "transgression of desolation" will overrun the 1,260-day Great

---

[3] Revelation 9:1-5.

Tribulation by 1,040 days into the millennium. Accordingly, the wrath of the Lamb will be poured out during the interval of 1,040 days between the coming of Christ in the clouds at the opening of the sixth seal and the coming of Christ on a white horse for the Battle of Armageddon. The time interval between the rapture and the coming of Christ on a white horse will be 1,040 days--not seven years, as pretribulationism teaches. The doctrine of a two-stage or two-phase coming of Christ is made necessary by the 1,040-day interval, during which the wrath of the Lamb will be poured out.

WHAT EVENTS MUST OCCUR BETWEEN THE TWO STAGES OF CHRIST'S SECOND COMING?

We have just seen that the reason time is needed between the first and second stages of Christ's coming is to accommodate many events that must occur between the two stages. The first stage of Christ's coming in power and great glory will occur when the sun and moon are darkened at the opening of the sixth seal, immediately after the Great Tribulation. Following is a list of events which the Bible says will occur during the interval *after* the coming of Christ in the clouds, and *before* the coming of Christ on a white horse for the Battle of Armageddon:

1. The 144,000 Israelites will be sealed.

2. The seventh seal will be opened.

3. There will be silence in heaven for about the space of half an hour.

4. The seven trumpet judgments will be poured out. They will be as follows:

First Trumpet	- The third part of trees will be burned up, and all green grass will be burned up.
Second Trumpet	- The third part of the sea will become blood; the third part of creatures which are in the sea will die; and the third part of ships will be destroyed.
Third Trumpet	- The third part of the rivers and the fountains of waters will become wormwood, and many men will die of the waters, because they will be made bitter.
Fourth Trumpet	- The third part of the sun and moon will be smitten, so the third part of them will be darkened.
Fifth Trumpet	- The bottomless pit will be opened, and smoke will arise out of pit. Locusts will arise out of smoke, and the locusts will torment men for five months.
Sixth Trumpet	- The third part of men will be killed.

Seventh Trumpet   - There will be lightnings, and voices, and thunderings, and an earthquake, and great hail.

5. The seven angels will be given seven vials of wrath, in preparation for the continued outpouring of judgment.

6. The seven vials of wrath will be poured out upon the earth and its inhabitants. The seven vials of wrath will be as follows:

First Vial   - Noisome and grievous sores will fall upon the men which have received the mark of the beast.

Second Vial   - The sea will become as blood, and every living soul in the sea will die.

Third Vial   - The rivers and fountains of waters will become blood, and those who will have shed the blood of saints will be given blood to drink.

Fourth Vial   - Power will be given unto the sun to scorch men with fire and great heat.

Fifth Vial   - Darkness and pain and sores will afflict the kingdom of the beast and the wicked.

Sixth Vial   - The Euphrates River will be dried up that the way of the kings of the east might be prepared; three unclean spirits will gather the kings of the earth to the battle of that great day of God Almighty.

Seventh Vial - There will be voices, and thunders, and lightnings, and a great earthquake; and the great city will be divided into three parts, and the cities of nations will fall; great Babylon will come into remembrance before God, to give unto her the cup of his wrath; there will fall upon men a great hail, every stone about the weight of a talent.

7. The great whore, Mystery Babylon, will be destroyed.

8. The sanctuary will be cleansed at the end of the 2,300 days of the transgression of desolation.

According to Daniel and Revelation, all of these events must occur during the interval *after* the coming of Christ in the clouds with power and great glory, at the opening of the sixth seal, and *before* the coming of Christ on a white horse for the Battle of Armageddon.

IS THE COMING OF CHRIST ON A WHITE HORSE A MANIFESTATION OF GOD'S WRATH?

The answer to this question is found in Revelation 19:11-21 and other passages dealing with the Battle of Armageddon. In Revelation 19:15, we read the following words: "And out of his mouth goeth a sharp sword, that with it he should smite the nations: and he shall rule them with a rod of iron: and *he treadeth the winepress of the fierceness and wrath of Almighty God.*" This verse reveals clearly that the coming of Christ on a white horse is a manifestation of the wrath of the Lamb.

The truth that the coming of Christ on a white horse is a manifestation of God's wrath is confirmed by another passage which deals with the Battle of Armageddon. In Revelation fourteen, John writes:

> And I looked, and behold a white cloud, and upon the cloud one sat like unto the Son of man, having on his head a golden crown, and in his hand a sharp sickle. And another angel came out of the temple, crying with a loud voice to him that sat on the cloud, Thrust in thy sickle, and reap: for the time is come for thee to reap; for the harvest of the earth is ripe. And he that sat on the cloud thrust in his sickle on the earth; and the earth was reaped. And another angel came out of the temple which is in heaven, he also having a sharp sickle. And another angel came out from the altar, which had power over fire; and cried with a loud cry to him that had the sharp sickle, saying, Thrust in thy sharp sickle, and gather the clusters of the vine of the earth . . . *and cast it into the great winepress of the wrath of God. And the winepress was trodden without the city, and blood came out of the winepress, even unto the horse bridles, by the space of a thousand and six hundred furlongs.*[4]

Verse 19 in the above passage states plainly that the coming of Christ on a white horse for the Battle of Armageddon is a manifestation of God's wrath. This Scripture says, *"and the angel thrust in his sickle into the earth, and gathered the vine of the earth, and cast it into the great winepress of the wrath of God."*

---

[4] Revelation 14:14-20.

The truth that the coming of Christ on a white horse with His saints is a manifestation of God's wrath is further confirmed by Jude 14, 15. This Scripture says,

And Enoch also, the seventh from Adam, prophesied of these, saying, Behold, the Lord cometh *with* ten thousands of his saints, *to execute judgment upon all*, and to convince all that are ungodly among them of all their ungodly deeds which they have ungodly committed, and of all their hard speeches which ungodly sinners have spoken against him.

It is evident that the coming of Christ on a white horse is a manifestation of God's wrath. The second phase of Christ's coming is distinct from the coming of Christ in the clouds with power and great glory, when the sun and moon are darkened immediately after the Great Tribulation, at the opening of the sixth seal. When Christ comes in the clouds with power and great glory, it will be to gather His elect *from* the uttermost part of the earth to the uttermost part of heaven, that is, to catch up His saints to Himself.

The Bible teaches plainly that there are two phases to Christ's second coming. The two phases are clearly distinct. The two phases are separated by a time interval of 1,040 days. The two phases will have several momentous events occur between them. In the first phase, Christ will come to catch up His saints. In the second phase, Christ will come to pour out His wrath and "to execute judgment upon all . . . ."

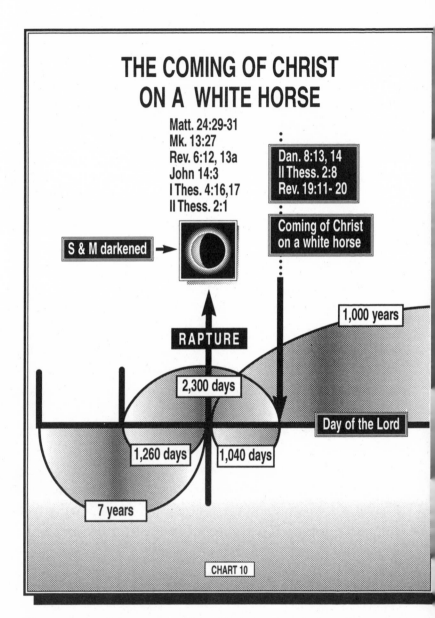

The coming of Christ on a white horse is identified as the second advent or second stage of Christ's coming.

ELEVEN

PRETRIBULATIONISM'S PREPOSTEROUS PILLARS

"Lo, this only have I found, that God hath made man upright; but they have sought out many inventions."

— *Ecclesiastes 7:29*

In his chapter entitled "The Pretribulation Rapture *Theory*," Pentecost lists twenty-eight arguments in favor of the pretribulational rapture. The arguments are lettered A-Z, AA, and BB.[1] First, we shall observe how easily the Bible refutes all twenty-eight of Pentecost's arguments. Second, we shall notice how the Bible also disproves Hal Lindsey's favorite arguments for a pretribulational rapture. Third, we will note how easily the Bible explodes Al Lacy's arguments for a pretribulational rapture.

PENTECOST'S PILLARS

Under the heading "The Essential Arguments of the Pretribulation Rapturist," Pentecost marshals his arguments as follows:

---

[1] Pentecost, pp. 193-213.

A. THE LITERAL METHOD OF INTERPRETATION.

Pentecost writes:

> Pretribulation rapturism rests essentially on one major premise
> — the literal method of interpretation of the Scriptures . . . . It
> can easily be seen that the literal method of interpretation de-
> mands a pretribulation rapture of the church. The posttribula-
> tionist must either interpret the book of Revelation historically,
> which is basically a spiritualizing method, or else treat it as yet
> future, but spiritualize away the literalness of the events in an
> attempt to harmonize these events with other scriptures in the
> light of his interpretation. Either explanation violates the prin-
> ciple of literal interpretation.[2]

Contrary to what Pentecost writes, this writer interprets the Bible more literally than any pretribulationist he
has read; he does not interpret the book of Revelation
historically; he does not use a spiritualizing method; when
it comes to the book of Revelation, he is a futurist, and he
does not "spiritualize away" the literalness of the events.

Pentecost writes, "The literal method of interpretation, consistently employed can lead to no other conclusion than that the church will be raptured before the
seventieth week."[3] The truth of the matter is that the
literal method of interpretation, consistently employed,
can lead to no other conclusion than that the church will
go through the Great Tribulation and be raptured at the
end of the Seventieth Week. The post-trib, pre-wrath
rapture of the church has been established in earlier chapters of this book. Pentecost's pillar does not support a
pretribulational rapture.

---

[2] Ibid., pp. 193, 194.
[3] Ibid., p. 194.

B. THE NATURE OF THE SEVENTIETH WEEK.

Pentecost writes, "There are a number of words used in both the Old and New Testaments to describe the seventieth week period, which, when considered together, give us the essential nature or character of this period . . . ."[4] Pentecost then listed the following words and references:

wrath - (Revelation 6:16, 17; 11:18; 14:19; 15:1, 7; 16:1, 19; I Thessalonians 1:9, 10; 5:9; Zephaniah 1:15, 18);

judgment - (Revelation 14:7; 15:4; 16:5-7; 19:2);

indignation - (Isaiah 26:20, 21; 34:1-3);

punishment - (Isaiah 24:20, 21);

destruction - (Joel 1:15);

darkness - (Joel 2:2; Zephaniah 1:14-18; Amos 5:18).[5]

Every reference listed by Pentecost is weighty. However, the *fatal flaw* in Pentecost's argument is that every one of the references he lists describes events that will take place *in the Day of the Lord* — not in the Seventieth Week. The Seventieth Week will be completed *before* the Day of the Lord begins, for the Day of the Lord cannot begin until *after* the sun and moon are darkened immediately *after* the Great Tribulation (Joel 2:31, Matthew 24:29). Therefore, no part of the Seventieth Week is concurrent with any part of the Day of the Lord. The above scriptures listed by Pentecost will be fulfilled *in* the

---

[4] Ibid.
[5] Ibid., pp. 194, 195.

1,040 days, that is, in the great day of His wrath in the Day of the Lord — *not* in the Seventieth Week. This pillar does not support pretribulationism.

C. THE SCOPE OF THE SEVENTIETH WEEK.

In this argument, Pentecost writes:

> There can be no question that this period will see the *wrath* of God poured out upon the whole earth. Revelation 3:10; Isaiah 34:2; 24:1, 4-5, 16-17, 18-21, and many other passages make this very clear . . . . The events of the seventieth week are events of the 'Day of the Lord' or 'Day of Jehovah.'[6]

Pentecost is as confused as a termite in a yo-yo when he writes, "There can be no question that this period [the Seventieth Week] will see the wrath of God poured out upon the whole earth . . . . The events of the seventieth week are the events of the 'Day of the Lord' or 'Day of Jehovah.'"[7] As in his previous argument, Pentecost misuses scriptures that pertain *only* to the Day of the Lord, and he erroneously moves events that will take place in the Day of the Lord *into* the Seventieth Week. Once again, we must keep in mind that the Day of the Lord will not begin until *after* the sun and moon are darkened immediately *after* the Great Tribulation. Joel 2:31 says, "The sun shall be turned into darkness, and the moon into blood, *before* the great and the terrible day of the Lord come." In Matthew 24:29, Jesus said, "Immediately after the tribulation of those days shall the sun be darkened, and the moon shall not give her light, and the stars shall fall from heaven, and the powers of the heavens shall be

---

[6] Ibid., p. 195.
[7] Ibid.

shaken . . . ." Pentecost's pillar does not support a pretribulational rapture.

D. THE PURPOSE OF THE SEVENTIETH WEEK.

Pentecost writes:

> The first purpose is stated in Revelation 3:10, 'I also will keep thee from the hour of temptation, which shall come upon all the world, to *try* them that dwell upon the earth.' . . . this period has in view 'them that dwell upon the earth' and not the church. This same expression occurs in Revelation 6:10; 11:10; 13:8, 12, 14; 14:6; and 17:8.[8]

In the above verses cited by Pentecost, the phrase "them that dwell upon the earth" refers to "them" who are the murderers of the saints, "them" who are deceived by Satan, and "them" who follow and worship the beast. Thayer says that the term "dwell," in Greek, has the idea of permanence in it. Thiessen writes, "Thus the judgment referred to in Rev. 3:10 is directed against the earthdwellers of that day, against those who have settled down in the earth as their real home, who have identified themselves with the earth's commerce and religion."[9] According to Thayer, the word "try," when God is the subject, means "*to inflict evil* upon one in order to prove his character . . . ."[10]

Pentecost's argument is easily answered. The *evil inflicted*, that is, the seven trumpet judgments, the seven

---

[8] Ibid., p. 197.

[9] Henry C. Thiessen, *Will the Church Pass Through the Tribulation?* (New York: Loizeaux Bro., 1941), pp. 28, 29.

[10] Joseph Henry Thayer, *A Greek-English Lexicon of the New Testament* (New York: American Book Co., 1886), p. 498.

vial judgments, and the wrath at Armageddon, will be inflicted upon "them that dwell upon the earth" *in* the early part of the Day of the Lord, which is called "the great day of his wrath." The *evil* mentioned by Thayer will be inflicted upon "them that dwell upon the earth" during the 1,040-day period that will *follow* the ending of the Great Tribulation and the darkening of the sun and moon. *If* Revelation 3:10 refers to a future *hour* and not merely to the historical church in Philadelphia to which the letter was addressed, the purpose mentioned would be accomplished upon "them that dwell upon the earth" during the 1,040 days of wrath, which will *follow* the darkening of the sun and moon immediately *after* the Great Tribulation. This pillar in no way supports a pretribulational rapture.

Furthermore, where is the Scripture that says "*the hour*" of Revelation 3:10 is equivalent to the Seventieth Week? Gundry writes:

> The word 'hour' appears many times in the gospels with reference to the passion of Jesus (Matthew 26:45; Mark 14:35, 41; John 2:4; 7:30; 8:20; 12:23, 27; 13:1; 17:1). The emphasis falls on *the experience* within the time, *not the period* as such. In the request, 'Father, save me from this hour,' Jesus would not have been praying for deliverance from the period of time, through which he would have gone even had he not died. Rather, he contemplates asking for deliverance from the events within the period of time (John 12:27). This is a common way of speaking. To pray, say, for deliverance from a time of illness is not to ask that one should be taken out of the world before he becomes ill— he is already ill—but that the Lord should preserve and bring him safely out of the period of illness. Stress does not lie on the

period of time per se, but upon the prominent characteristics of the period.[11]

If Revelation 3:10 should refer to the future as well as to the historical church in Philadelphia, *the evil* inflicted upon "them that dwell upon the earth" would be poured out upon "them" *during* the 1,040 days of "the great day of his wrath." The church would be kept "from the hour," even though it will go through the Great Tribulation. The church would be kept "from the hour," even though the rapture will be posttribulational, for the wrath of the Lamb will not be poured out until *after* the Day of the Lord begins, *after* the sun and moon are darkened immediately after the Great Tribulation. Pentecost's pillar does not prove pretribulationism.

Pentecost continues:

> The second major purpose of the seventieth week is in relation to Israel . . . . It can only be concluded then that Elijah, who is to come before the great and terrible day of the Lord, can have only one ministry: that of preparing a remnant in Israel for the advent of the Lord. It is evident that no such ministry is needed by the church . . . .[12]

The Bible does indeed teach that Elijah will come to prepare the remnant of Israel for the advent of Christ. Malachi 4:5, 6a says, "Behold, I will send you Elijah the prophet *before* the coming of the great and dreadful day of the Lord: and he shall turn the heart of the fathers to the children, and the heart of the children to their fathers . . . ." When Elijah comes, he will prepare the remnant of Israel to receive her Saviour and King, even as

---

[11] Gundry, pp. 59, 60.
[12] Pentecost, pp. 197, 198.

John the Baptist, who came in the spirit and power of Elijah, prepared a remnant of Israel to receive Christ at His first coming.

If Elijah is one of the two witnesses in Revelation eleven, as most pretribulationists believe, he will not begin his ministry until *the latter part* of the Great Tribulation. In Revelation 11:7-14, the Bible reveals that the two witnesses will be killed after the sixth trumpet judgment and before the seventh trumpet judgment. Also, Revelation 11:3 says, ". . . my two witnesses . . . shall prophesy a thousand two hundred and threescore days . . . ." Because the two witnesses will prophesy 1,260 days, *their ministry will begin* 1,260 days before they are killed *after* the sixth trumpet judgment; that is, their ministry will begin somewhere *near the middle of the last half* of the Seventieth Week. Remember, the fifth trumpet judgment alone will last five months. Since the two witnesses will be killed after the sixth trumpet judgment, *their deaths* will occur somewhere near the middle of the 1,040-day overrun of the 2,300 days into the Day of the Lord. Therefore, the two witnesses will prophesy during the latter half of the Great Tribulation, and they will continue to prophesy into the Day of the Lord, namely, the millennial kingdom, until they are killed *after* the sixth trumpet judgment. Just *after* the sun and moon are darkened *when* Christ comes in the clouds with power and great glory, all the tribes of the earth will mourn. Then, God will pour upon the house of David, and upon the inhabitants of Jerusalem, the spirit of grace and supplications; and they shall look upon Him Whom they have pierced. The 144,000 Israelites will be converted in a day (Zechariah 3:8-10; 12:9-13:1; Hosea 5:15-6:2).

Elijah, if he is one of the two witnesses, will not begin his ministry until somewhere near the middle of the Great Tribulation. The late commencement of Elijah's ministry and the sealing of the 144,000 just *after* the Day of the Lord begins gives no support whatever to a supposed pretribulational rapture. Consequently, the Bible's teaching about the coming of Elijah is not "supporting evidence that the church will not be in the seventieth week," as Pentecost erroneously teaches.[13] Pentecost's pillar does not support a pretribulational rapture.

E. THE UNITY OF THE SEVENTIETH WEEK.

Pentecost writes:

It should be observed from the three preceding considerations that the entire seventieth week is in view when it is described and predicted in prophecy. While *all* would agree . . . that the seventieth week is divided into two parts of three and one-half years each, yet the *nature and character* of the seventieth week is one, permeating both parts in their entirety.[14]

Pentecost's egregious error is revealed in his argument B which deals with "The Nature of the Seventieth Week." He writes, ". . . the essential *nature* or *character* of this period: 1) wrath . . . 2) judgment . . . 3) indignation . . . 4) punishment . . . ."[15]
Pentecost's error, like that of other pretribulationists, is his putting the wrath, judgment, indignation, and punishment of "the great day of his wrath" *in* the Seventieth Week. The unparalleled wrath of "the great day of his

---

[13] Ibid., p. 198.
[14] Ibid.
[15] Ibid, p. 194.

wrath" will *not* be poured out in the Seventieth Week; it will be poured out *in* the Day of the Lord, *after* the sixth seal is opened, and *after* the sun and moon are darkened immediately *after* the Great Tribulation. The divine wrath of "the great day of his wrath" will be poured out *in* the 1,040-day overrun of the 2,300 days of "the transgression of desolation" *in* the Day of the Lord. This teaching has been explained in our chapter entitled, "The Transgression of Desolation." Pentecost's pillar does not support a pre-tribulational rapture.

F. THE NATURE OF THE CHURCH.

Pentecost writes:

> Since the church is the body, of which Christ is the head . . . there exists between the believer and the Lord a union and a unity . . . . *If the church is in the seventieth week, she is sub-jected to the wrath, judgment, and indignation which character-izes the period*, and because of her oneness with Christ, He, likewise, would be subjected to that same visitation. This is impossible . . . for He cannot be brought into judgment again . . . . Again, Revelation 13:7 makes it clear that *all* who are in the seventieth week are brought into *subjection* to the Beast and through him to Satan, who gives the Beast His power. If the church were in this period, she would be subjected to Satan and Christ would either lose His place as head, or He, Himself, because of the union with the church, would be likewise subject to Satan's authority. Such a thing is unthinkable. Thus it is concluded that the nature of the church . . . prevents her from being in the seventieth week . . . .[16]

Pentecost's flagrant mistake is his placing the wrath of the Lamb in the Seventieth Week of Daniel. The un-

---

[16] Ibid., p. 200.

paralleled wrath of "the great day of his wrath" will *not* be poured out upon them that dwell upon the earth *in* the Seventieth Week of Daniel; that *wrath* of the Lamb will be poured out on them that dwell upon the earth *in* the Day of the Lord, which cannot begin until *after* the sun and moon are darkened, immediately *after* the Great Tribulation. Accordingly, when the church is raptured at the end of the Great Tribulation, it will not have experienced any of the divine wrath of "the great day of his wrath," for the wrath of the Lamb will be poured out *in the Day of the Lord.*

Revelation 13:7, 8 refutes the final part of this argument by Pentecost, saying:

> And it was given unto him [namely, the Antichrist] to make war with the saints, and to overcome them: and *power* was given him over all kindreds, and tongues, and nations. And *all* that dwell upon the earth *shall worship him, whose names are not written in the book of life of the Lamb* . . . .

Notice that this passage does *not* say, as Pentecost said it does, that *all* who are in the Seventieth Week are brought into subjection to the beast. It does say that the beast will make war with the saints and overcome them. It further says that "*All* that dwell upon the earth shall worship him, *whose names are not written in the book of life of the Lamb.*" Did you get that? The Bible says plainly that *those whose names are not written in the book of life* of the Lamb are the ones who will worship the beast. The implication is very clear. Those whose names are *in* the book of life of the Lamb will *not* worship the beast, and they will not subject themselves to the beast. Rather, they will be faithful unto death. Some believers will survive the Great Tribulation, for Jesus said,

". . . he that shall endure unto the end, the same shall be saved."[17] Those believers who endure unto the end of the Great Tribulation will be raptured when Christ comes in the clouds with great power and glory. Pentecost's pillar does not support a pretribulational rapture.

G. THE CONCEPT OF THE CHURCH AS A MYSTERY.

Pentecost writes:

> The church is manifestly an interruption of God's program for Israel, which was not brought into being until Israel's rejection of the offered kingdom. It must logically follow that this mystery program must itself be brought to a conclusion before God can resume His dealing with the nation Israel . . . . This mystery concept of the church makes a pretribulational rapture a necessity.[18]

The answer to this argument is found in Daniel 9:24, which says,

> "*Seventy weeks are determined upon thy people* and upon thy holy city, *to finish the transgression, and to make an end of sins, and to make reconciliation for iniquity, and to bring in everlasting righteousness*, and to seal up the vision and prophecy, *and to anoint the most Holy*."

It will not be *until* the seventy weeks are past that these blessings to Israel will occur. Daniel 9:25 says, "Know therefore and understand, that from the going forth of the commandment to restore and to build Jerusalem unto the Messiah the Prince shall be seven

---

[17] Matthew 24:13.
[18] Pentecost, p. 201.

weeks, and threescore and two weeks [that is, sixty-nine weeks] ...." The Messiah did not come at the end of sixty-eight weeks; He came at the end of sixty-nine weeks, precisely as Daniel 9:25 says.

Even so, God will resume His program with the remnant of Israel *at the end* of the Seventieth Week, *not at the beginning* of the Seventieth Week. The church will be raptured after the Great Tribulation, when Christ comes in the clouds with great power and glory, that is, *at the end of the seventy weeks*. As we have seen before, God will resume His dealing with Israel after the sixth seal is opened, for Revelation 7:1-4 says, "And *after these things* ... the number of them which were sealed ... were ... an hundred and forty four thousand ...." It is at *this* time that God will resume His dealing with Israel. God will not resume His dealing with Israel at the beginning of the Seventieth Week, but the 144,000 will be sealed after the sixth seal is opened, when the seventy weeks are completed. Accordingly, they will be protected from the wrath of God, which will be poured out during the seven trumpet judgments, the seven vial judgments, and the Battle of Armageddon.

In Revelation 14:1, 4, John wrote:

And I looked, and, lo, a Lamb stood on the mount Sion, and with him an hundred forty and four thousand, having his Father's name written in their foreheads .... These were redeemed from among men, being the first fruits unto God and to the Lamb.

These 144,000 comprise *the first fruits of a new order in the millennial kingdom,* namely, the Day of the Lord. Therefore, the mystery concept of the church does not make a pretribulational rapture a necessity. Pentecost's pillar does not support a pretribulational rapture.

H. THE DISTINCTIONS BETWEEN ISRAEL AND THE CHURCH.

Pentecost writes, "These clear contrasts, which show the distinction between Israel and the church, make it impossible to identify the two in one program, which it is necessary to do if the church goes through the seventieth week."[19] This argument is refuted by the writer's answer to Pentecost's argument G. In short, the writer does not identify Israel and the church in one program. The church and *unsaved* Israelites will go through the Great Tribulation together. The church will be raptured when the sun and moon are darkened immediately *after* the Great Tribulation, when Christ comes in the clouds with great power and glory. Then, Revelation 7:1 says, "And *after these things . . . .*" the 144,000 Israelites are sealed and called the servants of God. The conversion of the 144,000 and their sealing will occur just *after* the posttribulational rapture. Therefore, the distinction between Israel and the church is not proof of a pretribulational rapture. Pentecost's pillar does not support a pretribulational rapture.

I. THE DOCTRINE OF IMMINENCE.

In defining imminency, Stanton writes, "As applied to the coming of the Lord, imminency consists of three things: the certainty that He may come at any moment, the uncertainty of the time of that arrival, and the fact that no prophesied event stands between the believer and that

---

[19] Ibid., p. 202.

hour."[20] Just how important is the pillar of imminency to pretribulationism? Walvoord writes, *"The central feature of pretribulationism* [is] the doctrine of imminency."[21] Walvoord further writes, ". . . the doctrine of imminency is *the heart* of pretribulationism."[22] It is obvious that Walvoord considers imminency to be the primary pillar upon which pretribulationism stands.

Pretribulationists use verses such as the following to support their theory of imminency:

1. *"Watch* therefore: for ye know not what hour your Lord doth come" (Matthew 24:42).

2. "Therefore *be ye* also *ready*: for in such an hour as ye think not the Son of man cometh" (Matthew 24:44).

3. "So that ye come behind in no gift; *waiting* for the coming of our Lord Jesus Christ . . . ." (I Corinthians 1:7, 8).

4. *"Looking* for that blessed hope, and the glorious appearing of the great God and our Saviour Jesus Christ" (Titus 2:13).

In the above verses we have the words "*watch*," "*be ready*," "*waiting*," and "*looking*." In our chapter, "Posttribulationism Is the Historical Position," we will show that Walvoord, Stanton, and Pentecost all try to convince

---

[20] Stanton, p. 108.

[21] Walvoord, *Rapture Question: Revised*, p. 51.

[22] Ibid, p. 53.

their readers that the early church fathers taught imminency. They did *not* teach imminency; they taught expectancy. It is one thing to eagerly *expect* Christ's coming, but it is an entirely different thing to believe that
Christ may come at any moment.

When the writer was a boy, he enjoyed summer vaca-
tions. As soon as a summer vacation ended, he immediately began to *watch* for, be *ready* for, *wait* for, and
look for the new school year to end and the next summer
vacation to begin. Although he knew that Thanksgiving
Day, Christmas Day, and Easter Sunday all had to occur
first, he still *watched* for, was *ready* for, *waited* for, and
looked for the next summer vacation. One of the writer's
favorite holidays was the Fourth of July. In those days,
people were allowed to shoot firecrackers on the Fourth,
and as a youth he thought that was one of the most exciting things a person could do. People shot firecrackers of
all sizes — from lady fingers to cherry bombs. When the
Fourth of July was past, on the fifth of July, he began to
watch for, be *ready* for, *wait* for, and *look* for the next
Fourth of July. He knew that before the Fourth of July
could come again, summer vacation would have to end,
the next school year would begin, Thanksgiving would
come, Christmas would come, Easter would come, his
birthday would come, and then, finally the Fourth of July
would come again. Although he knew that all those
events had to occur prior to the coming of the Fourth of
July, he was nonetheless *watching* for, *ready* for, *waiting*
for, and *looking* for the coming of the next Fourth of July.

When the writer and his late wife were engaged to be
married in the summertime, they set their wedding date
for the following December 28. Prior to the day of the
wedding, he was *watching* for, *ready* for, *waiting* for, and

looking for the wedding day to come. However, he knew
that before that day could come, Thanksgiving Day and
Christmas Day had to come first. Although he knew certain events had to take place before their wedding day
could come, he was nonetheless *watching* for, *ready* for,
waiting for, and *looking* for their wedding day. In short,
his attitude toward the approaching wedding day was one
of *expectancy*. Not once did he believe that their wedding
day was *imminent*, that is, that their wedding day could
occur at any moment. The postapostolic fathers taught
expectancy; they did *not* teach imminency.

The scriptures pretribulationists use to support imminency simply do not teach imminency. For example,
Stanton uses the following verses in support of imminency: John 14:2, 3; Acts 1:11; I Corinthians 15:51, 52;
Philippians 3:20; Colossians 3:4; I Thessalonians 1:9, 10;
I Timothy 4:16; Hebrews 10:37; James 5:8; II Peter 3:4,
5; Revelation 22:20.[23] If one reads these verses carefully,
interprets the words literally, and if one does not read
imminency into these verses, he will see that *not one of
them teaches that Christ may come at any moment.*

After citing the above verses, Stanton writes, "These
. . . precious promises were given . . . to the entire church,
and for the entire age. This alone is sufficient ground to
prove . . . the coming of Christ as imminent."[24] However,
Stanton is as confused as a termite in a yo-yo, for these
verses do not teach imminency. If these verses truly teach
imminency, Walvoord would not concede, *"Pretribulationism . . . is an induction . . . rather than an explicit*

---

[23] Stanton, pp. 124, 125.
[24] Ibid., p. 125.

statement of the Bible."[25]   If these verses really teach imminency, Walvoord would never admit, "*While . . . pretribulationists . . . have strained to find some specific reference in support of their views . . . most adherents . . . concede that there is no explicit reference . . . .*"[26] If these verses truly teach imminency, Pentecost would not confess, "The pretribulation doctrine *is* not based on these arguments singly [individually, single-handedly], but rather they are considered as cumulative evidence . . . ."[27]

   Now let us consider some plain truth from the Bible which destroys the pretribulational concept of imminency. First, let us ponder Peter's case. Jesus said to Peter:

> Verily, verily, I say unto thee, when thou wast young, thou girdest thyself, and walkedst whither thou wouldest: but when *thou shalt be old*, thou shalt stretch forth thy hands, *and another shall gird thee, and carry thee whither thou wouldest not.* This spake he, signifying by what death he [Peter] should glorify God.[28]

   This prophecy teaches that *Peter would grow old.* Furthermore, it teaches that *when* Peter grew old, *he would die as a martyr.* Jesus said, ". . . *when thou shalt be old* . . . ." (Jesus did *not* say, *if* you grow old.) Further, Jesus said, ". . . *another shall gird thee, and carry thee whither thou wouldest not.*" (Jesus did not say that another shall carry thee whither thou wouldest not *if* you grow old.) Verse nineteen explains verse eighteen, for it says, "This spake he, signifying by what death he [Peter] should glorify God." After Peter had grown old, he wrote

---

[25] Walvoord, *Rapture Question: Revised*, p. 181.

[26] Ibid, p. 182.

[27] Pentecost, p. 218.

[28] John 21:18, 19.

II Peter in A.D. 66 or early 67.[29]   Accordingly, Peter wrote his second epistle approximately thirty-five years *after* Jesus had told him that he would grow old and that another would gird him and carry him where he did not want to go. Jesus had told him that he would grow old and die a martyr's death.

In Peter's second epistle, he wrote, "Knowing that shortly I must put off this my tabernacle, *even as our Lord Jesus Christ hath shewed me.*"[30]   Peter understood clearly what Jesus had said to him on the shore of the Sea of Galilee in A.D. 32, just after the resurrection. This prophecy by our Lord must have been a tremendous source of comfort to Peter, for he knew that he would not die *until* he reached old age. Ponder this passage further.

Peter had to grow old in order for Christ's prophecy to be fulfilled. Consequently, Peter *could not* have been raptured before he grew old, for if he had been raptured before he grew old, Christ's prophecy would not have been fulfilled. Then, Christ would have become a false prophet, according to Deuteronomy 18:22. To teach that Christ could have raptured the church during the lifetime of Peter by coming at any moment prior to Peter's becoming old and dying as a martyr is to teach that Christ could have become a false prophet. The possibility of our Lord's becoming a false prophet is unthinkable for all thinking Bible believers. Therefore, *the rapture could not have occurred* during the time between Christ's giving the prophecy in A.D. 32 and Peter's dying a martyr's death in

---

[29] Henry C. Thiessen, *Introduction to the New Testament* (Grand Rapids. Mich.: Wm. B. Eerdmans Publishing Co., 1943), p. 291.

[30] II Peter 1:14.

his old age. This fact means that *the rapture could not have been imminent* during Peter's lifetime. This conclusion is as simple as two plus two equals four.

Since Peter had to grow old and die a martyr's death, an imminent rapture would have been an impossibility during Peter's lifetime. But something of even greater magnitude is true in the light of the preceding facts. The Holy Spirit would never have moved a writer to record two contradictory prophecies. The Holy Spirit certainly knew of Christ's prophecy to Peter in A.D. 32. Accordingly, the Holy Spirit knew that *Peter had to grow old* and die a martyr's death in order to fulfill Christ's prophecy. Hence, the Holy Spirit knew that Christ's coming to rapture the church *could not be imminent* during the interval between Christ's prophecy in A.D. 32 and Peter's death about A.D. 68. Regarding the time of Peter's death, Thiessen writes, ". . . he died a martyr's death in 67 or 68."[31] Because the Holy Spirit knew these facts, *He would never have given any inspired words teaching imminency to any New Testament writer prior to the death of Peter in his old age.*

Therefore, this fact means that the epistles of Paul do not teach imminency. This fact means that the epistles of Peter do not teach imminency. This fact means Matthew, Mark, and Luke do not teach imminency. It is apparent that the gospel of John was written before the destruction of Jerusalem in A.D. 70, for John 5:2 says, "Now there *is* at Jerusalem by the sheep market a pool, which *is* called in the Hebrew tongue Bethesda . . . ." The Scripture here says there *is* at Jerusalem — not there *was* at Jerusalem. Hence, when the gospel of John was written, Jerusalem

---

[31] Thiessen, *Introduction to the New Testament*, p. 282.

had not yet been destroyed. This fact means that the gospel of John was written before A.D. 70. If John was written before Peter died, then the fourth gospel could not have taught imminency. Again, James, probably the earliest New Testament book written, cannot teach imminency. In short, the four gospels, the book of Acts (written in A.D. 61), the Pauline epistles, James, and I and II Peter cannot possibly teach imminency, for the Holy Spirit is the Spirit of truth. Knowing that *Peter had to grow old and die a martyr's death*, the Holy Spirit would never have taught that Christ could come at any moment in the above-mentioned New Testament books. If the Holy Spirit had taught an any-moment coming of Christ in the in the above books, He would have been a Spirit of falsehood. For the Holy Spirit to teach falsehood is an impossibility, as every Bible believer knows, for the Holy Spirit is the Spirit of truth.

Stanton attempts to neutralize the devastating effect of Christ's prophecy to Peter, when he writes, ". . . it is certain that the believers expected Peter's death, for when Rhoda bore the news of his release, they said unto her, 'Thou are mad,' and when they saw Peter, 'they were astonished' (Acts 12:15, 16)."[32] Now, isn't Stanton something? If those believers did not know of Christ's prophecy to Peter and expected Peter's death, it still would have made absolutely no difference. Christ gave the prophecy, and the prophecy had to be fulfilled, even if the believers expected Peter's death. What the believers expected could never alter the sure words of Christ's prophecy. In short, an imminent coming of Christ was

---

[32] Stanton, p. 113.

impossible during the interval between the prophecy given in A.D. 32 and Peter's death about A.D. 68.

Even more importantly, *imminency could not be taught in any of the books of the New Testament written during that interval.* All of the verses Stanton lists to prove imminency, with one exception, were written prior to Peter's martyrdom. The one exception (Revelation 22:20) does not prove imminency either. Stanton's answer is preposterous. When a person gets hooked on a theory, it certainly does mess up his mind, doesn't it?

Let us look at more clear truth from the Bible which also destroys the pretribulational concept of imminency. The case of Paul in A.D. 60 is similar to the case of Peter. Paul was in Jerusalem, and he was in danger of being killed in a riot. The chief captain ordered the soldiers to take Paul into the castle. The Bible says, "And the night following the Lord stood by him, and said, Be of good cheer, Paul: for as thou hast testified of me in Jerusalem, *so must thou bear witness also at Rome.*"[33] In order for this prophecy to be fulfilled, *Paul had to go to Rome.* Therefore, the rapture could not have occurred until Paul reached Rome in A.D. 63. During the voyage to Rome, Paul's ship was caught in a terrible tempest. In the midst of the storm, the angel of God came to Paul and said, ". . . Fear not, Paul; thou must be brought before Caesar."[34] Consequently, Paul could not have been raptured until he was brought before Caesar. After arriving in Rome in A.D. 63, Paul spent two years in Rome in his own hired house. The two years in Rome takes Paul to A.D. 65.

---

[33] Acts 23:11.
[34] Acts 27:24.

The rapture could not have been imminent before Paul appeared before Caesar. If the rapture had occurred before Paul had been brought before Caesar, the Lord's prophecy would have been untrue. The possibility of the Lord's becoming a false prophet is unthinkable for Bible believers. Therefore, none of the New Testament books written before Paul saw Caesar could possibly teach imminency. If any do, then the Holy Spirit was teaching imminency when He knew Christ could not come at any moment. To say that the Holy Spirit would teach a falsehood is absolutely unthinkable for thinking Bible believers. It is not just unthinkable; it is blasphemous.

Consider still more transparent truth from the Bible which refutes the pretribulational concept of imminency. Notice the case of the apostle John. Scofield says that Revelation was written in A.D. 96 by the aged apostle John, exiled on the isle of Patmos. Most Bible scholars agree that Revelation was the last of the New Testament books written. Keeping in mind this fact, we find something very interesting in the tenth chapter of Revelation. In Revelation ten, a statement relevant to John's future ministry is made. The verse says, *"Thou [John] must prophesy again* before many peoples, and nations, and tongues, and kings."[35] Therefore, *no book of the Bible written prior to John's fulfilling this prophetic command can teach imminency.* Revelation 10:11 does to the pretribulational concept of imminency what the atomic bomb did to Hiroshima. Remember that Walvoord wrote, *"The central feature* of pretribulationism [is] the doctrine of imminency . . . ."[36] The pretribulational doctrine of immi-

---

[35] Revelation 10:11.
[36] Walvoord, *Rapture Question: Revised*, p. 51.

nency is about as sound as a Confederate dollar. So much for the doctrine of imminency, which Walvoord says "is *the heart* of pretribulationism."[37]

J. THE WORK OF THE RESTRAINER IN II THESSALONIANS 2.

Pentecost writes:

> Paul's argument in verse 7 is that . . . this lawless one could not be manifested until the Restrainer was taken out of the way . . . while this is essentially an exegetical problem, it would *seem* that the only One who could do such a restraining ministry would be the Holy Spirit . . . thus, this ministry of the Restrainer . . . which must cease before the lawless can be revealed, requires the pretribulation rapture of the church . . . .[38]

Dr. Peter Ruckman, who is the smartest pretribulationist that the writer knows, gave him the answer to this argument in a telephonic conversation in the fall of 1981. Ruckman said that the restrainer cannot be the Holy Spirit, for the rule of grammar requires that the restrainer must be *the antecedent* of the pronouns "he," which are used in verse seven. He said that the only antecedent for the pronouns "he" in verse seven is "the man of sin" referred to in verse three. The man of sin will be the restrainer until he is wounded to death. Then, a spirit from the bottomless pit will enter into his body, and the body will be restored to life. The man of sin, who will be wounded to death and revivified, will be revealed as *the son of perdition* when he breaks the covenant in the midst of the Seventieth Week (Daniel 9:27). When the man of

---

[37] Ibid., p. 53.
[38] Pentecost, p. 204.

sin is *revealed* as the son of perdition, there will be no more restraining *of* iniquity. This interpretation also fits well with the historical view, which teaches that the restraining influence is human government. This interpretation also fits the restrainer "what" in verse six, for the "what" in verse six is in the neuter gender—not the masculine gender, as are the pronouns "he" in verse seven. The neuter "what" (apparently, human government) is the withholding or restraining influence referred to in verse six.

Pentecost admitted, "... *this is essentially an exegetical problem . . . .*"[39] To read the Holy Spirit as the meaning of the pronouns "he" into the text of verse seven is *not* exegesis—it is a reading of one's own view into the text of Scripture. An interpreter has as much exegetical authority to say that the "he" means Donald Duck, Mickey Mouse, or Goofy, as he does to say that the "he" means the Holy Spirit. If one follows the *grammatical*, historical method of interpretation and interprets the Bible *literally*, he must determine the meaning of the pronouns "he" in verse seven by finding the antecedent in the preceding context. Since the Holy Spirit is not mentioned in II Thessalonians prior to chapter two and verse seven, it is grammatically impossible for the Holy Spirit to be the antecedent of the pronouns "he" in verse seven.

Accordingly, the restrainer of verse seven is not the Holy Spirit. Therefore, the work of the restrainer in II Thessalonians two does *not* support a pretribulational rapture of the church. Pentecost's pillar does not support pretribulationism.

---

[39] Ibid., p. 205.

K. THE NECESSITY OF AN INTERVAL.

We have demonstrated in previous chapters that *there is an interval* of 1,040 days between the coming of Christ in the clouds with power and great glory and His coming on a white horse for the Battle of Armageddon. An interval requires only a two-phase coming, *not* a pretribulational coming. Therefore, the necessity of an interval does *not* prove a pretribulational rapture of the church. Pentecost's pillar does not support pretribulationism.

L. THE DISTINCTION BETWEEN THE RAPTURE AND THE SECOND ADVENT.

As mentioned in the refutation of Pentecost's previous argument, the writer has taught plainly in this book that *there is a distinction* between the rapture and the second advent. It has been demonstrated by this writer that there is a distinction between the coming of Christ in the clouds with power and great glory to rapture the church at the end of the Great Tribulation, and the coming of Christ on a white horse for the Battle of Armageddon 1,040 days later. Therefore, the distinction between the rapture and the second advent does *not* require a pretribulational rapture; it merely requires a two-phase second coming. Pentecost's pillar does not support a pretribulational rapture.

M. THE TWENTY-FOUR ELDERS.

Pentecost writes:

Scofield presents evidence to support the view that these are the representatives of the church. He writes, 'The elders are, *sym-*

bolically, the church, and they are seen in heaven in the place which the Scriptures assign to the church before a seal is opened or a woe uttered, and before a vial of the wrath of God is poured out.'[40]

Pentecost continues:

... these must be *representatives* of the saints of this present age. Since they are seen to be resurrected, in heaven, judged, rewarded, enthroned at the beginning of the seventieth week, it is concluded that the church must have been raptured before the seventieth week begins.[41]

Now let us watch Pentecost and Scofield work. As Pentecost develops his argument, he writes, ". . . Scofield presents evidence to support the view that these are *the representatives* of the church."[42] Then Pentecost quotes Scofield, who wrote, "The elders are, *symbolically*, the church . . . ."[43] Ain't that somethin'? After Pentecost tells us that the *literal* interpretation of Scripture proves a pretribulational rapture of the church, he uses the *symbolical* interpretation of the twenty-four elders to support a pretribulational rapture.

Because the writer believes in "the literal method of interpretation," he holds that the twenty-four elders must be interpreted literally. If a person interprets literally, as the writer does, the twenty-four elders are twenty-four elders; they are *not symbolical* of anything—just as the *one* sitting on the throne is *not symbolical* of anything. In Revelation four, there is one throne, and there are twenty-

---

[40] Ibid., p. 208.
[41] Ibid., p. 209.
[42] Ibid., p. 208.
[43] Ibid.

four seats. The one throne is literal, and the twenty-four seats are literal. There is *one God* on the one throne, and there are twenty-four elders on the twenty-four seats. The one God is literal, and the twenty-four elders are literal. Nothing in the context requires a person to believe that the twenty-four elders are symbolical—that is, nothing except a theological necessity.

If anyone wonders where these "resurrected, in heaven, judged, rewarded, enthroned-at-the-beginning-of-the-seventieth-week," twenty-four elders come from, a little careful Bible study can answer that question. Matthew writes, "And the graves were opened; and *many bodies of the saints which slept arose*, and came out of the graves after his resurrection, and went into the holy city, and appeared unto many."[44]

Accordingly, the Bible teaches that there was a resurrection of the saints just after Christ's resurrection. This truth is confirmed in Paul's first letter to the Corinthians, where he writes:

> For as in Adam all die, even so in Christ shall all be made alive. But every man in his own order: *Christ the firstfruits; afterward* they that are Christ's at his coming. *Then* cometh the end, when he shall have delivered up the kingdom to God, even the Father; when he shall have put down all rule and all authority and power. For he must reign, till he hath put all enemies under his feet.[45]

Here Paul teaches that there are three stages to the first resurrection, namely, the resurrection of life (John 5:28). The first stage was at the time of Christ's resur-

---

[44] Matthew 27:52, 53.
[45] I Corinthians 15:22-25.

rection (Matthew 27:52, 53); the second stage will be at His coming; the third stage will be at the end of the millennium.

The resurrection mentioned in Matthew 27:52, 53 was a resurrection of *many* of the just, and Jesus said to His disciples, ". . . thou shalt be recompensed *at* the resurrection of the just."[46] The twenty-four *elders* of Revelation, chapters four and five, are twenty-four *elders* (literal interpretation) who were resurrected and rewarded just after Christ's resurrection. This view is mandatory for all who truly adhere to *a literal interpretation* of the Bible.

The Bible confirms the truth that the *twenty-four elders are distinct from the church*. The twenty-four elders in Revelation four and five are seen to be "resurrected, in heaven, judged, rewarded [and] enthroned before the first seal is opened." However, the church will not be rewarded until after the seventh trumpet sounds. Accordingly, the judging and rewarding of the saints who constitute the church will not take place until *after* the Great Tribulation. *At the sounding of the seventh trumpet, it is the twenty-four elders themselves who call for the judging and rewarding of the saints, namely, the church* (Revelation 11:18). Since the twenty-four elders are the ones calling for the judging and rewarding of the saints after the sounding of the seventh trumpet in Revelation eleven, it must be concluded that *the twenty-four elders are not the church*. This truth is more fully explained in Appendix C.

Pentecost, in dealing with the twenty-four elders, abandons the literal method of interpretation which he

---

[46] Luke 14:14.

says is vital, *and he follows the symbolical interpretation* of Scofield. Think about that. The twenty-four elders of Revelation do not support pretribulationism; hence, Pentecost's pillar does not support a pretribulational rapture.

N. THE PROBLEM BEHIND I THESSALONIANS 4:12-18.

Pentecost writes, "Paul writes . . . to teach . . . the fact that at the rapture the living would not have advantage over the dead in Christ."[47] This fact, however, does not support a pretribulational rapture. Attempting to build his futile argument on *assumptions*, Pentecost writes, ". . . these Christians *evidently* believed that the church would not go through the Seventieth Week and in their anticipation of the return of Christ, mourned for their brethren, whom they thought had missed the blessing of this event."[48]

Contrary to Pentecost's assumption, postapostolic Christians *did* believe the church would go through the Seventieth Week. Even Walvoord admits, ". . . the early fathers were not specifically pretribulational . . . the early church did not teach Twentieth-Century pretribulationism."[49] Despite his specious reasoning and false assumptions, Pentecost does not prove a pretribulational rapture. No wonder Pentecost conceded, *"The pretribulation doctrine is not based on these arguments singly . . . ."*[50]

While I Thessalonians 4:13-18 is indeed a great rapture passage, *it does not teach the time of the rapture.* In

---

[47] Pentecost, p. 209.
[48] Ibid.
[49] Walvoord, *Rapture Question: Revised*, pp. 156, 157.
[50] Pentecost, p. 218.

1980, Allen Beechick wrote *The Pretribulation Rapture*.
In his imprimatur on the back cover of the book,
Walvoord said, "The book offers many solid and unanswerable arguments for the pretribulation rapture." In
the book, Beechick wrote, *"I believe that Paul was
neither Pre-trib, nor Post-trib, and . . . I can prove it
from I and II Thessalonians."*[51] Walvoord said Beechick's book contained many "solid and unanswerable
arguments for the pretribulation rapture," but Beechick
himself said Paul was "neither Pre-trib nor Post-trib . . . ,"
and that he could "prove it from I and II Thessalonians."
Beechick's words do not correspond with Walvoord's
words found in the imprimatur of the book, and I Thessalonians four does not prove a pretribulational rapture. It
is no wonder that Walvoord conceded in one of his own
books:

> . . . pretribulationism . . . is an induction . . . rather than an ex-
> plicit statement of the Bible . . . . While . . . pretribulationists
> . . . have strained to find some specific reference in support of
> their views, most adherents . . . concede that there is no explicit
> reference . . . ."[52]

Neither I Thessalonians four nor the supposed problem
behind the text, as propagated by Pentecost, gives any
support to pretribulationism. Pentecost's pillar does not
support a pretribulational rapture.

---

[51] Allen Beechick, *The Pretribulation Rapture* (Denver, Colo.:
Accent Books, 1980), p. 81.

[52] Walvoord, *Rapture Question: Revised*, pp. 181, 182.

O. THE ANNOUNCEMENT OF PEACE AND SAFETY.

Pentecost writes:

> In I Thessalonians 5:3 Paul tells the Thessalonian church that *the day of the Lord* will come after the announcement of 'peace and safety.' . . . If the church were in the seventieth week there would be no possibility that, during the period when believers are being persecuted by the beast to an unprecedented degree, such a message [namely, peace and safety] could be preached and find acceptation so that men would be lulled into complacency . . . . The fact that *the visitation of wrath, judgment* and *darkness* is preceded by the announcement of such a message indicates that the church must be raptured before that period can begin.[53]

The writer has pointed out many times that *the unparalleled wrath* of *the great day of His wrath* will be poured out *in* the Day of the Lord, *after* the sun and moon are darkened. Jesus said that the sun and moon will be darkened immediately *after* the Great Tribulation, that is, after the Seventieth Week is completed. A little careful Bible study shows that *it is not the believers* who are lulled into complacency; *it is the unbelievers.* In I Thessalonians 5:1-4, Paul wrote,

> But of the times and the seasons, brethren, *ye* have no need that I write unto *you. For yourselves know perfectly that the day of the Lord so cometh as a thief in the night.* For when *they* shall say, Peace and safety; then sudden destruction cometh upon *them*, as travail upon a woman with child; and *they* shall not escape. But *ye, brethren*, are not in darkness, that that day should overtake *you* as a thief.

---

[53] Pentecost, pp. 209, 210.

This passage is as clear as day. While *believers* are suffering great tribulation during the reign of Antichrist, *they*
will know that the Day of the Lord is fast approaching,
for *they* are not in darkness. The *unbelievers* will be in
darkness and will be lulled into complacency by the cry of
"peace and safety." It is upon the *ungodly* that the Day of
the Lord will come as a thief in the night. Paul makes that
crystal-clear in verse four by saying, "But *ye, brethren,*
are not in darkness, that *that day* should overtake *you* as a
thief." Pentecost needs to do some serious Bible study in
I Thessalonians 5:1-4. No wonder Pentecost conceded,
"The pretribulation doctrine is not based on these
arguments singly . . . ."[54] Pentecost's pillar does not support a pretribulational rapture.

P. THE RELATION OF THE CHURCH TO GOVERNMENTS.

Pentecost writes:

> . . . the church is . . . instructed to be in subjection to such
> powers . . . Romans 13:1-7, because these governments are
> God's representatives to carry out His will. According to Reve-
> lation 13:4 the government during the seventieth week is con-
> trolled by Satan and is carrying out his will . . . . The church
> could not subject herself to such a government.[55]

Pentecost really scrapes the bottom of the barrel here.
The *general rule* is submission to the government, but if
the government compels God's people to violate God's
laws, God's people must obey God, even if it means
disobeying the government. Has Pentecost forgotten

---

[54] Ibid., p. 218.
[55] Ibid., p. 210.

about the three Hebrew children? Has Pentecost forgotten about Peter and John's saying (when they were commanded to stop teaching in the name of Jesus), "Whether it be right in the sight of God to hearken unto you more than unto God, judge ye." Has Pentecost forgotten about the thousands of Christians whose blood reddened the mouths of lions in the Colosseum because they would *not* subject themselves to the government's command to bow down before Caesar or his image? Has Pentecost forgotten about the millions of martyrs who would not subject themselves to church-controlled governments that ordered Christians to recant. Has Pentecost forgotten about the believers who were burned at the stake during the Inquisition because they would not renounce their faith in Christ? Has Pentecost forgotten about the millions of believers who were martyred for their faith in Red Russia, Red China, Red Cuba, and all of the other communist countries of the world?

In this argument, Pentecost made *one* true statement when he said, "The church could not subject herself to such a government."[56] Precisely — and that is why many of the saints will be martyred under the reign of Antichrist during the Great Tribulation. The saints will not subject themselves to such a government; they will choose martyrdom instead. Regarding the elect who will be martyred by the Antichrist, John writes, ". . . and I saw the souls of them that were beheaded for the witness of Jesus, and for the Word of God, and which had not worshipped the beast, neither his image, neither had received his mark upon their foreheads, or in their hands; and they lived and

---

[56] Ibid.

reigned with Christ a thousand years."[57] As we ponder Pentecost's pitiful pillar, we can see why he conceded, "The pretribulation doctrine is not based on these arguments singly . . . ."[58] He was not kidding.

Q. THE SILENCE CONCERNING THE TRIBULATION IN THE EPISTLES.

Pentecost writes, *"Evidently* the writers of the epistles had no knowledge that the church would endure the seventieth week, for they certainly would have given help and guidance to meet the most severe persecution men will ever have known . . . ."[59]

Paul, who wrote fourteen of the twenty-seven books of the New Testament, wrote most of the epistles, and he gave clear "help and guidance" by informing the church that it would face the son of perdition before the rapture came. Paul wrote, "Let no man deceive you by any means: for that day [the Day of Christ] shall not come, except there come a falling away first, and that man of sin be revealed, the son of perdition."[60] Furthermore, post-apostolic fathers who immediately succeeded the apostles believed that the church would go through the Great Tribulation and that it would face the Antichrist. These early fathers warned the church that it would face great persecution from the Antichrist during the Great Tribulation. For example, Justin Martyr wrote, "The man of apostasy [Antichrist] . . . shall venture to do unlawful

---

[57] Revelation 20:4.
[58] Pentecost, p. 218.
[59] Ibid, p. 211.
[60] II Thessalonians 2:3.

deeds on the earth *against us the Christians . . . .*"⁶¹ The
Shepherd of Hermas wrote, "Happy *ye who endure the
great tribulation* that is coming on . . . ."⁶² Twice in *The
Teaching of the Twelve Apostles*, Matthew 24:31, which
describes the gathering together of the elect, is quoted
with the substitution of "church" *for* "elect."⁶³ Believers
are then urged to stand true through Antichrist's reign of
terror until the posttribulational coming of Christ in the
clouds with power and great glory. Irenaeus wrote, "And
they [the ten kings] shall . . . give their kingdom to *the
beast, and put the church to flight.*"⁶⁴ Again, Irenaeus
wrote, "But he [John] indicates the number of the name
now, that when this man comes *we may avoid him, being
aware who he is.*"⁶⁵ Hippolytus wrote, "Now concerning
the tribulation of the persecution which is to fall upon the
church from *the Adversary . . .* that refers to the one
thousand two hundred and threescore days [the second
half of the Seventieth Week] *during which the Tyrant is
to reign and persecute the church.*"⁶⁶ Tertullian wrote,
". . . that *the beast Antichrist with his false prophet may
wage war on the church of God . . . .*"⁶⁷ It is obvious that
these postapostolic fathers who immediately followed the

---

⁶¹ James Donaldson and Alexander Roberts, *The Ante-Nicene
Fathers* (Grand Rapids, Mich.: Wm. B. Eerdmans Publishing Co.,
1989), Volume 1, *Trypho CX*, pp. 253, 254.

⁶² Ibid, Volume 2, *Shepherd of Hermas, Vision II*, p. 11.

⁶³ Gundry, p 175.

⁶⁴ Donaldson and Roberts, Volume 1, Irenaeus, *Against
Heresies*, p. 555.

⁶⁵ Ibid., p. 560.

⁶⁶ Ibid., Volume 5, Hippolytus, *Treatise on Christ and
Antichrist*, p. 217.

⁶⁷ Ibid., Volume 3, Tertullian, *On the Resurrection Flesh*,
p. 563.

apostles, believed that the church would endure the Great
Tribulation and that it would face the Antichrist.

Pentecost continues:

> They would not prepare [the church] for the persecutions
> common to all *and neglect the outpouring of wrath* in which the
> believer would need special help and assistance if he were to be
> in it . . . . Inasmuch as the persecutions of this age and the *wrath
> of the seventieth week* vary in character, not just in intensity
> . . . . The silence in the Epistles . . . would leave the church
> unprepared for the tribulation . . . .[68]

Here again, Pentecost is guilty of one of the most
egregious errors of pretribulationism—putting the wrath
of the Lamb *in* the Seventieth Week. The writer has
pointed out again and again that the unparalleled wrath of
the great day of His wrath will not be poured out *until*
the Day of the Lord comes. And, the Day of the Lord
will not come until *after* the sun and moon are darkened
immediately *after* the Great Tribulation. Therefore, although the church will go through the Great Tribulation,
it will not experience any of the wrath of the Lamb, which
will be poured out during the trumpet judgments, the vial
judgments, and the Battle of Armageddon.

Pentecost quoted Scofield, who wrote, ". . . there is
no syllable of Scripture which affirms that the church will
enter the great tribulation . . . ."[69] The truth of the matter
is that there is no syllable of Scripture which affirms that
the church will *not* enter the Great Tribulation. If there
were a syllable of Scripture which affirms that the church
will not enter the Great Tribulation, Pentecost would not

---

[68] Pentecost, p. 211.
[69] Ibid.

have admitted, *"The pretribulation doctrine is not based on these arguments singly . . . ."*[70] If there were a syllable of Scripture which affirms the church will not enter the Great Tribulation, Walvoord would not concede:

> . . . pretribulationism . . . is an induction . . . rather than an explicit statement of the Bible . . . .While . . . pretribulationists . . . have strained to find some specific reference in support of their views, most adherents . . . concede that there is no explicit reference . . . ."[71]

Pentecost's pillar does not support a pretribulational rapture.

R. THE MESSAGE OF THE TWO WITNESSES.

Pentecost writes:

> The substance of their preaching is not revealed, but its content may be seen as suggested by the clothing of those messengers . . . . It may be concluded, from their distinctive dress, that *the two witnesses are announcing the same message as John did, that of repentance* because the King is coming . . . . *The message committed to the church is the message of grace. The church has no other message.* The fact that the message announced is one of judgment, repentance, and preparation in view of the coming of the King indicates that *the church must no longer be present for no such message is committed to her.*[72]

It must be pointed out that Pentecost is in deadly theological error, for the message of repentance was committed to the church also (cf. Luke 24:45-48; Acts 3:19; 17:30; 20:21; 26:20). The Bible plainly teaches that the

---

[70] Ibid., p. 218.

[71] Walvoord, *Rapture Question: Revised*, pp. 181, 182.

[72] Pentecost, p. 211.

church was commanded to preach repentance as well as remission of sins by grace through faith. Paul, whose example the church is commanded to follow, preached repentance as well as grace (cf. Acts 17:31; Acts 24:25; Hebrews 9:27).

William Booth, the great Christian leader of a century ago, in one of his last major addresses said, "I fear the day will come when preachers will preach heaven without hell, and faith without repentance." The day that Booth feared would come, has come.

Pentecost's argument does not prove that the church must no longer be present. The two witnesses will not begin their ministry until approximately halfway through the last half of Daniel's Seventieth Week. This is evident, for their ministry of 1,260 days ends after the sixth trumpet judgment and before the seventh trumpet judgment. This fact is revealed in Revelation 11:7-14. It is undoubtedly true that the two witnesses, one of whom most commentators believe is Elijah, will preach repentance to prepare the 144,000 Israelites for the coming of their King. Malachi 4:5 says that Elijah will come before the great and dreadful Day of the Lord. The two witnesses will prophesy for 1,260 days, beginning somewhere near the middle of the Great Tribulation and continuing until they are killed after the sixth trumpet judgment in the Day of the Lord. Their deaths will occur somewhere near the middle of the 1,040-day overrun of the 2,300-day "transgression of desolation" into the Day of the Lord. Since the church has been commanded to preach repentance as well as faith in Christ, this argument of Pentecost's in no way proves that the church must no longer be present. If it did, Pentecost would not have conceded, "The pretribulation doctrine is not based on these arguments singly . . . ."[73] And Walvoord would not confess, ". . . pretribulationism . . . is an induction . . . rather than an explicit statement of the Bible . . . ." [74] Pentecost's pillar does not support a pretribulational rapture.

S. THE DESTINY OF THE CHURCH.

Pentecost writes:

> No one will deny that the destiny of the church is a heavenly destiny . . . . If the rapture did not take place till the end of the seventieth week, and part of the saved went into an earthly blessing and part into a heavenly destiny, the body of Christ would be dismembered and the unity destroyed. Such dismemberment is impossible. This can only indicate that those saved during this seventieth week to go into the millennium must have been saved after the termination of the program for the church.[75]

The writer has demonstrated that the 144,000 Israelites who will go into the millennium will not be *sealed* or called the *servants* of God until *after* the posttribulational rapture. Therefore, they will not be part of the church. As we have shown previously, the entire church will be raptured at the end of the Great Tribulation, when Christ comes in the clouds with power and great glory to gather His elect to the uttermost part of heaven. When the posttribulational rapture occurs, there will be no believers left on earth. John writes, "And I beheld when he had opened the sixth seal, and, lo, there was a great earthquake; and the sun became black as sackcloth of hair, and the moon

---

[73] Ibid., p. 218.

[74] Walvoord, *Rapture Question: Revised*, p. 182.

[75] Pentecost, p. 212.

became as blood; and the stars of heaven fell unto the earth . . . ."[76] It will be at this time (Matthew 24:30, 31 and Mark 13:26, 27) that the coming of Christ in the clouds will take place, and it will be at this time that the rapture of the church takes place. It will be *after these things* that the 144,000 will be saved and sealed, for John writes, "And *after these things* (that is, *after* the darkening of the sun and moon, and *after* the coming of Christ in the clouds, and *after* the gathering of the elect to the uttermost part of heaven) I saw four angels standing on the four corners of the earth . . . ."[77] It will be at this time, that is, *after these things*, that the 144,000 Israelites will be sealed and called the servants of God. They will continue on the earth during the millennial kingdom. Therefore, the "destiny of the church" in no way supports pretribulationism. Pentecost's pillar does not support a pretribulational rapture.

T. THE MESSAGE TO LAODICEA.

Pentecost says:

In Revelation 3:14-22 John gives a message to the church in Laodicea. This church represents the final form of *the professing church, which is rejected by the Lord* and vomited out of His mouth *because of the unreality of its profession.* If the church goes into the seventieth week in its entirety and not just the professing portion of it, it would have to be concluded that this Laodicean Church is the picture of the true church.[78]

---

[76] Revlation 6:12, 13.

[77] Revelation 7:1.

[78] Pentecost, p. 212.

302 ■ THE POST-TRIB, PRE-WRATH RAPTURE

There was a historical Laodicean Church, for in Colossians 4:16, Paul wrote, "And when this epistle is read among you, cause that it be read also in *the church of the Laodiceans*; and that ye likewise read the epistle from Laodicea." The Laodicean Church was indeed a true church. This fact is confirmed by Revelation 1:4, which says, "John to the *seven* churches [including the church of Laodicea] which *are* in Asia: Grace be unto you, and peace, from him which is, and which was, and which is to come . . . ." This truth is further confirmed by Revelation 1:11, where Jesus says, "What thou seest, write in a book, and send it unto the *seven* churches which *are* in Asia; unto Ephesus . . . and *unto Laodicea.*" This truth is yet further confirmed by Revelation 1:20, where Jesus says, "*The seven stars are the angels of the seven churches,* and *the seven candlesticks* which thou sawest *are the seven churches.*" Again, the *reality* of the Laodicean Church is evidenced by Revelation 3:14, where Jesus says, "And unto the angel of *the church of the Laodiceans* write . . . He that hath an hear, let him hear what the Spirit saith unto the churches." This argument by Pentecost is built on sand, for the Laodicean Church was a *real* church.

Furthermore, if the seven churches depict the history of the church age, as many pretribulationists believe, the Laodicean Church must be *a real church*, for the first six churches are real churches. It is the height of inconsistency to say that the first six churches are real churches, but the seventh church is *a mere professing church*. In short, Paul and Jesus taught that the Laodicean Church was a real church, but Pentecost says, "This church *represents* the final form of the professing church, which is rejected . . . because of the *unreality of its profession.*"[79] Think about that for five minutes. Pentecost's pillar does not support pretribulationism.

U. THE TIMES OF THE GENTILES.

In this argument, Pentecost points out that Jerusalem will continue under Gentile dominion "until the times of the Gentiles be fulfilled" (Luke 21:24), and that this fact necessitates a pretribulational rapture.

Pentecost writes:

> In Luke 21:14 the Lord indicates that Jerusalem will continue in Gentile dominion 'until the times of the Gentiles be fulfilled.' Zechariah 12:2; 14:2, 3 indicate that this will not be until the second advent, when the armies of the Beast are destroyed by the Lord, as he is seen to do in Revelation 19:17-19.[80]

This argument by Pentecost has no effect whatever against the posttribulationism set forth in this book. This writer agrees that Jerusalem will be delivered from Gentile dominion by the coming of Christ on a white horse for the Battle of Armageddon. Pentecost's pillar does not prove a pretribulational rapture.

V. THE WAITING REMNANT AT THE SECOND ADVENT.

Pentecost writes:

> Passages such as . . . Revelation 7:1-8, and many others, indicate clearly that when the Lord returns to earth there will be a believing remnant in Israel awaiting His return . . . . In order for

---

[79] Ibid.
[80] Ibid., p. 213.

the Lord to fulfill the promises made in the Abrahamic, Davidic, Palestinic, and New Covenants at His second advent, it is necessary that there be a believing remnant over whom He can reign and to whom the covenants can be fulfilled.[81]

The writer also believes there will be a believing remnant waiting for the return of the King *when He comes on a white horse* with His army for the Battle of Armageddon at the end of the 1,040 days. Pentecost continues:

> These groups go into the millennium in their natural bodies, saved, but not having experienced death and resurrection. If the church were on earth until the time of the second advent, these saved individuals would have been saved to a position in the church, would have been raptured at that time, and consequently there would not be one saved person left on the earth.[82]

Here Pentecost is unscriptural. The entire church will be raptured after the Great Tribulation, immediately after the sun and moon are darkened. *After these things* (Revelation 7:1-8), the 144,000 Israelites will be saved, sealed, and called the servants of God. Their sealing will protect them from the wrath of the Lamb, which will be poured out during the 1,040 days of the great day of His wrath in the Day of the Lord. When Christ returns on a white horse at the end of the 1,040 days for the Battle of Armageddon, the 144,000 will be waiting for Him. Pentecost's pillar does not support a pretribulational rapture.

---

[81] Ibid., p. 214.
[82] Ibid.

W. THE SEALED ONE HUNDRED AND FORTY-FOUR THOUSAND FROM ISRAEL.

Pentecost writes, "As long as the church is on the earth there are none saved to a special Jewish relationship. All who are saved are saved to a position in the body of Christ . . . ."[83]

Pentecost is correct here, but this fact does *not* prove a pretribulational rapture. The church will be gathered from the earth to the uttermost part of heaven immediately *after* the darkening of the sun and moon, immediately *after* the Great Tribulation, when Christ comes in the clouds with power and great glory. At that time, there will not be one saved person left on earth with the exception of the two witnesses. (Their ministry will continue until they are killed after the sixth trumpet judgment.) Then the Bible says, *"After these things . . . ."*[84] Yes, *after these things*, that is, after the posttribulational rapture, the 144,000 Israelites, who will not yet be saved when the rapture occurs, will be *saved, sealed,* and called the *servants* of God just *after* the posttribulational rapture. It has been explained previously that the 144,000 Israelites would be raptured at the posttribulational rapture *if* they were saved prior to its occurrence.

The 144,000 will not be saved, sealed and called servants, however, until *after* the posttribulational rapture. It is after the posttribulational rapture, that is, *"after these things"* (Revelation 7:1-3), that the Israelites will be saved, *sealed,* and called the *servants* of God. Pentecost's pillar does not prove a pretribulational rapture.

---

[83] Ibid.
[84] Revelation 7:1.

X. THE CHRONOLOGY OF THE BOOK OF REVELATION.

Pentecost writes:

> Chapters 4-11 cover the events of the entire seventieth week period and conclude with the return of Christ to the earth to reign . . . . Thus the seals are the events of the first three and one-half years and the trumpets the events of the last three and one-half years.[85]

These statements by Pentecost show that he did not understand the chronology of the book of Revelation. The seals do not cover merely the events of the first three and one-half years of the Seventieth Week, for when *the sixth seal is opened, the end of the Great Tribulation will have been reached.* This fact of eschatology was established firmly by Christ, Who said, "Immediately *after* the tribulation of those days shall the sun be darkened, and the moon shall not give her light, and the stars shall fall from heaven, and the powers of the heavens shall be shaken."[86] The Bible teaches clearly that these momentous events will occur *when the sixth seal is opened,* for it says, "And I beheld *when he had opened the sixth seal,* and, lo, there was a great earthquake; and the sun became black as sackcloth of hair, and the moon became as blood; and the stars of heaven fell unto the earth . . . ."[87]

When it comes to the chronology of the book of Revelation, Pentecost is as confused as a termite in a yo-yo. Relevant to Pentecost's saying that the trumpets are the events of the *last* three and one-half years of the

---

[85] Pentecost, p. 215.
[86] Matthew 24:29.
[87] Revelation 6:12, 13.

Seventieth Week, it must be pointed out that Pentecost's
teaching here is outrageously unscriptural. His teaching is
indeed unscriptural, for *the sixth seal takes us to the end
of the Great Tribulation,* when the sun and moon are
darkened. The seven trumpet judgments will not begin
until *after* the sixth and seventh seals are opened *after* the
Great Tribulation. It is not until after the sixth seal is
opened that the phrase "after these things" (meta tauta)
occurs in Revelation 7:1, and it is not until "after these
things" that the seventh seal is opened and the events of
the seven trumpets occur.

Regarding the phrase "after these things" (meta tauta),
Ken Johnson, in his sermon entitled "The Imminent Pre-
trib Coming of Christ," writes the following:

This phrase, 'meta tauta' [which] equals 'after these things,' is
the sequential key to the book of Revelation.

1. It denies there being seven repeated visions.

2. It establishes the continuity of the book.

3. It is used 10 [times] in the book of Revelation:
   1:19; 4:1; 7:1, 9; 9:12; 15:5; 18:1; 19:1; and 20:3.

This is the key to lead us through the book of Revelation in the
Divine sequence God has established for the outline he gave in
1:19 . . . . There must be a continued sequence for the 7 seals of
6:1 goes to 8:1 which has the 7 trumpets *in the 7th seal.* The *7th
trumpet* is heard in 11:15 and contains the parenthesis of explanation up to 15:5, 6, where the 7 vials of wrath are seen.
Included in the vision of the 7th vial are the events leading up to

19:1 which reveals the things heard by John *after these things* which are the [events of the] preceding chapters of Revelation.[88]

The seven trumpet judgments, the seven vial judgments, and the Battle of Armageddon all occur in the 1,040-day overrun of the 2,300-day "transgression of desolation" into the Day of the Lord. The wrath of the Lamb will be poured out upon the worshipers of the beast and his image *in* the Day of the Lord during the 1,040 days. The chronology of the book of Revelation gives no support to pretribulationism. Pentecost's pillar does not support a pretribulational rapture.

Y. THE GREAT OBJECT OF SATANIC ATTACK.

Pentecost writes:

> According to Revelation 12, the object of satanic attack during the tribulation period is 'the woman' who produced the child . . . . The church must not be here, for, since it is the 'body of Christ' and the 'bride of Christ' and consequently precious to Christ, it would be the object of satanic attack then as it has been all through the age (Ephesians 6:12) if it were present. The reason Satan turns against Israel can only be explained by the absence of the church from that scene.[89]

The answer to this argument by Pentecost is as easy as falling off a log. Jesus said, "Immediately *after* the tribulation of those days shall the sun be darkened, and the moon shall not give her light, and the stars shall fall from heaven . . . ."[90] The darkening of the sun and moon

---

[88] Ken Johnson, "The Imminent Pre-Trib Coming of Christ." *Plains Baptist Challenger*, March 1995, p 6.

[89] Pentecost, p. 215.

[90] Matthew 24:29.

occurs in conjunction with the opening of the sixth seal, for John writes: "And I beheld *when* he had opened the sixth seal, and, lo, there was a great earthquake; and *the sun became black as sackcloth of hair*, and the moon became as blood; and *the stars of heaven fell unto the earth . . . .*"[91]

As it has been explained previously, these stars are angels (Revelation 1:20; Revelation 9:1; and Revelation 12:4). The Bible says, *"And his tail drew the third part of the stars of heaven . . .* And the great dragon was cast out, that old serpent, called the Devil, and Satan . . . he was cast out into the earth, *and his angels* [stars in Revelation 12:4] *were cast out with him."*[92] We know from Matthew 24:29-31 that when the sun and moon are darkened, Christ will come in the clouds with power and great glory and will gather His elect, that is, the church from the four winds to the uttermost part of heaven. As it has been shown previously, the coming of Christ in the clouds after the Great Tribulation is for the posttribulational rapture of the church. When the stars fall from heaven to the earth, that is, when Satan and his angels are cast out into the earth, the Bible says, ". . . *now is come . . . the kingdom of our God,* and the power of his Christ: *for the accuser of our brethren is cast down . . . .*"[93]

At this time, the church will be in the uttermost part of heaven. Then the 144,000 Israelites will be saved, sealed, and called servants after the posttribulational rapture of the church. Therefore, with the church raptured and in

---

[91] Revelation 6:12, 13.
[92] Revelation 12:4, 9.
[93] Revelation 12:10.

heaven with Christ, the only object of attack left for Satan is the sealed Israelites who are the servants of God. Pentecost's statement, "The reason Satan turns against Israel can only be explained by the absence of the church from that scene," does not prove a pretribulational rapture. Pentecost's pillar does not support pretribulationism.

Z. THE APOSTASY OF THE PERIOD.

Pentecost writes, "The complete apostasy of the period on the part of the professing church *prevents* the church from being in the world."[94]

On the contrary, the complete apostasy of the period *will not prevent* the church from being in the world. Everyone acknowledges that there will be tribulation saints who will be martyred and come out of the tribulation in great numbers, according to Revelation 7:14. *The tribulation saints will not become a part of that apostasy.* Their refusal to become a part of that apostasy is why they will be martyred.

Pentecost continues, "The only organized church ever mentioned in *the* tribulation period is the Jezebel system (Revelation 2:22) . . . ."[95] Notice that Pentecost sticks the article "the" before the word "tribulation." The tribulation referred to in Revelation 2:22 is "great tribulation"—not *the* Great Tribulation. That this passage does not refer to *the* Great Tribulation is proved by the fact that *a person could escape that* great tribulation *by repenting* of his deeds. Pentecost writes, "Since the church is not mentioned as also having kept herself from this system it must be concluded that the church is not

---

[94] Pentecost, p. 215.
[95] Ibid.

there."[96] This argument is merely a lot of hot air. The church will keep herself from the apostasy of the period by refusing to receive the mark of the beast and by refusing to worship the beast or his image. For refusing to worship the beast, many will be martyred and will comprise the great unnumbered multitude which John saw coming out of great tribulation (Rev. 7:13-17). This argument does not prove a pretribulational rapture.

AA. THE PROMISES TO THE TRUE CHURCH.

1. REVELATION 3:10. "I WILL KEEP THEE FROM THE HOUR OF TEMPTATION."

In Revelation 3:10 Jesus said, "Because thou hast kept the word of my patience, I also will keep thee from *the hour* of temptation, which shall come upon all the world, to try them that dwell upon the earth."

Observe how flimsy this pillar is as a support for pretribulationism. Walvoord writes, "The primary promise to the church of Philadelphia was that *they* would not enter this hour of trial. Historically, it meant just that. The Church at Philadelphia was not to enter *the tribulation period.*"[97]

Notice that Revelation 3:10 does *not* say "the tribulation period," as Walvoord says it does; the verse says, "the hour of temptation." It is crucial to observe these subtle alterations of the Word of God. Walvoord continues:

By application, *if* expositors are correct who find in the seven churches a foreshadowing of the entire church age, the Phila-

---

[96] Ibid., p. 216.
[97] Walvoord, *Rapture Question: Revised*, pp. 66, 67.

delphia church representing the true and faithful church, is promised deliverance before the hour comes. While *it may be debatable to what extent this constitutes absolute proof for pretribulationism*, it gives no comfort whatever to posttribulationism. [98]

This writer hastens to add that it gives no comfort whatever to *pretribulationism*. First, many expositors do not believe that the seven churches mentioned in Revelation two and three foreshadow the entire church age. This fact means that this pillar is shaky from the start. Second, if the seven churches do foreshadow the entire church age, this fact by itself destroys the pretribulational doctrine of imminency. Al Lacy said that the seven letters are *prophetic*. *If* the seven letters are prophetic of the church age, the church age must run its course to fulfill the prophecy. Accordingly, the rapture cannot occur until the church age ends. Therefore, according to Lacy's view (the seven letters are prophetic), the rapture cannot occur at any moment. This is especially devastating when one recalls Walvoord's words regarding pretribulationism and imminency: "The *central feature* of pretribulationism . . . [is] the doctrine of imminency . . . ."[99] The pretribulationists cannot have their cake and eat it too.

Another question pretribulationists must answer is what chapter and verse teaches that "*the hour of temptation*" mentioned in Revelation 3:10 is equivalent to *the Great Tribulation?* In Revelation 14:7, there is a statement about "*the hour* of his judgment." The angel having the everlasting gospel says, ". . . Fear God, and give glory

---

[98] Ibid., p. 67.
[99] Ibid., p. 51.

to him; for *the hour* of his judgment is come . . . ."[100] It has been pointed out that *the church is not appointed to wrath*, for even though it will go through the Great Tribulation, it will be raptured prior to the beginning of the Day of the Lord. It is *during* the Day of the Lord that the wrath of the Lamb will be poured out upon those who reject Christ, receive the mark, and worship the beast and his image.

Furthermore, we have noticed previously that the Greek preposition "<u>ek</u>", which is rendered "from" in Revelation 3:10 ("I also keep thee *from* the hour of temptation"), *denotes emergence*. The meaning of "<u>ek</u>" (from) was discussed in our chapter entitled "The Coming of Christ in the Clouds." *If* the hour of temptation does mean the Great Tribulation, which no pretribulationist has proved, the word "<u>ek</u>" denotes that the Philadelphia church will be *in* the Great Tribulation and *then emerge out of it*, for "<u>ek</u>" denotes emergence. In the account of Philip and the eunuch, Scripture says, ". . . and they went down both *into* the water, both Philip and the eunuch; and he baptized him. And when they were come up *out of* [<u>ek</u>] the water, the Spirit . . . caught away Philip."[101] Here, the sense of emergence out of the water is clearly seen. Christ's promise ("I will keep thee *from* [<u>ek</u>] the hour of temptation") perfectly describes emergence from the 2,300-day period of *the transgression of desolation*. The church will go through the 1,260 days of the Great Tribulation; *then*, it will be raptured *out of* the 2,300-day reign of terror by the Antichrist. It will be kept from the

---

[100] Revelation 14:7.
[101] Acts 8:38, 39.

1,040-day period, which will be *"the hour* of his judgment" (Revelation 14:7).

Revelation 3:10 is another preposterous pillar used for the support of pretribulationism. Walvoord admits that this passage *"may be debatable"* as proof for pretribulationism.[102] Remember, Walvoord concedes that ". . . pretribulationism is an *induction* . . . rather than an explicit statement of the Bible."[103] He also confesses, "While . . . pretribulationists . . . have strained to find some specific reference in support of their views, most adherents . . . concede that *there is no explicit reference* . . . ."[104] Keep in mind that Pentecost admitted, "The pretribulation doctrine is not based on these arguments singly, but rather they are considered as cumulative evidence . . . ."[105] Both Walvoord and Pentecost concede that there is *no single argument or explicit reference* that proves a pretribulational rapture. This admission means that Revelation 3:10 *does not prove* a pretribulational rapture. Think about that for five minutes.

2. "GOD HATH NOT APPOINTED US TO WRATH."

Another preposterous pillar of pretribulationism is its outrageously erroneous use of *the Bible truth* that the church is not appointed to wrath. It is true that *the church is not appointed to wrath,* but this truth in no way supports a pretribulational rapture. To the Thessalonians, Paul wrote:

---

[102] Walvoord, *Rapture Question: Revised,* p. 67.
[103] Ibid., pp. 181, 182.
[104] Ibid.
[105] Pentecost, p. 218.

But of the times and seasons, *brethren*, *ye* have no need that I write unto *you*. For *yourselves* know perfectly that the day of the Lord so cometh as a thief in the night. For when *they* shall say, Peace and safety; then sudden destruction cometh upon *them*, as travail upon a woman with child; and *they* shall not escape. But *ye*, *brethren*, are not in darkness, that that day should overtake *you* as a thief . . . *for God hath not appointed us to wrath*, but to obtain salvation by our Lord Jesus Christ . . . .[106]

Again to the Thessalonians, Paul wrote, ". . . wait for his Son from heaven, whom he raised from the dead, even *Jesus, which delivered us from the wrath to come.*"[107]

God's wrath will be poured out upon those who worship the beast and his image *in the Day of the Lord.* This extremely important fact has been established in our chapters entitled "The Day of the Lord" and "The Great Day of His Wrath." The Day of the Lord will not begin until *after* the sun and moon are darkened, for Joel says, "The sun shall be turned into darkness, and the moon into blood, *before* the great and the terrible day of the Lord come."[108] The sun and moon will not be darkened *until* immediately *after* the Great Tribulation, for Jesus said, "Immediately *after* the tribulation of those days *shall the sun be darkened*, and the moon shall not give her light . . . ."[109] Therefore, although the church will go through all of the Great Tribulation, *it will not experience God's unparalleled wrath.* The church will not exper- ience the wrath of the Lamb, for that wrath will not be poured out *until after* the Day of the Lord begins. Con- sequently, the truth that the church is not appointed to

---

[106] I Thessalonians 5:1-9.
[107] I Thessalonians 1:10.
[108] Joel 2:31.
[109] Matthew 24:29.

wrath in no way supports a pretribulational rapture. To erroneously use the truth that the church is not appointed to wrath as a pillar for pretribulationism is preposterous. Pentecost's pillar does not support a pretribulational rapture.

3. I THESSALONIANS 1:9-10 – AGAIN PAUL CLEARLY INDICATED THAT OUR EXPECTATION IS NOT WRATH.

This argument is answered under AA. 2.

BB. THE AGREEMENT OF TYPOLOGY.

Pentecost writes, "While argument from analogy is a *weak* argument in itself, yet if a teaching is contrary to all typology it can not be a true interpretation."[110] Notice that Pentecost conceded that the argument from typology is a *weak* argument in itself. Also, notice the types Pentecost gave as illustrations of a pretribulational rapture. He listed the following persons: *Noah, Rahab, and Lot. Not one* of these three was *delivered* from judgment *by being raptured* and taken to heaven, but all three were delivered while remaining on the earth. Pentecost continues, "If the presence of one righteous man [Lot] prevented the outpouring of deserved judgment on the city of Sodom, how much more will the presence of the church on earth prevent the outpouring of *divine wrath* until after her removal."[111] The writer has previously pointed out that the wrath of the Lamb will be poured out during the trumpet judgments, the vial judgments, and the Battle of Armageddon *in* the Day of the Lord, *after* the sun and

---

[110] Pentecost, p. 217.

[111] Ibid., p. 218.

moon are darkened, immediately *after* the Great Tribulation and the posttribulational rapture of the church. It is no wonder that the last sentence in Pentecost's chapter begins with the words, "The pretribulation doctrine is not based on these arguments singly . . . ."[112]

LINDSEY'S PILLARS

Now, let us consider Hal Lindsey's favorite pretribulational rapture arguments.

1. THE CHURCH'S ABSENCE FROM THE EARTH FROM REVELATION 6-19.

Hal Lindsey writes:

The largest descriptive volume of *the tribulation* is found in Revelation 6-19. Here is a fascinating revelation about Revelation. In the first five chapters of this book, the church is mentioned thirty times. In fact, in chapters 2 and 3, at the end of each letter to the churches, John says, 'Let him hear what the Spirit saith unto the churches.' This is repeated seven times. Then we have the beginning of the description of the Tribulation, and there is not one mention of the churches. The church is conspicuous by its absence. Why? Because the church will be in heaven at that time.[113]

There is a *fatal flaw* in Lindsey's teaching. Lindsey *equates* "the tribulation" with Revelation 6-19. Lindsey's equating "the tribulation" with Revelation 6-19 is like equating the martyrdom of Stephen with the pouring out of God's wrath upon the sodomites in Sodom and

---

[112] Ibid.

[113] Hal Lindsey, *The Late Great Planet Earth* (Grand Rapids, Mich.: Zondervan Publishing House, 1970), pp. 143, 144.

Gomorrah. Lindsey's equating "the Tribulation" with
Revelation 6-19 is *flagrantly false teaching*, for the Great
Tribulation ends at Revelation 6:12, 13, with the opening
of the sixth seal. John writes, "And I beheld when he had
opened the sixth seal, and, lo, there was a great earthquake; and *the sun became black as sackcloth of hair*,
and the moon became as blood." Remember, the sun and
moon will not be darkened until immediately *after* the
Great Tribulation, for Jesus said, "Immediately *after* the
tribulation of those days shall the sun be darkened,
and the moon shall not give her light . . . ."[114] What is
described in Revelation 6:14-19:21 is *not* "the Tribulation;" what is described therein is "the great day of his
wrath."[115] During this 1,040-day period of time, the
unparalleled wrath of the Lamb will be poured out upon
the worshipers of the beast and his image through the
seven trumpet judgments, the seven vial judgments, and
the Battle of Armageddon. This explains why the church
is not found on earth from Revelation 6:14-19:21. The
church will be raptured just *after* the sun and moon are
darkened (Revelation 6:12, 13), as was demonstrated in
our chapter entitled "The Coming of Christ in the
Clouds." This pillar of pretribulationism is preposterous.

2. THERE WILL BE NO ONE TO GO INTO THE KINGDOM.

Lindsey writes:

Here is the *chief reason* why we believe the Rapture occurs
before the Tribulation: the prophets have said that God will set

---

[114] Revelation 6:12; Matthew 24:29.
[115] Revelation 6:14-17.

up a Kingdom on earth over which the Messiah will rule. There
will be mortal people in that kingdom. If the Rapture took place
at the same time as the second coming, there would be no
mortals left who would be believers; therefore, there would be no
one to go into the Kingdom and repopulate the earth.[116]

The writer has shown that the coming of Christ in the
clouds to rapture the church will not occur at the same
time as the coming of Christ on a white horse. Consider
further Lindsey's *chief reason* for believing in a pretribulational rapture, in the light of what Jesus said:

> Immediately *after the tribulation* of those days shall the sun be
> darkened, and the moon shall not give her light . . . . And *then*
> shall appear the sign of the Son of man in heaven: and *then*
> shall all the tribes of the earth mourn (Matthew 24:29, 30). And
> *then* shall they see the Son of man coming in the clouds with
> great power and glory. And *then* shall he send his angels, and
> shall gather together his elect from the four winds, from the
> uttermost part of the earth to the uttermost part of heaven (Mark
> 13:26, 27).

*All of these things will happen when the sixth seal is
opened,* and the sun and moon are darkened. These
things include the darkening of the sun and moon, the
mourning of all the tribes on earth, the coming of Christ in
the clouds, and the gathering of His elect to the uttermost
part of heaven. After the opening of the sixth seal, John
says:

> And *after these things* I saw four angels standing on the four
> corners of the earth, holding the four winds of the earth, that the
> wind should not blow on the earth, nor on the sea, nor on any
> tree. And I saw another angel ascending from the east, having

---

[116] Lindsey, p. 143.

the seal of the living God: and he cried with a loud voice to the four angels, to whom it was given to hurt the earth and the sea, Saying, *Hurt not the earth, neither the sea, nor the trees, till we have sealed the servants of our God* in their foreheads.[117]

The thing to observe here is that *the sealing of the 144,000 Israelites will occur "after these things."* After what things? *After the things that will take place when the sixth seal is opened.* The 144,000 will be sealed so that they will be protected from the wrath of God which will be poured out upon those who worship the beast and his image. For example, in Revelation 9:4, *the locusts* that come out of the bottomless pit *are commanded not to hurt those which have the seal of God in their foreheads.* This Scripture says, "And it was commanded them that *they should not hurt the grass* of the earth, neither any green thing, neither any tree; *but only those men which have not the seal of God in their foreheads.*"[118] The 144,000 sealed Israelites will be protected from God's wrath. Notice that they will not be sealed until *after* the sun and moon are darkened, and they will not be sealed until *after* the elect (the church) are gathered "to the uttermost part of heaven."[119] Because they will be sealed *after* the darkening of the sun and moon and after the posttribulational rapture of the church, the 144,000 Israelites will be alive *on* planet earth *when Christ returns on a white horse.* As a support for pretribulationism, Lindsey's chief pillar is preposterous.

---

[117] Revelation 7:1-3.
[118] Revelation 9:4.
[119] Mark 13:27.

LACY'S PILLARS

In his attempt to prove pretribulationism, Dr. Al Lacy uses some old and some new arguments. Let us consider Lacy's pillars for pretribulationism.

1. IF THE RAPTURE IS POSTTRIBULATIONAL, THERE IS NO BLESSED HOPE.

In his sermon entitled "The Blasted Hope," Lacy says: "There are people who don't believe in the blessed hope; they believe in a blasted hope . . . . People who believe they will go through great tribulation have no blessed hope; they have a blasted hope."

Lacy teaches that the blessed hope is deliverance from the Great Tribulation by means of a pretribulational rapture. He equates the blessed hope with *escape* from "the tribulation." The pretribulationists who hold this view do so on the basis of their incorrect understanding of Titus 2:13.

Paul wrote, "Looking for that blessed hope, and the glorious appearing of the great God and our Saviour Jesus Christ."[120] This passage does *not* teach that the blessed hope is deliverance from "the tribulation." This passage teaches that *the blessed hope is the glorious appearing* of the great God and our Saviour Jesus Christ.

This truth is established by a rule of Greek grammar known as the Granville-Sharp rule. Greek grammarians Dana and Mantey wrote:

> When the copulative kai [and] connects two nouns of the same case, the article ὁ [the] or any of its cases precedes the first of the said nouns or participles, and is not repeated before the second

---

[120] Titus 2:13.

322 ■ THE POST-TRIB, PRE-WRATH RAPTURE

noun or participle . . . it denotes a further description of the first-named person.[121]

Dana and Mantey gave as an example of the rule the last half of Titus 2:13, which says, ". . . the great *God and* [kai] our *Saviour* Jesus Christ." In this case, the Granville-Sharp rule means that "the . . . God" is equivalent to "our Saviour Jesus Christ." This verse forcefully proves the deity of Jesus Christ. Furthermore, this rule of Greek grammar establishes the truth that *the* blessed *hope is the* glorious *appearing*, regardless of the time of the rapture, for the Granville-Sharp rule applies to the first half of Titus 2:13, just as it does to the last half of the verse. Both halves of the verse meet the requirements of the rule. Therefore, *the blessed hope is equivalent to the glorious appearing.* Consequently, the blessed hope is *not* equivalent to *escape* from "the tribulation."

If, as pretribulationists teach, the blessed hope means escape from the Great Tribulation by means of a pretribulational rapture, then only those saints living at the end of the age can experience the blessed hope. This would mean that all the saints who died prior to the rapture of the church cannot experience the blessed hope, that is, escape from "the tribulation" by means of the rapture. The truth of the matter is that the blessed hope is for the saints of all ages. The blessed hope, once again, is the glorious appearing of Christ with all of its attendant blessings.

At the glorious appearing, the dead in Christ will be raised first, then we which are alive and remain will be caught up together with them to meet the Lord in the air.

---

[121] Dana and Mantey, p. 147.

At the glorious appearing, not only will the dead in Christ be raised and the living saints raptured, but all saints will experience total sanctification. This is clearly seen in I John 3:2, which says, "Beloved, now are we the sons of God, and it doth not yet appear what we shall be: but we know that, *when he shall appear, we shall be like him*; for we shall see him as he is." This, namely, the glorious appearing, is the blessed hope, and Christians of all ages will experience the blessed hope with all the attendant blessings that accompany the glorious appearing of the great God and our Saviour Jesus Christ.

2. THE RAPTURE OCCURS AT REVELATION 4:1.

In his sermon "The Blasted Hope," Lacy read Revelation 4:1, which says,

> After this I looked, and, behold, a door was opened in heaven: and the first voice which I heard was as it were of a trumpet talking with *me*; which said, *Come up* hither, and I will shew *thee* things which must be hereafter.

After reading the verse, Lacy said, *"There is the rapture right there . . . . If you can't see the rapture here, you have got some shades on your eyes."*

Lacy and other pretribulationists, who say Revelation 4:1 teaches that the rapture occurs at this point, must interpret this verse *symbolically*, for Revelation 4:1 interpreted literally does not teach the rapture at all. A careful reading of the verse reveals that *the voice spoke to John*, not the church. The voice said, "Come up hither" to John, not the church. The command *"Come up hither,"* in the Greek, *is* in *the second person singular*. This means that the command was given to John, not to the church. Then the voice said, "I will shew thee things which must be hereafter." The word "thee" *is singular*. All would agree that more than one person belongs to the church. Accordingly, this verse pertains to John's being shown things which must be hereafter. This verse says *literally* nothing about the rapture.

In chapter six of this book, it was shown that the rapture will occur at the opening of the sixth seal. Revelation 4:1 pertains to John's being given the revelation of the throne scene in heaven. It is not until Revelation 5:7 that the Lamb of God takes the seven-sealed book out of the hand of God Who is sitting upon the throne, and it is not until Revelation 6:1 that the first seal is opened. Then it is not until Revelation 6:12, 13, when the sixth seal is opened, that the rapture occurs. This truth was established in chapter six. Therefore, the rapture does not occur at Revelation 4:1.

3. THE EVENTS OF THE FOURTH SEAL ARE THE WRATH OF GOD.

In his effort to prove that the wrath of the Day of the Lord will be present during "the Tribulation," Lacy says that the events of the fourth seal consist of the same divine wrath as that of the trumpet and vial judgments.

The events of the fourth seal are described in Revelation 6:7, 8:

> And when he had opened the fourth seal, I heard the voice of the fourth beast say, Come and see. And I looked, and behold a pale horse: and his name that sat on him was Death, and Hell followed with him. And power was given unto them *over the*

fourth part of the earth, to kill with sword, and with hunger, and with death, and with the beasts of the earth.

Lacy insists that since God has power over death and hell, the events of the fourth seal must be the wrath of the Day of the Lord. However, people died in the flood and in Sodom and Gomorrah without experiencing *the wrath of the Lamb*, which will be poured out in the Day of the Lord. Pretribulationists exaggerate the severity of the events of the fourth seal. The passage says, ". . . power was given unto them *over the fourth part of the earth, to kill* . . . ." However, the passage does *not* say that a fourth part of men *are* killed, as pretribulationists like Walvoord and Fruchtenbaum falsely teach. Compare the wording of Revelation 6:8 with Revelation 9:18, which says, "By these three was the third part of men killed . . . ." The Bible does not say that a fourth part of men will be killed at the opening of the fourth seal. Pretribulationists are guilty of grossly exaggerating the severity of the events of the fourth seal, for they have a theological necessity to move the wrath of the Lamb *from* the Day of the Lord *into* "the Tribulation."

Despite Lacy's huffing and puffing about the events of the fourth seal, the Scripture teaches plainly that the events of the fourth seal are *not* equivalent to the wrath of the Lamb, which will be poured out *in* the Day of the Lord *after* the Great Tribulation. Revelation 6:9-11 records the events which follow the opening of the fifth seal, and the events sequentially follow the opening of the fourth seal. This passage says:

And when he had opened the fifth seal, I saw under the altar the souls of them that were slain for the word of God, and for the testimony which they held: And they cried with a loud voice, saying, *How long*, O Lord, holy and true, *dost thou not judge and avenge our blood on them that dwell on the earth?* And white robes were given unto every one of them; *and it was said unto them, that they should rest yet for a little season, until their fellowservants also and their brethren, that should be killed as they were, should be fulfilled.*

When the fifth seal is opened, the martyred saints are seen crying for God's *forthcoming* judgment and vengeance, for they know that the wrath of the Lamb has not yet been poured out. This Scripture teaches clearly that the wrath of the Lamb has not yet fallen when the fifth seal is opened. This truth was discussed in detail in chapter nine. In short, the Bible clearly teaches that *the events of the fourth seal are not equivalent to the wrath of the Lamb*, which will be poured out during the trumpet judgments, the vial judgments, and the Battle of Armageddon *after* "the Tribulation" is past.

Hence, Lacy is wrong when he says that the events of the fourth seal are equivalent to the wrath of the Lamb, which will be poured out during the trumpet and vial judgments. Therefore, Lacy, like all other pretribulationists, has failed to prove that the events of the fourth seal are equivalent to the unparalleled wrath of God, which will be poured out *in* the Day of the Lord, *after* the sun and moon are darkened immediately *after* the Great Tribulation.

4. IF THE RAPTURE IS POSTTRIBULATIONAL, ALL CHRISTIANS WILL BE KILLED.

Lacy bases his argument on Revelation 13:15, which says, "And he had power to give life unto the image of the beast, that the image of the beast should both speak, and cause that as many as would not worship the image of the beast should be killed." Lacy says this verse teaches that if Christians were living during "the Tribulation," they would all be killed, and there would be no Christians left to be raptured by a posttribulational rapture.

However, Lacy's interpretation of this verse is incorrect, for the verbs "cause" and "should be killed" are in the subjunctive mood in the Greek. Huddliston said, "The subjunctive mood, as in English, denotes a *doubt* or *contingency*."[122]

Again, Dana and Mantey said:

"[The] subjunctive is the mood of mild contingency; the mood of probability. While the indicative assumes reality, *the subjunctive assumes unreality*. It is the first step away from that which is actual in the direction of that which is only conceivable, and, therefore, properly leads the list of the potential moods."[123]

A.T. Robertson said that the subjunctive is the mode of "doubtful assertion."[124] In English grammar, the subjunctive mood is called the "contrary-to-fact" mood.

The Greek use of the subjunctive mood in Revelation 13:15 refutes Lacy's argument, based on his incorrect interpretation. Because of its use of the subjunctive mood, this verse does *not* teach that all who refuse to worship the image of the beast will be killed. Furthermore, pretribulationists believe the 144,000 Israelites will survive "the Tribulation" without worshiping the image of the beast. In short, this verse does *not* teach that every

---

[122] John Homer Huddliston, *Essentials of New Testament Greek* (New York: MacMillian Co., 1949), p. 35.

[123] Dana and Mantey, p. 170.

[124] A.T. Robertson, *A New Short Grammar of the Greek New Testament* (New York: Harper and Bro. Publishers, 1931), p. 309.

person who refuses to worship the image of the beast will be killed. Therefore, this verse does not make a pretribulational rapture necessary.

5. IN "THE TRIBULATION," ALL WILL TAKE THE MARK.

Lacy gets his argument from Revelation 13:16, which says, "And he *causeth* all, both small and great, rich and poor, free and bond, to receive a mark in their right hand, or in their foreheads." Lacy says, "All will take the mark." Based on his *private interpretation* of this verse, Lacy's conclusion is that Christians must be raptured prior to "the Tribulation," or they will take the mark. Lacy's argument, however, is built on an incorrect interpretation of Revelation 13:16. In this verse, "causeth" is a present indicative active in the Greek. The present denotes durative, that is, continued or repeated action. This verse does *not* say that he (the beast) *will* cause all . . . to receive a mark. This verse says, ". . . he *causeth* [that is, he is causing] all . . . to receive a mark . . . ." If a person had been living in Hitler's Germany, he could have said, "Hitler is causing all Jews to be put to death." This statement would not mean that Hitler killed all Jews, for although Hitler was causing Jews to be killed, he did not kill all Jews. During the time Antichrist is *causing* all to receive a mark, he will not succeed in getting all to take it. A great unnumbered multitude will not take the mark, and they will be martyred (Revelation 20:4). Furthermore, the 144,000 Israelites will not take the mark. The fact that the beast causeth (is causing) all to take the mark does not mean that he will succeed in forcing all to take it.

Since not all will take the mark, Revelation 13:16 does not make a pretribulational rapture necessary.

6. MATTHEW 24:36 REQUIRES A PRETRIBULATIONAL RAPTURE.

In his sermon entitled "The Blasted Hope," Lacy says: "If Matthew 24:36 is talking about the rapture and the rapture is posttribulational, you could know exactly the day. If the rapture is posttribulational, you can multiply three hundred sixty times seven years and know the day of the rapture." Because of his incorrect interpretation of Matthew 24:36, Lacy teaches that no man can know the day, and, therefore, the rapture must be imminent and pretribulational.

The truth of the matter is that Jesus did *not* say of that day and hour no man *shall* [future tense] *know*. Jesus said, "But of that day and hour knoweth [oiden] no man, no, not the angels of heaven, but my father only." Concerning the word oiden ("knoweth"), *The Analytical Greek Lexicon* says, "2 perf. from obsol. [obsolete] eido, with the sense of the present . . . ."[125] Now the sense of the present means that Jesus said, "But of that day and hour *knoweth* no man (namely, no man *is knowing,* that is, no man is knowing at this time)." The correct interpretation of this verse is confirmed by Mark 13:32, which says, "But of that day and that hour knoweth [oiden] no man, no, not the angels which are in heaven, *neither the Son,* but the Father." Did you get that? When Jesus made this statement during His Olivet Discourse, not even He knew the day or the hour. Jesus did not know the day

---

[125] Samuel Baxter, ed., *The Analytical Greek Lexicon* (Grand Rapids, Mich.: Zondervan Publishing House, 1970), p. 283.

or the hour at that time, for He was in His state of humiliation (Philippians 2:5-8), and He had laid aside the voluntary use of His attributes, such as omniscience. However, when He was later glorified (John 17:4, 5), He most certainly knew the day and the hour. These scriptures show clearly that Jesus did *not* say of that day and hour no man *shall know*.

Pretribulationist Alan Beechick saw, independently of this writer, that tribulation saints could know the very Day of Christ's posttribulational coming. In his book *The Pretribulation Rapture*, which was endorsed strongly by John Walvoord, Beechick wrote:

So far we have seen that it is the abomination of desolation which begins the three and one-half years, and it is the abomination which begins the forty-two months. But what about the twelve hundred sixty days? Does the abomination begin that too? Revelation 12:6 does not reveal the occasion of the fleeing for safety for the twelve hundred sixty days. But if you are thinking ahead, you know already what I'm getting at. If not, Matthew 24:15-16 will give it away. 'When ye therefore shall see the abomination of desolation spoken of by Daniel the prophet, stand in the holy place, (whoso readeth, let him understand:) then let them which be in Judaea flee into the mountains.' Amazing, isn't it? Jesus pinpoints the moment of fleeing for safety, namely, the abomination of desolation. Revelation 12 and Matthew 24 make a great team. Matthew 24 names the event ("abomination of desolation") while Revelation 12 dates the event (1260 days). Yes, if I were going through the tribulation and spotted the abomination, you can be sure I would calculate the twelve hundred sixty days very carefully on my calendar or on the wall of my cave.[126]

---

[126] Allen Beechick, *The Pretribulation Rapture* (Denver, Colo.: Accent Books, 1980), pp. 17, 18.

Regarding Matthew 24:36, Beechick wrote:

How can we find out what this verse is really saying? Let's begin with the tense of the word "know." It is present tense [sic. the word is <u>oiden</u>, and it is a second perfect from the obsolete <u>eido</u>, with the sense of the present]. No one knows *now*, in the *present*, but some may know later. This interpretation solves the problem . . . .[127]

In conclusion, this pillar of Lacy's, like Lacy's other pillars for pretribulationism, does not support a pretribulational rapture.

---

[127] Beechick, p. 259.

TWELVE

HERMENEUTICAL HYPOCRISY

"Consistency, thou art a jewel . . . ."

— *Shakespeare*

H ermeneutics, according to Webster's, is "the science of interpretation and explanation; that branch of theology which defines the laws applied by exegesis." *Hypocrisy*, according to Webster's, is "the act or practice of feigning to be what one is not . . . ." Now let us see if pretribulationists are as literal in their interpretation of the Scriptures as they say they are.

Pentecost writes:

> *Pretribulation rapturism rests essentially on one major premise—the literal method of interpretation of the Scriptures . . . .* The literal method of interpretation, consistently employed, can lead to no other conclusion than that the church will be raptured before the seventieth week.[1]

Let us consider some of the leading pretribulationists of this century to see if they have consistently followed the literal method of interpretation.

---

[1] Pentecost, pp. 193, 194.

334 **■** THE POST-TRIB, PRE-WRATH RAPTURE

Concerning the twenty-four elders, Scofield writes, "The elders are *symbolically*, the church . . . ."[2] Did you get that? Scofield interpreted the twenty-four elders in Revelation chapters four and five *symbolically*. Think about that for five minutes.

Regarding the twenty-four elders, Arno Gaebelein, a consulting editor of the Scofield Reference Bible, writes, "Who is *represented* by these twenty-four elders? . . . They *represent* the redeemed, the Saints in glory."[3]

According to Webster's, "represent" means "to serve as a sign or *symbol* of." Did you get that? Gaebelein, like Scofield, made the twenty-four elders *representative* or *symbolical.*

Pertaining to Revelation 4:1, Gaebelein writes, "The open door and the voice which calls 'Come up hither' and John's presence in glory in the spirit, clearly indicates *symbolically* the fulfillment of I Thessalonians 4:15-17."[4] Here Gaebelein made the call to John ("Come up hither") *symbolical* of the rapture of the church.

Commenting on the first trumpet judgment, Gaebelein writes, "Hail (heat withdrawn), fire and blood are all *symbols* of divine wrath . . . . The green things are *symbols* of agricultural and commercial prosperity."[5]

Commenting on the second trumpet judgment, Gaebelein writes:

---

[2] C.I. Scofield, *Will The Church Pass Through The Tribulation?* (Philadelphia. Pa.: Philadelphia School of the Bible, 1917), p. 24.

[3] Arno Gaebelein, *The Revelation* (Neptune, N.J.: Loizeaux Bro., 1961), pp. 45, 46.

[4] Ibid., p. 44.

[5] Ibid., p. 61.

"That *this is not a literal mountain* is obvious. A mountain in scripture language *represents* a kingdom . . . . The sea is *typical* of nations . . . . The result will be a still greater destruction of life and commerce, which is *represented* by the ships."[6]

Explaining the fourth trumpet, Gaebelein writes:

The sun is a *symbol* of the highest authority, the moon, who has not her own light, is *symbolical* of derived authority and the stars are *symbolical* of subordinate authority. The *symbolical* meaning of this trumpet judgment is that all authority within the revived Roman Empire will be smitten by the hand from above . . . .[7]

Speaking of the fifth trumpet, Gaebelein said, "The smoke first, *symbolical* of darkening; the locusts next, *symbolical* of these demon powers."[8]

Interpreting the two witnesses of Revelation eleven, Gaebelein said, "We take it then that these two witnesses *represent* the great testimony to be given in Jerusalem during the 1,260 days of the great tribulation . . . *a large number of witnesses is unquestionably in view here.*"[9]

Commenting on the 144,000 Israelites of Revelation seven, Gaebelein said, "The number 144,000 being *symbolical* and *not actual* permits such interpretation."[10]

Respecting the vial judgments of Revelation sixteen, Gaebelein said, " . . . it is undoubtedly true that we have *symbols* also in these vial judgments . . . ."[11] Interpreting the second vial, Gaebelein said, "The sea *represents* the

---

[6] Ibid.
[7] Ibid., p. 62.
[8] Ibid., p. 63.
[9] Ibid., p. 70.
[10] Ibid., p. 86.
[11] Ibid.

Gentiles. . . . See the plague in Egypt . . . *that was a literal thing*; but *not so here*."[12] Commenting on the fourth vial, Gaebelein said,

> The fourth vial is poured into the sun and men are scorched with great heat . . . the *symbolical* meaning is to be preferred . . . the sun here is *not the physical sun*, but *means*, as unto the fourth trumpet, the supreme authority governing them . . . ."[13]

Did you see the *symbolical method of interpretation* used by Gaebelein? Remember, Pentecost said that pretribulation rapturism rests essentially on this major premise--the literal method of interpretation of the Scriptures.[14]

Now let us check pretribulationist Walter Scott. He wrote *Exposition of the Revelation of Jesus Christ*. This is one of the most influential pretribulational commentaries on the book of Revelation. Notice just how literal Scott was in his interpretation of Revelation. With the opening of the sixth seal, the Bible says, ". . . the sun became black as sackcloth of hair, and the moon be came as blood; And the stars of heaven fell unto the earth . . . ."[15] Commenting on this passage, Scott writes, "The sun *symbolizes* the supreme governing authority."[16] Commenting on the moon becoming as blood, Scott writes, "All authority immediately derived from and dependent on the supreme authority is here *figured* by the

---

[12] Ibid., p. 93.
[13] Ibid.
[14] Pentecost, pp. 193, 194.
[15] Revelation 6:12, 13.
[16] Walter Scott, *Exposition of the Revelation of Jesus Christ* (Westwood, N.J.: Fleming H. Revell Co., n.d.), p. 158.

'whole moon.'"[17]   Speaking of the stars falling from heaven unto the earth, Scott writes, "*All lesser authorities, as individual rulers,* civil and ecclesiastical, morally fell from their exalted stations."[18]

Interpreting the first trumpet judgment, Scott writes, "These are *not* to be understood as *literal* destructive agencies. They are *symbols*."[19] Pertaining to the second trumpet judgment, Scott writes: "Does blood here *symbolize* a violent natural death, or does it refer to the spiritual death of apostasy? In our judgment these two forms of death are here combined."[20]

Respecting the fourth trumpet, Scott writes, "The sun, moon, and stars collectively *symbolize* the whole *governing body*, from the supreme head down to all lesser authorities--a complete system of government in all its parts."[21] Commenting on the fallen star of Revelation 9:1, Scott writes: "The key *symbolizes* competent authority . . . . Smoke, not spirits, rose up out of the pit, and out of the smoke emerges a devastating swarm of *symbolic locusts.*" [22] Commenting on the locusts that come out of the smoke, Scott writes:

Neither the smoke nor the locusts are literal . . . that the locust army is a *symbolical* representation of judgment of a super-human kind is evident from the whole description . . . the duration of the satanic scourge is limited to five months . . . . The

---

[17] Ibid., p. 159.
[18] Ibid.
[19] Ibid., p. 187.
[20] Ibid.
[21] Ibid., p. 190.
[22] Ibid., p. 203.

time specified points to a brief and determinate period of woe, *not necessarily* one of five *literal* months.[23]

Explaining the fire, smoke, and brimstone that comes out of the mouths of the horses of Revelation 9:13-21, Scott writes, "To fire and brimstone, the *symbols* of inconceivable anguish . . . ."[24]

Regarding the vials of wrath, Scott writes, ". . . we judge that the plagues of our chapter must be understood *symbolically* in keeping with the general character and design of the book."[25] Concerning the second vial of wrath, Scott writes, "It is important to lay hold of the force of the *symbols* . . . the sea 'became blood' *is not a physical fact* . . . but in the vial plague the sea becoming *blood* points *symbolically* to a scene of moral death."[26]

Respecting the third vial of wrath, Scott writes, "'The fountain of waters,' the source of our prosperity and well being, are all turned into blood, *symbolical* of course."[27] Pertaining to the fourth vial of wrath, Scott writes:

> The power of the sun is increased to such an intense degree that men are scorched or burnt with its fire. *It is not*, of course, a *physical judgment* produced by the great celestial luminary; we must therefore seek to ascertain what is *the* moral significance and *symbolic* meaning of the sign.[28]

Concerning the fifth vial of wrath, Scott writes, "No

[23] Ibid., p. 204.
[24] Ibid., p. 213.
[25] Ibid., p. 323.
[26] Ibid., p. 324.
[27] Ibid., p. 325.
[28] Ibid., p. 328.

doubt there is here an allusion to Exodus ... *there, however, the darkness was physical, here it is moral.*"[29]

Regarding the seventh vial of wrath, Scott writes, "This judgment falls upon the moral life-breath of the world. The air, essential to natural life, is *symbolically* visited in judgment."[30] Did you see the symbolical method of interpretation used by Scott? Remember, Pentecost said that *pretribulation rapturism rests on the literal method of interpretation of the Scriptures.*

Harry Ironside was one of the most famous pretribulationists of the twentieth century. Concerning the darkening of the sun and the moon when the sixth seal is opened, Ironside writes:

> The sun, we are told, became black as sackcloth of hair. The sun, the source of light and life for this planet, *speaks* of supreme authority . . . . Naturally enough this will mean the complete destruction of all derived authority, so we next read, 'the moon became as blood.' . . . The stars falling from heaven *indicate*, I take it, the downfall and apostasy of great religious leaders . . . .[31]

Respecting the first trumpet judgment, Ironside writes, "I cannot explain this *symbol* fully, but I think I can see a hint . . . *grass is man* in its weakness, man in his littleness; the *tree is man* in his dignity, in his greatness, in his independence--man lifting himself up against God."[32] Concerning the smoke and the locusts that come out of the bottomless pit, Ironside writes:

[29] Ibid., p. 330.

[30] Ibid., p. 336.

[31] H.A. Ironside, *Lectures on the Book of Revelation* (New York: Loizeaux Bro., 1920), p. 116.

[32] Ibid., p. 148.

... It is clear that a *key implies a system of teaching* ... we can readily understand what follows .... This arch apostate, by a system of erroneous teaching opens up the bottomless pit, from whence issues a blinding *smoke* as the smoke of a great furnace .... It *is the strong delusion* ... Their whole spiritual sky will be made dark by the false system with which they will be deluded .... They aptly ... *symbolize* the spiritual plague of the last days. The *symbol* of the locusts is coupled with that of the scorpion, because of the torment these evil teachings eventually bring to those who accept them.[33]

Regarding the two witnesses of Revelation eleven, Ironside writes:

I do not know that we need limit the witness to two individuals. Two is the number of testimony, and we need to remember that *we are dealing here with symbols, not* necessarily with the *literal* personalities. Therefore the two witnesses might well *symbolize* the witnessing remnant of Judah as a whole.[34]

Pertaining to the winepress of Revelation fourteen, Ironside writes:

And we are told the winepress was trodden without the city, and blood came out of the winepress, even unto the horse bridles, by the space of a thousand and six hundred furlongs .... The *picture [representation]* is that of the entire land drenched in blood up to the horse bridles. What will *the reality* be?"[35]

Respecting the seven vial judgments of Revelation sixteen, Ironside writes, "As in the case of the seven trumpets, and, in measure, of the seven seals, I do not profess to be able to tell you just how much we are to

---

[33] Ibid., pp. 156-158.
[34] Ibid., p. 192.
[35] Ibid., pp. 267, 268.

take as *symbolic,* and how much as literal . . . ."[36] Concerning the *first vial* of wrath, Ironside writes,

"It perhaps *symbolizes* a spiritual plague which will cause those who have received the mark of the beast . . . as great annoyance as the physical suffering which would follow such a noisome and grievous sore upon the bodies of men."[37]

Did you notice the *symbolical method of interpretation* used by Ironside? Remember, Pentecost said that *pretribulation rapturism rests on the literal method of interpretation of the Scriptures.* Think about that for five minutes in the light of Ironside's method of interpretation.

Now let us consider Hal Lindsey's best-selling book *There's A New World Coming.* Regarding the stars of heaven falling to the earth with the opening of the sixth seal, Hal Lindsey writes:

Verse 13 states that 'the stars of heaven fell to the earth.' This word for *star* can refer to *either a star or a meteor* [The Greek word means star--not meteor, according to Barry's Lexicon]. In this verse it seems more likely that meteors are intended . . . however, verse 13 may be referring to more than ordinary meteors. Russia now has a weapon called a 'fractional orbital bomb' . . . when these missiles streak through the air they'll look like *meteors* showering the atmosphere![38]

Concerning the *locusts* that come out of the bottomless pit, Lindsey writes:

---

[36] Ibid., p. 275.
[37] Ibid., p. 276.
[38] Hal Lindsey, *There's A New World Coming* (Santa Ana, Calif.: Vision House Publishers, 1973), p. 110.

There are diverse opinions among Bible teachers as to whether these creatures are actually going to be a supernatural, mutant locust . . . or whether they *symbolize* some modern device of warfare. I have a Christian friend who . . . said, 'I know what those are. I've seen hundreds of them in Viet Nam. They're Cobra helicopters!' . . . *A cobra helicopter does fit* the composite description very well. They also make the sound of 'many chariots.'[39]

Commenting on the 200 million horsemen of Revelation 9:13-21, Lindsey writes, "The four angels . . . will mobilize an army of 200 million *soldiers* from east of the Euphrates . . . I believe these 200 million troops are *Red Chinese soldiers* accompanied by other Eastern allies."[40]

We have read Lindsey; now let us read the Bible. Revelation 9:17 says of them that sit on the horses that *they have breastplates of fire and brimstone*; it further says that *fire, smoke, and brimstone come out of the mouths of the horses.* Since when do *Red Chinese soldiers* and their horses fit the description given in Revelation 9:17? Did you notice Lindsey's *symbolical* method of interpretation?

Pentecost himself quoted and used Scofield's *symbolical* interpretation of the twenty-four elders of Revelation chapters four and five. Pentecost writes, "Scofield presents evidence to support the view that these [twenty-four elders] are the *representatives* of the church."[41]

Pentecost then quoted Scofield, who said, "The elders are, *symbolically*, the church . . . ."[42] Did you see the

---

[39] Ibid., pp. 138, 139.
[40] Ibid., p. 140.
[41] Pentecost, p. 208.
[42] Ibid., p. 200.

symbolical method of interpretation used by Pentecost? Remember, it was *Pentecost* who wrote:

> *Pretribulation rapturism rests essentially on one major premise— the literal method of interpretation of the Scriptures* . . . the literal method of interpretation, consistently employed, can lead to no other conclusion than that the church will be raptured before the seventieth week.[43]

[43] Ibid., pp. 193, 194.

THIRTEEN

POSTTRIBULATIONISM IS THE HISTORICAL POSITION

"For inquire, I pray thee, of the former age, and prepare thyself to the search of their fathers."

— Job 8:8

As a student and faculty member at a pretribulational university, the writer acquired the false view that pretribulationism was taught by the early church fathers. However, the early fathers were not pretribulational; they were posttribulational. Accordingly, pretribulationism is not the historical position; *posttribulationism is the historical position.*

Let us consider some of the famous Baptist confessions. As we ponder what they say about Christ's return, it is apparent that the classic Baptist confessions are as posttribulational as Charles Haddon Spurgeon, who said:

> When the Lord Jesus shall come, the heavens shall tell us: 'There shall be signs in the sun, and in the moon, and in the stars.' And then, . . . our own eyes shall tell us, for they shall see 'the Son of Man coming in a cloud with power and great glory.' . . . 'Look up, and lift up your heads' . . . because the graves are opening . . . . You will quit the grave never more to die.

The Waterland Confession of 1580 says:

Lastly, *we believe and teach that Jesus Christ, our glorious King and Lord, visibly just as He ascended . . . will return from heaven . . . with power and great glory*, and with him all the holy angels . . . *at that time . . . all men just and unjust*, who have lived upon the earth and have died, *will rise from the dead* (with incorruption . . .) . . . *but those who are alive in that day and have not died, changed in a moment and in a twinkling of an eye, will put on incorruption* . . . and the whole multitude of the human race will stand before the tribunal of Christ . . . .[1]

The Second London Confession of 1677 and 1688 says:

At the last day such of the saints as are found alive shall not sleep but be changed; and all the dead shall be raised up with the self same bodies . . . although with different qualities, which shall be united again to their souls for ever. The bodies of the unjust shall by the power of Christ, be raised to dishonour; *the bodies of the just by his spirit unto honour, and be made conformable to his own glorious body*.[2]

The Second London Confession is as posttribulational as Charles Haddon Spurgeon, who wrote:

And we are told that *his coming will be attended by a peculiar sign*. 'Behold, he cometh with clouds.' We shall have no need to question whether it is the Son of man who has come, or whether he is indeed come. *This is to be no secret matter: his coming will be as manifest as yonder clouds* . . . So it is written, 'And *then shall appear the sign of the Son of man in heaven:* and then shall all the tribes of the earth mourn, *and they shall see the Son of man coming in the clouds of heaven with power and great*

---

[1] William L. Lumpkin, *Baptist Confessions of Faith: Revised* (Valley Forge. Pa.: Judson Press, 1969), p. 65.
[2] Ibid., p. 294.

glory.' . . . With clouds of angels, cherubim and seraphim, and all the armies of heaven He comes. *With all the forces of nature,* thundercloud and blackness of tempest, *the Lord of all makes His triumphant entrance to judge the world. The clouds are the dust of his feet in that dread day of battle when He shall ease Him of His adversaries,* shaking them out of the earth with his thunder, and consuming them with the devouring flame of his lightning . . . Not as the man of sorrows, despised and rejected of men, shall Jesus come; but as Jehovah came upon Sinai in the midst of thick clouds and a terrible darkness, so shall he come, whose coming shall be the final judgment . . . . The clouds, also, denote the terror of his coming to the ungodly. *His saints shall be caught up together with him in the clouds, to meet the Lord in the air . . . .* [3]

The statement of faith of the Southern Baptist Convention of 1925 says:

According to His promise, *Jesus Christ will return personally and visibly in glory to the earth; the dead will be raised; and Christ will judge all men in righteousness. The unrighteous will be consigned to hell,* the place of everlasting punishment. *The righteous in their resurrected and glorified bodies will receive their reward* and will dwell forever in heaven with the Lord. [4]

The 1925 Southern Baptist Convention statement of faith is as posttribulational as J. A. Broadus, Herschel Hobbs, E. Y. Mullins, A. T. Robertson, and William T. Bruner.

Gundry writes:

. . . The antiquity of the view [posttribulationism] weighs in its

---

[3] Charles H. Spurgeon, *12 Sermons on the Second Coming* (Grand Rapids, Mich.: Baker Book House, 1976), pp. 116, 117.
[4] Lumpkin, p. 397.

favor, especially when that antiquity reaches back to the apostolic age. For those who received their doctrine firsthand from the apostles and from those who heard them stood in a better position to judge what was apostolic doctrine than we who are many centuries removed.[5]

Gundry continues:

Until Augustine in the fourth century, the early Church generally held to the premillenarian understanding of Biblical eschatology. This *chiliasm* entailed a futuristic interpretation of Daniel's seventieth week, the abomination of desolation, and the personal Antichrist. And it *was posttribulational*. Neither mentioned nor considered, the possibility of a pretribulational rapture seems never to have occurred to anyone in the early Church.[6]

Next, consider the evidence from postapostolic fathers. In *The Epistle of Barnabas*, Christians are exhorted to stand for the Lord in the coming Great Tribulation. Barnabas wrote:

The final stumblingblock (or source of danger) approaches . . . . [At this point, Barnabas begins a discussion of the Antichrist.] We take earnest heed in these last days; for the whole time of your faith will profit you nothing, unless now in this wicked time we also withstand coming sources of danger, as becometh sons of God. That the Black One may find no means of entrance, let us flee from every vanity, let us utterly hate the works of the way of wickedness.[7]

Justin Martyr believed the resurrection and the gathering together of Christians is *at the beginning of the mil-*

---

[5] Gundry, p. 172.
[6] Gundry, p. 173.
[7] Donaldson and Roberts, Volume 1, *Epistle of Barnabas*, IV, pp. 138, 139.

XIII Posttribulationism Is the Historical Position ■ 349

lennium, and he equated their hope not with a pretribulational rapture, but with Christ's return to earth as prophesied in the Old Testament. Justin Martyr wrote, "The man of apostasy [namely, the Antichrist] . . . shall venture to do unlawful deeds on the earth against us the Christians . . . ."[8]

Now, get ready for a jolt. It is disgusting to see what some pretribulational leaders have done with the historical writings of some of the early church fathers. Here is an example from Stanton in *Kept from the Hour.* He quotes *The Shepherd of Hermas,* and he says that Hermas was told the following:

> You have escaped from great tribulation on account of your faith, because you did not doubt in the presence of such a beast. Go, therefore, and tell the elect of the Lord His mighty deeds, and say to them that this beast is a type of the great tribulation that is coming. If then ye prepare yourselves, and repent with all your heart, and turn to the Lord, it will be possible for you to escape it . . . .[9]

Commenting on the quotation from *The Shepherd of Hermas,* Stanton writes,

> While pretribulationists get their doctrine directly from the Bible and not from early Christian writers such as Hermas, this passage direct from the turn of the first century completely voids the argument that the concept of escaping the tribulation is something 'new and novel' originating with Darby and Tweedy. . . .[10]

---

[8] Ibid., Volume 1, *Trypho CX,* pp. 253, 254.

[9] Ibid., Volume 2, *The Shepherd of Hermas, Vision Four,* p. 18.

[10] Stanton, p. 222.

It is appalling to see that Stanton breaks off his quotation from *The Shepherd Of Hermas* before the real view of Hermas is revealed. To be truthful, Stanton should not have broken off his quotation where he did, for Hermas continues:

> ... *those*, therefore, who continue steadfast, and *who are put through the fire, will be purified by means of it* . . . . Wherefore cease not speaking these things in the ears of the saints. This then is the type of the great tribulation that is yet to come. *If ye wish it, it will be nothing* . . . .[11]

In his second vision, *the Shepherd of Hermas* says, *"Happy ye who endure the great tribulation that is coming on* . . . .[12] Why, the Shepherd of Hermas was as posttribulational as Oswald T. Allis, Matthew Arnold, Rowland V. Bingham, Horatius Bonar, William Booth, William Carey, Adam Clarke, Alexander Cruden, Jonathan Edwards, Charles R. Erdman, W.J. Erdman, John Foxe, John Gill, A.J. Gordon, Charles Hodge, Frank Houghton, John Huss, Cotton Mather, Philip Melancthon, W.G. Moorehead, George Müller, Isaac Newton, Alexander Reese, Harry Rimmer, A.B. Simpson, H. W. Soltau, A.H. Strong, William Tyndale, B.B. Warfield, Robert Dick Wilson, and John Wycliffe.

In view of what Hermas actually wrote, how could Stanton dare say, "This passage direct from the turn of the first century completely voids the argument that the concept of escaping the tribulation is something 'new and

---

[11] Donaldson and Roberts, Volume 2, *The Shepherd of Hermas, Vision Four*, p. 18.

[12] Ibid., *The Shepherd of Hermas, Vision Two*, p. 11.

novel,' originating with Darby and Tweedy . . . ." There it is, like a dead skunk.

Let us consider Stanton once again. He says that Cyprian, bishop of Carthage, who flourished as a writer from A.D. 220-250, wrote, ". . . let us ever in anxiety and cautiousness be waiting for the second coming of the Lord." After quoting Cyprian, Stanton writes:

> . . . It is apparent that not a few of them [early fathers] looked upon the return of Christ as imminent, expressing a definite conviction that the church may escape the great tribulation . . . . A belief in imminence implies a belief that the rapture will precede the tribulation . . . in light of such evidence from the early church and from representative apostolic fathers and Ante-Nicene Fathers, it can hardly be sustained that pretribulational beliefs are 'new and novel' . . . .[13]

Now, notice something Cyprian taught of which Stanton did not tell you. Cyprian wrote, ". . . the day of affliction has begun to hang over our heads, and the end of the world and the time of the Antichrist to draw near, so that *we must all stand prepared for the battle* . . . ."[14] Stanton suggests strongly that Cyprian was pretribulational, but Cyprian was as posttribulational as Augustus Hopkins Strong, Louis Berkhof, and Dave MacPherson.

Next, consider the Ante-Nicene authority entitled, *The Teaching of the Twelve Apostles*. Gundry writes:

> Twice in The Teaching of the Twelve Apostles, Matthew 24:31, which concerns the gathering of the elect at the posttribulational advent, is quoted with the substitution of 'Church' for 'elect'

---

[13] Stanton, p. 222.

[14] Donaldson and Roberts, Volume 5, Cyprian, *Epistle 55*, p. 347.

(IX, X). *Christians are then exhorted to stand fast through the reign of the Antichrist until the posttribulational advent and resurrection.*[15]

The Teaching of the Twelve Apostles says: "Watch for your life's sake. Let not your lamps be quenched, nor your loins unloosed; but be ye ready, for ye know not the hour in which our Lord cometh."[16] At this point, Walvoord, Stanton, and Pentecost break off the quotation too abruptly. In so doing, they give the impression that some of the church fathers believed in imminency. The remainder of the paragraph, which the three heavyweights of pretribulationism did not quote, reads as follows:

> For the whole time of your faith will not profit you, if ye be not made perfect in the last time . . . *then shall appear the world-deceiver as Son of God,* and shall do signs and wonders . . . . Then shall the creation of men come into the fire of trial, and many shall be made to stumble and perish; but *they that endure in their faith shall be saved from under the curse itself.*[17]

Imagine that. Can you believe that these three leading pretribulational scholars all did the same thing in their books. Why, it's incredible — absolutely incredible!

Irenaeus, a posttribulationist like David Baron, Franz Delitzsch, Alfred Edersheim, and Adolph Saphir (all Hebrew Christian scholars) wrote, *"And they shall . . . give their kingdom to the beast, and put the Church to*

---

[15] Gundry, p. 175.

[16] John Walvoord, ed., "A Survey of the Eschatology of the Olivet Discourse," *Bibliotheca Sacra,* Volume 113, p. 200; Stanton, p. 221; Pentecost, p. 169.

[17] Gundry, p. 175.

flight."[18]   Again, Irenaeus wrote, "But he indicates the number of the name now, that when this man comes *we* may avoid him, being aware who he is . . . ."[19]   Gundry writes, "Irenaeus also places the resurrection of the Church after the rule of the Antichrist and in conjunction with the resurrection of Old Testament saints."[20]

Hippolytus wrote:

> Now concerning the tribulation of the persecution which is to fall upon the Church from the adversary . . . . That refers to one thousand two hundred and threescore days (the half of the seventieth week) during which *the tyrant is to reign and persecute the Church* . . . .[21]

Gundry writes, "*Methodius makes the resurrection of Christians* coincident with the millennial renewal of nature *after the tribulation.* (Discourse on the Resurrection, i, 8)"[22]

Again Gundry writes, "Tertullian identifies the rapture à la I Thessalonians 4 with Christ's coming to earth to destroy the Antichrist and to establish His kingdom."[23]

Tertullian wrote:

> *Now the privilege of this favor* [being raptured] *awaits those who* shall at the coming of the Lord be found in the flesh, and who shall *owing to the oppressions of the time of Antichrist, deserve by an instantaneous death* [Tertullian's definition of the rap-

---

[18] Donaldson and Roberts, Volume 1, *Against Heresies, V*, p. 555.

[19] Ibid., p. 560.

[20] Gundry, p. 175.

[21] Donaldson and Roberts, Volume 5, Hippolytus, *Treatise on Christ and Antichrist*, p. 217.

[22] Gundry, p. 176.

[23] Ibid.

ture], *which is accomplished by a sudden change, to become qualified to join the rising saints . . . . the beast Antichrist with his false prophet may wage war on the Church of God . . . .*[24]

Gundry further writes, ". . . in his outline of coming events, Lactantius gives but one advent and one resurrection of the righteous, both after the tribulation."[25]

Again, Gundry writes, "Commodianus places the resurrection of Christians after the reign of the Antichrist, between the great tribulation and the millennium."[26]

The Constitutions of the Holy Apostles says:

Let your loins be girded about, and your lights burning, and ye like unto men who wait for their Lord, when He will come, at even, or in the morning, or at cock-crowing, or at midnight. For at what hour they think not, the Lord will come; and if they open to him, blessed are those servants, because they were found watching.

At this point, Walvoord breaks off the above quotation, after quoting just enough to make his readers think that this early writing teaches imminence. Incredibly, Walvoord does it again.

The remainder of the quotation (which Walvoord omitted) from *The Constitutions of the Holy Apostles* continues:

. . . for through the abounding of iniquity the love of many shall wax cold. For men shall hate, and persecute, and betray one another. And *then shall appear the deceiver of the world*, the enemy of the truth, the prince of lies, *whom the Lord Jesus 'shall*

---

[24] Donaldson and Roberts, Volume 3, Tertullian, *On the Resurrection of the Flesh*, p. 575.

[25] Gundry, p. 178.

[26] Ibid., p. 177.

destroy with the spirit of His mouth, who takes away the wicked with his lips; *and many shall be offended at Him. But they that endure to the end, the same shall be saved.* And then shall appear the sign of the Son of man in heaven' and afterwards shall be the voice of a trumpet by the archangel; and in that interval shall be the revival of those that were asleep.[27]

This brief survey of early fathers shows that they were as posttribulational as Eric C. Peters, A.W. Pink, Oswald J. Smith, J. Barton Payne, Charles Brokenshire, and Ian Paisley.

Robert Cameron wrote, "Dr. Tregelles, B.W. Newton and others say there is not a hint of this doctrine [pretribulationism] in any writing extant, from the days of Polycarp to the days of Irving [*Morning Watch*, September 1830]."[28] Significantly, Samuel P. Tregelles has been called the greatest Brethren scholar of the nineteenth century.

No wonder Walvoord concedes, ". . . the early Fathers were not specifically pretribulational . . . *the early church did not teach twentieth-century pretribulationism . . . .*"[29]

---

[27] Donaldson and Roberts, Volume 7, *The Constitutions of the Holy Apostles*, *VII*, p. 471.
[28] MacPherson, *The Rapture Plot*, p. 173.
[29] Walvoord, *Rapture Question: Revised*, pp. 156, 157.

FOURTEEN

ENDEAVORING TO KEEP THE UNITY OF THE SPIRIT

"Endeavouring to keep the unity of the Spirit in the bond of peace."

— Ephesians 4:3

T he apostle Paul writes:

I therefore, the prisoner of the Lord, beseech you that ye walk worthy of the vocation wherewith ye are called, with all lowliness and meekness, with longsuffering, forbearing one another in love; *endeavouring to keep the unity of the Spirit* . . . . Till we all come in the unity of the faith . . . .[1]

While pondering Paul's exhortation to the Ephesians, let us consider what some of the leading pretribulationists have written relevant to Paul's exhortation, *"endeavouring to keep the unity of the Spirit . . . ."*
   Ladd writes:

One of America's outstanding pretribulationists was H.A. Ironside; we would do well to imitate his words of charity toward those who differed with him. Speaking of Baptist theologian A.H. Strong's accusation of heresy in Brethren doctrine, Ironside replied, 'It passes our comprehension how any man, or set of

---

[1] Ephesians 4:1-3, 13.

men, with an atom of genuine love for the Lord and His people, can deliberately brand as heretics fellow-believers whose lives are generally fragrant with Christian graces, who stand unflinchingly for the inspiration of the entire Bible, simply because they hold different views on prophecy. Dr. Strong evidently does not believe in the secret rapture of the saints, but in the coming of the Lord in judgment at the end of the world. 'Brethren' would not brand him as a heretic for this, though they feel he has lost much by his defective views.[2]

Lewis Sperry Chafer writes:

Certain phases of prophecy find good men taking positions which are opposed the one to the other. The prophetic word has come plainly enough for all to agree on it, but just the same its meaning cannot always be ascertained to the satisfaction of all conservative minds. There is room for a difference of viewpoint on prophetic points where none exist in the realm of salvation truth, basic as that doctrine must be for all time.[3]

John Walvoord of Dallas Theological Seminary writes:

Before the first coming of the Lord, there was confusion even among the prophets concerning the distinction between the first and second comings (I Peter 1:10-11). At the present time, there is similar confusion between the translation of the church and the second coming to establish the millennial kingdom. An attitude of Christian tolerance is called for toward those who differ on this doctrine. But may we all 'love his appearing.'[4]

---

[2] Ladd, pp. 58, 59.
[3] Ibid, p. 160.
[4] Ibid.

Harold Lindsell and Charles Woodbridge write:

Differences of interpretation exist. They are not basic to salvation, but deal with matters which have perplexed countless generations of Christians and about which good men have always differed. Christian liberty and forbearance must be allowed to operate . . . . Many premillennialists believe in the pretribulational rapture of the church, other premillennialists believe in the midtribulation rapture. Still others hold that the church will go through the great tribulation . . . . There seems to be no plain statement in the Bible dealing with the precise time of the rapture . . . . The time of the rapture should never be made a test of orthodoxy . . . .[5]

Charles E. Fuller on the Old-Fashioned Revival Hour said:

A word of warning, sweetly given: do not make this difference a test of orthodoxy. Be tolerant in this matter. If a truly born again believer differs with you, don't withdraw your fellowship because of this difference on this matter; it is not a test of orthodoxy. Churches should not be divided over this point of doctrine. The test of orthodoxy, beloved--listen, and I will give my life for it--is based on the Virgin Birth, the Incarnation: God manifest in the flesh, the atoning sacrifice, the bodily resurrection of Christ from among the dead, His ascension, His intercession and His coming again. If a man bring any doctrine other than I have stated, receive him not into your home. It gives me grief to see the contention over some secondary--shall I put it--point of doctrine. Satan loves to divide and bring division in the body of believers. If you believe one point, or the second point, or the third point, of this pre-mid-and posttribulation rapture, God bless you.[6]

---

[5] Harold Lindsell and Charles Woodbridge, *A Handbook of Christian Truth* (Westwood, N. J.: Fleming H. Revell Co., 1935), pp. 166, 167, 169, 170.
[6] Ladd, p. 161.

Bob Jones University's close fellowship with Dr. Ian Paisley of Northern Ireland for a quarter of a century is an example of how pretribulationists and posttribulationists can keep the unity of the Spirit. Bob Jones University is pretribulational; Ian Paisley is posttribulational. Nevertheless, Ian Paisley has appeared on Bob Jones University's platform time after time for a quarter of a century. In order to heed Paul's plea, we must *endeavor "to keep the unity of the Spirit . . . . Till we all come in the unity of the faith . . . ."*[7]

---

[7] Ephesians 4:3, 13.

APPENDIX A

"Posttribulationism . . . is the majority view."(Walvoord)

Walvoord writes, "Posttribulationism has long been a common doctrine held by the majority of the church . . . *posttribulationism*, as far as the church as a whole is concerned, *is the majority view.*"[1]

MacPherson writes:

> Many pretribulationists and posttribulationists agree on at least one point. They *think* that the pretribulational rapture view is the majority view among Bible-believing Christians . . . . It may come as a surprise that many Bible scholars, including those of pretribulational persuasion, have admitted in their writings that the posttribulational rapture view is the majority view and always has been.[2]

Herman Hoyt, while president of Grace Theological Seminary in Winona Lake, Indiana, in *The End Times*, page 86, stated that the posttribulational view has had much greater acceptance than pretribulationism.

An article in the November 1973, *Moody Monthly* entitled "Curious about the Future?", written by Moody Bible Institute professor Louis A. Barbieri, Jr., declared that pretribulationists are probably in the minority at the present time.[3]

---

[1] Walvoord, *Rapture Question: Revised*, p. 131.
[2] MacPherson, *The Late Great Pre-Trib Rapture*, p. 37.
[3] Ibid., p. 38.

Again, MacPherson writes:

A top British scholar, who is also a member of the Brethren, revealed in a letter a few weeks ago: 'In Brethren circles in Great Britain there are *more* younger men who do not hold the [pretribulational] view than older ones who will not give up the cherished notion passed on by JND [John Nelson Darby] through Margaret MacDonald.'[4]

Once again, MacPherson writes:

Biederwolf was definitely a posttrib. I should also point out that *the list of several hundred eminent scholars in the back of the Second Coming Bible is almost solidly posttrib*; in fact, I could find only about a dozen Pre-tribs out of *hundreds* of names![5]

Missionary leader Oswald J. Smith of Toronto, Canada, was a pretribulationist. In his testimony found in his pamphlet entitled "Tribulation or Rapture--Which?" He pointed out that as he read the Bible through the years, he began to see the holes in the pretribulation theory. After much consideration and prayer, he abandoned the pretribulation theory and became a posttribulationist by conviction. In his pamphlet, Smith said that he *knows* about seventy outstanding Bible teachers who are posttribulational. On page 13, he writes:

Among them . . . there are such names as W.J. Erdman, Charles R. Erdman, Dr. G. Campbell Morgan, Bishop Frank Houghton, Dr. A. B. Simpson, Dr. J.W. Thirtle, Dr. Charles T. Cook, Alexander Reese, Dr. Horatius Bonar, Dr. Adolph Saphir, Henry

---

[4] Ibid.
[5] Ibid, p. 39.

Varley, Dr. Nathaniel West, David Baron, H.W. Soltau, Dr. Bergin, Dr. Harold J. Ockenga, and many others.[6]

MacPherson says, "For about twenty-five years, I have diligently tracked down outstanding posttribs in all centuries from the time of Christ to the present day, and *the total so far is well over one thousand.*"[7]

Rosenthal writes:

Some of the Christian leaders who never embraced pretribulational rapturism or who initially embraced it only to eventually renounce it include:

Henry Alford	Oswald T. Allis
Matthew Arnold	David Baron
J. Sidlow Baxter	Louis Berkhof
Rowland V. Bingham	Horatius Bonar
William Booth	F.F. Bruce
John Bunyan	John Calvin
William Carey	Edward J. Carnell
Thomas Chalmers	Adam Clarke
Charles T. Cook	Samuel Cooper
Jon Cotton	Alexander Cruden
Franz Delitzsch	Alfred Edersheim
Jonathan Edwards	Charles R. Erdman
W.J. Erdman	Charles Finney
John Foxe	Alexander Fraser
John Gill	A.J. Gordon
Robert H. Gundry	William Hendriksen
Carl F.H. Henry	Matthew Henry
Herschel H. Hobbs	Charles Hodge
Frank Houghton	Thomas Houghton
John Huss	John Knox
Martin Luther	J. Gresham Machen
Norman S. MacPherson	Cotton Mather

---

[6] Ibid.

[7] Ibid., p. 40.

Philip Melancthon
W.G. Moorehead
George Müller
Isaac Newton
Harold J. Ockenga
A.W. Pink
Alexander Reese
Ed F. Sanders
A.B. Simpson
H.W. Soltau
A.H. Strong
William Tyndale
Charles Wesley
Nathaniel West
Robert Dick Wilson

Campbell Morgan
Leon Morris
Iain H. Murray
Thomas Newton
Eric C. Peters
Bernard Ramm
Harry Rimmer
Adolph Saphir
Oswald J. Smith
Charles H. Spurgeon
J.W. Thirtle
B.B. Warfield
John Wesley
George Whitefield
John Wycliffe

Among them are the men who gave us the Bible in the English language, some of the great puritan divines, the leading reformers, missionaries who pierced the darkness of heathen lands with the gospel, theologians of the first rank, some of history's greatest preachers, and authors whose books have stood the test of time to become classics within Bible-believing Christendom.[8]

P.O.S.T. provides the following list of posttribulational scholars from the time of the postapostolic fathers to the present:

George Abbott-Smith
William Albright
J.A. Alexander
Oswald T. Allis
Apollinaris
Francis Asbury
Augustine
H.A. Baker

Jay Adams
Archibald Alexander
Henry Alford
John A. Anderson
Matthew Arnold
Athanasius
Roger Bacon
Barnabas

---

[8] Marvin Rosenthal, "The Beginning of the End," *Zion's Fire*, January 1991, p. 20.

Albert Barnes
Clarence Bass
J. Sidlow Baxter
W.J. Ern Baxter
I.T. Beckwith
Louis Berkhof
Bernard of Clairvaux
E.H. Bickersteth
T.R. Birks
Loraine Boettner
David Brainerd
J.A. Broadus
Joshua Brooks
Thomas Broughton
Lionel Brown
F.F. Bruce
John Bunyan
C.W. Burpo
John Calvin
William Carey
B.H. Carroll
Thomas Chalmers
R.H. Charles
Chrysostom
Adam Clarke
Edmund Clowney
Harry Conn
C.T. Cook
Miles Coverdale
W.E. Cox
Thomas Cranmer
Hermann Cremer
Alexander Cruden
Cyprian
G.H. Dalman
Adolf Deissman
Gerald Derstine
Norman F. Douty
Alexander Duff

David Baron
Walter Bauer
Richard Baxter
George R. Beasley-Murray
J.A. Bengel
G.C. Berkouwer
Peter Beyerhaus
R.V. Bingham
J. Allen Blair
Horatius Bonar
Thomas Brightman
Charles Brokenshire
Brother Andrew
David Brown
W.G. Brown
William T. Bruner
William Burgh
Herbert Butt
Robert Cameron
Edward Carnell
Alexander Carson
Robert Chapman
Theodor Christlieb
R.W. Church
Clement of Rome
Commodianus
W.J. Conybeare
Coracion
William Cowper
Henry Craik
Dan Crawford
William Crews
William Cuninghame
Cyril of Jerusalem
Harvey Dana
Franz Delitzsch
J.D. Douglas
Murray Downey
F.H.C. Dusterdieck

Timothy Dwight
Alfred Edersheim
John Eliot
E.B. Elliott
Ephraim the Syrian
J.A. Ernesti
M.J. Evans
Charles Farah Jr.
Howard Ferrin
John Foxe
George Fromow
C.E. Fry
Daniel Fuller
John Gill
R.H. Glover
E.J. Goodspeed
S.D. Gordon
William Greathouse
W.J. Grier
Robert H. Gundry
Henry H. Halley
James Hastings
Hegisippus
William Hendriksen
Carl F.H. Henry
Hermas
Herschel Hobbs
Charles Hodge
J. Stuart Holden
Frank Houghton
John Huss
Irenaeus
Jerome
R.B. Jones
Justin Martyr
Arthur Katterjohn
Karl F. Keil
Ben Kinchlow
D.H. Kromminga

David Ebaugh
Jonathan Edwards
C.J. Ellicott
Walter Elwell
William J. Erdman
Eusebius
Patrick Fairbairn
A.R. Fausset
Charles Finney
Alexander Fraser
Henry Frost
Andrew Fuller
W. Ward Gasque
Arthur Glasser
F.L.. Godet
Thomas Goodwin
James R. Graham
Jack Green
H. Grattan Guinness
Robert Haldane
Floyd Hamilton
Roy Hayden
Shel Helsley
E.W. Hengstenberg
Matthew Henry
Hippolytus
A.A. Hodge
Anthony Hoekema
Edward Horne
Archibald Hughes
Ignatius
Paul G. Jackson
Orson Jones
Julius Africanus
Kenneth Kantzer
Arthur Katz
S.H. Kellogg
John Knox
Abraham Kuyper

Lactantius
Hugh Latimer
C.S. Lewis
J.B. Lightfoot
H.L. Lindsay-Young
Martyn Lloyd-Jones
William Lowe
Leslie Lyall
George W. MacPherson
Walter Maier
Dan Malachuk
J.C. Maris
Henry Martyn
Increase Mather
Richard McCartney
James McConkey
Alexander Mclaren
A. H. McNeile
Robert McQuilkain
Philipp Melanchthon
Will Meloon
Berkeley Mickelsen
Isaac Milner
Robert Moffat
Dale Moody
William G. Moorehead
Leon Morris
H.C.G. Moule
George Müeller
Andrew Murray
Nepos
Benjamin Newton
John Newton
W.O.E. Oesterley
C. Von Orelli
J. Edwin Orr
Francis Paget
Ian Paisley
Joseph Parker

George E. Ladd
R.C.H. Lenski
H. G. Liddell
John Lillie
David Livingstone
C.S. Lovett
Martin Luther
J. Gresham Machen
Norman S. MacPherson
S.R. Maitland
Julius Mantey
WalterR. Martin
Cotton Mather
Philip Mauro
Robert Murray McCheyne
Jim McKeever
S.I. McMillen
John McNichol
Joseph Mede
Melito
Methodius
George Milligan
John Milton
John Warwick Montgomery
G.F. Moore
G. Campbell Morgan
Robert Morrison
James Moulton
E.Y. Mullins
Iain H. Murray
Eberhard Nestle
Isaac Newton
Harold J. Ockenga
Lloyd J. Ogilvie
Origen
John Owen
James I. Packer
Papias
Blaise Pascal

John G. Paton
J. Barton Payne
A.S. Peake
J.B. Phillips
Clark Pinnock
Alfred Plummer
E.J. Poole-Conner
Bernard Ramm
Leonard Ravenhill
Paul Rees
H.N. Ridderbos
E.K. A. Riehm
A.T. Robertson
M.F. Roos
W.J. Rowlands
J.C. Ryle
George Salmon
William Sanday
Adolph Saphir
A. Von Schlatter
Robert Scott
J.J. Scruby
Demos Shakarian
T.T. Shields
Charles Simeon
David Smith
Paul B. Smith
A. Souter
Duane Edward Spencer
James Stephens
E.R. Stier
John R. W. Stott
Moses Stuart
Ray Summers
Henry B. Swete
Leslie K. Tarr
W. Theodore Taylor
Merrill C. Tenney
J.H. Thayer

Leroy Patterson
James Payne
Duane Pederson
Albertus Pieters
G.W. Playfair
Polycarp
Pothinus
Roland Rasmussen
Robert G. Rayburn
Alexander Reese
Nicholas Ridley
J.C.H. Rinck
Pat Robertson
Geroge Rose
R.J. Rushdoony
William Sailer
S.D.F. Salmond
Ed F. Sanders
G. Savonarola
Hermann Schultz
Thomas Scott
Edmund Shackleton
John Sharrit
Teignmouth Shore
Menno Simons
Oswald J. Smith
Henry Soltau
Charles H. Spurgeon
Francis Steele
W.A. Stevens
J.M. Stifler
A.H. Strong
C.T. Studd
J. Grant Swank Jr.
Iain Tait
Richard Taylor
Corrie Ten Boom
Tertullian
J.W. Thirtle

William C. Thomas
Arthur Thrush
James H. Todd
Edith Torrey (R.A.
Torrey's daughter)
William Tyndale
John Van der Hoeven
Cornelius Van Til
Victorinus
Vitringa
George W. Wade
Benjamin B. Warfield
Isaac Watts
G. Christian Weiss
Charles Wesley
Nathaniel West
Richard F. Weymouth
Daniel Whitby
Frank H. White
William Wilberforce
Roger Williams
G. B. Winer
A. Skevington Wood
Paul Woolley
James Wright
John Wycliffe
Edward J. Young
Robert Young
Theodore Zahn

D.A. Thompson
C. Von Tischendorf
Alan Toms
Samuel P. Tregelles
Richard C. Trench
James Ussher
J.J. Van Oosterzee
Venerable Bede
Marvin R. Vincent
Geerhardus Vos
C.T. Walrond
G. Henry Waterman
A.S. Way
John C. Wenger
John Wesley
Henry G. Weston
William Whiston
W.S. Whitcombe
George Whitefield
Charles B. Williams
Robert Dick Wilson
Richard Wolff
C. Stacey Woods
C.H.H. Wright
Richard Wurmbrand
M.J. Wyngaarden
Fred Young
Ronald F. Youngblood
Ulrich Zwingli.[9]

No wonder Walvoord said, "Posttribulationism, as far as the church as a whole is concerned, is the majority view."[10]

---

[9] Dave MacPherson, "A Long List of Post-Tribs," *P.O.S.T. Incorporated*, Box 49, Monticello, Utah 84535 USA.

[10] Walvoord, *Rapture Question: Revised*, p. 131.

APPENDIX B

The Aorist Indicative

The greatest of American Greek scholars, A.T. Robertson, writes:

> It is true that *in the expression of past time in the indicative . . . the aorist is the tense used as a matter of course . . . because of the time element in the indicative* (expressed by the augment and secondary endings) the real character of the aorist tense is best seen in the *other modes* where we do not have notes of time.[1]

Dana and Mantey write:

> The fundamental significance of the aorist is to denote action simply as occurring. . . . It is the indefinite tense . . . *its time relations being found only in the indicative, where it is used as past and hence augmented* . . . . The aorist signifies nothing as to completeness, but simply presents the action as attained. It states the fact of the action or event without regard to its duration . . . . The root idea of the aorist has been variously defined by Greek grammarians . . . Gildersleeve: '*The aorist states a past action* without reference to its duration simply as a thing attained.' This definition presents a defect in the emphasis it gives to the time element. Much more discriminating and accurate is the observation of Goodwin: '*The aorist indicative expresses the simple occurrence of an action in past time*' . . . . The observation of Winer that it signifies '*occurrence at some former time*' applies only to the *indicative*.[2]

---

[1] Robertson, *A Grammar of the Greek New Testament in Light of Historical Research*, pp. 831, 835.
[2] Dana and Mantey, pp. 193, 194.

Explaining the regular uses of the aorist, Dana and Mantey write:

> While the aorist views an action as a single whole, it may contemplate it from different angles. It may regard the action in its entirety, which we call the *constative* aorist ... *He lived.* The action may be regarded from the viewpoint of its initiation, which we call the *ingressive* aorist ... *He died.* When the action is viewed in its results, we call it the *culminative* aorist ... *He killed.*[3]

Speaking specifically about the *ingressive* aorist, Dana and Mantey write:

> The action signified by the aorist may be contemplated in its beginning. This use [*ingressive*] is commonly employed with verbs which signify a state or condition, and denote entrance into that state or condition ... 'for your sakes he became poor.' II Corinthians 8:9 [4]

There are three other (special) uses of the aorist in which the force of the aorist is rhetorically applied. They are the following: the gnomic aorist, the epistolary aorist, and the dramatic aorist. Commenting on the dramatic aorist, Dana and Mantey write:

> The aorist *may* be used for stating a present reality with the certitude of a past event. This *idism* is a device for emphasis. It is *commonly used* of a state which has just been realized, or a result which has just been accomplished ....[5]

---

[3] Dana and Mantey, p. 195, 196.
[4] Ibid., p. 196.
[5] Ibid., p. 198.

Huddliston writes, "The aorist is the most common tense in Greek to represent what has taken place."[6]

From the context of the aorist indicative verbs (used in Revelation 6:17; 11:15; 17, 18; and Revelation 12:10), it is apparent that these verbs are what we call the *ingressive* aorist. Therefore, these ingressive aorist verbs denote that the action of entrance into a condition had just occurred in past time.

[6] Huddliston, p. 55.

APPENDIX C

The Judgment Seat of Christ

Revelation 11:15-18 reveals that the judgment seat of Christ will not occur until after the sounding of the seventh trumpet. Prior to the declaration ("the kingdoms of this world are become the kingdoms of our Lord, and of his Christ") found in this passage, the kingdoms of this world will *have become* the kingdoms of our Lord, and of His Christ. This is proved by the word egenonto ("are become") in Revelation 11:15. The aorist *indicative* denotes action that occurred in past time. The significance of the aorist indicative egenonto ("are become"), as it is used in this passage, is explained in Appendix B.

It is evident that the seventh trumpet judgment consists of divine wrath, for in Revelation 11:18 the twenty-four elders say, "And the nations were angry, and *thy wrath is come* . . . ." The aorist *indicative* elthen ("is come") in this verse proves that at the time of the declaration ("thy Wrath is come"), the action of entrance into the condition of God's wrath had already occurred. The twenty-four elders say,

And the nations were angry, and *thy wrath is come*, and the time of the dead, that they should be judged, and that thou shouldest give reward unto thy servants the prophets, and to the saints, and them that fear thy name, small and great . . . .[1]

---

[1] Revelation 11:18.

Accordingly, Revelation 11:15-18 teaches that the judgment seat of Christ will occur *after* the kingdom of Christ has begun and *after* the wrath of the Lamb has begun to be poured out in "the great day of his wrath."

It has been shown that the millennial kingdom of Christ will begin when Satan is cast to the earth immediately after the Great Tribulation. This is confirmed by Revelation 12:4, 9, 10, which say:

> And his tail drew *the third part of the stars of heaven*, and did cast them to the earth . . . . *And the great dragon was cast out*, that old serpent, called the Devil, and Satan, which deceiveth the whole world: he was cast out into the earth, *and his angels were cast out with him*. And I heard a loud voice saying in heaven, *now is come . . . the kingdom of our God*, and the power of his Christ: *for the accuser of our brethren is cast down*, which accused them before our God day and night.

To be even more specific, the judgment seat of Christ will not occur until the time of the sounding of the seventh trumpet *in* the Day of the Lord, *after* the Great Tribulation is past. The aorist indicative <u>egenonto</u> ("are become") in Revelation 11:15 and the aorist indicative <u>elthen</u> ("is come") in Revelation 11:18 prove that both "the kingdoms of our Lord, and of his Christ" and the "wrath" of the Lamb will have begun before the declarations ("the kingdoms of this world are become the kingdoms of our Lord and of his Christ" and "thy wrath is come"), at the sounding of the seventh trumpet. While <u>egenonto</u> ("are become") and <u>elthen</u> ("is come") are both *aorist indicatives*, <u>krithenai</u> ("they should be judged") and <u>dounai</u> ("thou shouldest give reward") in Revelation 11:18 are both *aorist infinitives*. Regarding the infinitive, Robertson and Davis write, "*It* [the infinitive] *has no time* except in indirect discourse . . . ."[2] It is clearly apparent that the discourse of the twenty-four elders is *not* indirect discourse, for they are speaking *directly* to God.

Therefore, Revelation 11:15-18 reveals that the judgment seat of Christ will not occur during the Seventieth Week of Daniel after a supposed pretribulational rapture of the church. This passage proves that the judgment seat of Christ will take place *after* the posttribulational rapture of the church and after the sounding of the seventh trumpet.

---

[2] Robertson, *A New Short Grammar of the Greek New Testament*, p. 374.

APPENDIX D

Mythical Pre-tribs

Dave MacPherson's new book, *The Rapture Plot*, has focused attention on the origin of pretribulationism in 1830. Consequently, pretribulation leaders have been frantically trying to find evidence of pretribulationism before 1830.

Pretribulationists are now desperately claiming that the following writers taught a pretribulational rapture prior to 1830: Pseudo-Ephraem, Morgan Edwards, Benjamin Keach, and Hansord Knollys.

PSEUDO-EPHRAEM

Grant Jeffery, Timothy Demy, and Thomas Ice claim that a person known as Pseudo-Ephraem taught a pretribulational rapture more than a millennium ago.

Their case for Pseudo-Ephraem's having been a pretribulationist rests on the following quotations from this medieval writer:

1. 'Why therefore do we not reject every care of earthly actions and prepare ourselves for the meeting of the Lord Christ, so that He may draw us from the confusion, which overwhelms all the world?'

2. 'For all the saints and elect of God are gathered, prior to the tribulation that is to come, and are taken to the Lord lest they

see the confusion that is to overwhelm the world because of our sins.'[1]

MacPherson writes:

One can find a Pretribulational rapture in Pseudo-Ephraem (an early Catholic writer) only if one insists upon: 1. Ignoring or twisting Pseudo-Ephraem's explanation of the above quotes, and 2. Ignoring or twisting the interpretation given by Pseudo-Ephraem expert Paul Alexander, the author Demy and Ice quote selectively.[2]

Ice's pretribulation society has been disseminating the ten sections of Pseudo-Ephraem's sermon. The two crucial quotes are found in Section 2.

MacPherson writes:

In Section 2, after saying that many end-time signs have already been fulfilled, the writer declares that *only one thing is 'imminent'*: 'the advent of the wicked one' (Antichrist). He says that in light of 'the confusion that is to overwhelm the world because of our sins,' we at least stand in need of penance for our actions![3]

In Section 3, some Christians become part of an apostasy at the time of the end. In Section 4, gathered Christians are fleeing from the wicked.

MacPherson continues:

During the tribulation (Sections 5 through 9) Christians in wilderness areas 'bend their knees to God' .... *After the tribulation Christians are still on earth when the second coming arrives.*

---

[1] MacPherson, *The Rapture Plot*, p. 269.

[2] Ibid., pp. 269, 270.

[3] Ibid., p. 270.

So we see that Christians are *'gathered'* away from the wicked *in earthly settings* before the tribulation *and then are 'taken' closer to the Lord when the tribulation intensifies.*[4]

At the conclusion of their mid-1995 Bibliotheca Sacra article, Demy and Ice say that Pseudo-Ephraem "emphasizes imminence" and "two comings separated by the tribulation."[5] That is, they say that Pseudo-Ephraem taught an imminent coming of Christ, featuring a pretribulational rapture.

As MacPherson pointed out above, the only "imminent" event Pseudo-Ephraem expected was "'the advent of the wicked one,' (Antichrist)."

In answer to the claim of Demy and Ice that Pseudo-Ephraem taught "two comings," the first of which was a pretribulational coming, MacPherson writes:

In the before-the-tribulation sections in his sermon, P-E [Pseudo-Ephraem] mentions neither a descent of Christ, nor a shout, nor an angelic voice, nor a trumpet of God, nor a resurrection, nor any mention of air. He sees no coming of Christ before the tribulation. *The only coming of Christ he waits for is the non-imminent final advent which,* in section 2, *he ties to 'the end of the world' and to 'the harvest' and 'angels' who 'hold sickles in their hands'* (Rev. 14:14-19)![6]

Thomas Ice writes, "Paul Alexander [the Pseudo-Ephraem expert] clearly believed that Pseudo-Ephraem was teaching what we call today a Pre-Trib rapture."[7]

---

[4] Ibid., pp. 270, 271.
[5] Ibid., p. 271.
[6] Ibid., p. 271.
[7] Ibid., p. 272.

In response to this reckless pretribulational claim by Ice, MacPherson writes,

Alexander says (p. 210) *that 'taken to the Lord'* (which Demy/ Ice equate with 'draw' and 'gathered') *really means 'participate at least in some measure in the beatitude.'*

Demy / Ice avoid explaining the Catholic teaching of 'beatitude' and give the false impression that this expression refers to physical removal from the earth! But, *The New Catholic Encyclopedia* (1967, Vol. II, p. 195) states that *'beatitude'* meaning *'blessedness,'* has to do with 'the highest acts of virtue that can be performed in this life,'--*human action on earth* and not rapture action *away from* earth!

And when Alexander outlines P-E's order of end-time events (pp. 218-19), he shows that *this ancient writer spoke of only one coming*: the 'Second Coming of Christ' *following* the 'tibulatio magna lasting three and a half years'![8]

Paul Alexander outlined clearly Pseudo-Ephraem's order of end-time events in the following paragraph:

In Pseudo-Ephraem the sequence is as follows. After the attack of the *gentes nequissimae* or *bellicae* (1) there follows the surrender of the Christian Empire (2), the apparition of the Antichrist (3), an allusion to the Blessings of Moses and Jacob on the tribe of Dan (4), then the division of the Antichrist's career into a period of adolescence before his seizure of imperial power (5). Then comes his challenging God by sitting in the Jewish Temple at Jerusalem (6), the "great tribulation" of three and a half years (drought, famine, etc.): (7) and during it the mission of Enoch and Elijah (8), and finally, the Second Coming and the punishment of the Antichrist (9). This schedule may be presented schematically as follows:

---

[8] Ibid.

Pseudo-Ephraem

1.	Attack of *gentes bellicae* or *nequissimae*	212.13-213.17
2.	Surrender of the Empire	214.1
3.	*apparebit ille nequissimus et abominabilis draco*	214.4
4.	Blessings of Moses and Jacob on Dan	214.6
5.	*adulescens . . . antequam sumat imperium; factus legitimus sumet imperium*	216.2, 11
6.	Sitting in the Jewish Temple	217.1
7.	*tribulatio magna* lasting three and a half years	217.14
8.	Mission of Enoch and Elijah	219.10
9.	Second Coming of Christ and Punishment of the Antichrist[9]	220.2

Pseudo-Ephraem *was not* a pretribulationist; he *is* a mythical pretribulationist.

MORGAN EDWARDS

As a student at Bristol Baptist Seminary in England (1742-1744), Morgan Edwards wrote an essay for his Eschatology class. The essay was on the subject of his views of Bible prophecy. His essay was later published under the following title: Two Academical Exercises on Subjects Bearing the Following Titles: Millennium, Last-Novelties.

Morgan Edwards writes:

The distance between the first and second resurrection will be somewhat more than a thousand years. I say, somewhat more; because the dead saints will be raised, and the living changed at Christ's 'appearing in the air' (I Thes. iv. 17); and this will be

---

[9] Paul J. Alexander, *The Byzantine Apocalyptic Tradition* (Univ. of California Press, 1985), pp. 218, 219.

about three years and a half before the millennium, as we shall see hereafter: but will he and they abide in the air all that time? No: they will ascend to paradise, or to some one of those many 'mansions in the father's house' (John xiv. 2), and so disappear during the foresaid period of time. The design of this retreat and disappearing will be to judge the risen and change the saints; for 'now the time is come that judgment must begin,' and that will be 'at the house of God' (I Pet. iv. 17) . . . .[10]

To his earlier statement regarding Christ's "appearing in the air" (I Thessalonians 4:17), Edwards added:

Another event previous to the millennium will be the appearing of the son of man in the clouds, coming to raise the dead saints and change the living, and to catch them up to himself, and then withdraw with them, as observed before . . . *this event will come to pass when antichrist be arrived at Jerusalem in his conquest of the world* . . . .(P. 21)[11]

Edwards continues:

The last event, and the event that will usher in the millennium, will be, the coming of Christ from paradise to earth, with all the saints he had taken up thither (*about* three years and a half before) . . . (p. 24) millions and millions of saints will have been on earth from the days of the first Adam, to the coming of the second Adam. All these will Christ bring with him.[12]

Morgan Edwards was not a pretribulationist. This fact is clear to anyone who has no theological necessity

---

[10] Timothy Demy and Thomas Ice, "Morgan Edwards: Another Pre-Darby Rapturist," *Pre-Trib Perspectives*, September/October 1995, p. 2.

[11] Ibid.

[12] Ibid.

and reads carefully what he wrote. Ponder the following plain statement by Edwards,

> The last event [the coming of Christ on a white horse], and the event that will usher in the millennium, will be, the coming of Christ from paradise to earth, with all the saints He had taken up thither (*about three years and a half before*) . . . .(p. 24)

The above unclouded sentence proves that Edwards was not a pretribulationist, for he placed the rapture *"about three years and a half before"* the coming of Christ on a white horse. Furthermore, in our first quotation from Edwards, he wrote, "This [rapture] will be *about three years and a half before the millennium* . . . ."

Edwards' placing of the rapture *about three years and a half before the millennium* shows that his timing for the rapture is much closer to the position of midtribulationism than to that of pretribulationism. According to Webster's Ninth New Collegiate Dictionary, *about* means, "Reasonably close to . . . *almost* . . . ." Accordingly, it appears that Edwards was slightly *more* than a midtribulationist.

Furthermore, Edwards wrote, *"This event* ["the appearing of the Son of man in the clouds, coming to raise the dead saints and change the living, and to catch them up to Himself, and then withdraw with them . . . ."] *will come to pass when antichrist be arrived at Jerusalem in his conquest of the world* . . . ." The Antichrist's arrival "at Jerusalem in his conquest of the world" will be far too late on the historical timeline to coincide with a pretribulational rapture.

As does this writer, Morgan Edwards saw a two-stage coming of Christ. In conclusion, it must be stated emphatically that while Morgan Edwards saw a two-stage coming, *he was not* a pretribulationist; he *is* a mythical pretribulationist.

BENJAMIN KEACH

In *Exposition of the Parables*, Benjamin Keach (1649-1704) writes:

> Now this coming of Christ is either personal or precursory. 1. *His second personal coming I judge will be at the beginning of the 1,000-year reign* . . . 2. *There is a precursory coming of our Lord* (as one notes) or *a* most glorious *spiritual coming*, to set up a more visible and universal kingdom in this world, *which will precede His personal appearance*; which I take to be the beginning of the latterday glory, *and which will be at the sounding of the 'seventh trumpet,' for then Jesus Christ will begin His spiritual and more visible and glorious kingdom;* or 'when the kingdoms of this world shall become the kingdoms of our Lord and of his Christ' Rev. xi.15-18. *One design of this [precursory] coming of our Lord, is to destroy the son of perdition, and utterly to overthrow Mystery Babylon.* 'And then shall that wicked one be revealed, whom the Lord shall consume with the spirit of mouth and shall destroy the brightness of his coming.' 2 Thes. ii.8 Now it is partly this [precursory] coming of Christ (I conclude) our Lord in the first place intends, though I will not exclude His *personal* appearance; for I see no reason to doubt, but that the *precursory coming of the Lord Jesus is to prepare things for His personal appearance*; when, (as a bridegroom) He will appear to celebrate the marriage with His beloved spouse. *Yet His [precursory] coming upon Mystery Babylon, or by His bright appearance to destroy the son of perdition*, may be distinguished from the [personal] coming last mentioned, though both may be comprehended, or included by the bridegroom's coming.[13]

---

[13] Benjamin Keach, *Exposition of the Parables* (Grand Rapids, Mich.: Kregel Publications, 1974), p. 643.

A careful reading of this passage from Keach shows that Keach believed *Christ's second personal coming will be at the beginning of the one thousand years*, when He will appear to celebrate the marriage with His beloved spouse. Furthermore, a careful reading of this passage also reveals that Keach placed what he calls *the precursory or glorious spiritual coming at the sounding of the seventh trumpet.* More importantly, Keach said, *"One design of this [precursory] coming of our Lord is to destroy the son of perdition,* and utterly to overthrow Mystery Babylon." This *precursory* coming of Keach occurs far too late on the historical timeline to be considered a pretribulational coming to rapture the church before "the Tribulation."

As does this writer, Keach saw a two-stage coming of Christ. However, Keach *was not* a pretribulationist; he *is* a mythical pretribulationist.

HANSORD KNOLLYS

Knollys writes:

The next glorious appearing of the Lord Jesus Christ, will be His viritual and spiritual coming in His saints and sanction (*as the bridegroom of a church*) *to marry her sons* (Isaiah 62:4, 5) and by them to reign over the nations with power and great glory a 1,000 years here on earth, Daniel 7:27. *There are but three special kinds and times of Christ coming.* 1. His coming in the form of a servant in the days of His flesh, Phil. 2:9. 2. His coming as judge at the last day, when He shall judge the quick and the dead, (II Tim. 4:1) called His appearance the second time, Hebrews 9:29. *Both these are His personal appearances,* or His coming in His own person. But *between these two appearances, or comings of Christ in His own person,* there *is* witnessed by the holy prophets and apostles, and recorded in the Scripture of holy truth, *another kind of Christ's coming at another time. And that is His coming as the Bridegroom,* and as

388 ■ The Post-Trib, Pre-Wrath Rapture

the only Potentate, *King of Kings, and Lord of Lords*, (I Tim. 6:14, 15; *Rev.* 19:16) *which is His virtual, spiritual*, powerful, *and glorious coming* in His saints and sanction, and by them *to marry His Jerusalem*, Isaiah 62:4, 5.[14]

A careful reading of this passage from Knollys reveals that *Knollys associated the virtual* and *spiritual coming of Christ with the coming of Christ on a white horse* referred to in *Revelation* 19:16. Therefore, *the virtual and spiritual coming of Knollys is far too late to be a pretribulational rapture.*

As does this writer, Knollys saw a two-stage coming of Christ. However, Knollys *was not* a pretribulationist; he *is* mythical pretribulationist.

---

[14] Johnson, "The Imminent Pre-Trib Coming of Christ," pp. 5, 6.

BIBLIOGRAPHY

Armerding, Carl. "The Coming of the Son of Man." *Moody Monthly*, Volume 51, pp. 788, 809; cited by Rand Bibliotheca Sacra, Volume 113, p. 201.

Alexander, Paul J. *The Byzantine Apocalyptic Tradition.* Univ. of California Press, 1985.

Bauer, Walter. *A Greek-English Lexicon of the New Testament and other Early Christian Literature, Second Edition.* Chicago: The University of Chicago Press, 1958.

Beechick, Allen. *The Pretribulation Rapture.* Denver: Accent Books, 1980.

Biederwolf, William E. *The Second Coming Bible Commentary.* Grand Rapids, Mich.: Baker Book House, 1985.

Blair, Mike. "FEMA Connections Exposed." *The Spotlight*, Volume XX, 26 September 1994, p. 12.

Carr, Commander William Guy. *Pawns in the Game.* USA: printed privately.

Carroll, B.H. *An Interpretation of the English Bible, Volume 4.* Westwood, N. J.: Fleming Revell Co., 1913.

Chafer, Lewis S. *Systematic Theology, Volume 7.* Dallas: Dallas Seminary Press, 1948.

Dana, H.E., and Mantey, Julius R. *A Manual Grammar of the Greek New Testament.* New York: MacMillian Publishing Co., 1927.

Darby, John N. *Synopsis of the Books of the Bible, Volume V.* New York: Loizeaux Bro., 1942.

Demy, Timothy, and Ice, Thomas. "Morgan Edwards: Another Pre-Darby Rapturist." *Pre-Trib Perspectives*, September/October 1995, p. 2.

Donaldson, James, and Roberts, Alexander. *The Ante-Nicene Fathers*. Grand Rapids, Mich.: Wm. B. Eerdmans Publishing Co., 1989.

Edersheim, Alfred. *The Life and Times of Jesus the Messiah, Volume Two*. Grand Rapids, Mich.: Wm. B. Eerdmans Publishing Co., n.d.

Forbush, William, ed. *Foxe's Book of Martyrs*. Philadelphia, Pa.: The John C. Winston Co., 1926.

Foxe's Book of Martyrs. Philadelphia, Pa.: John D. Winston Co., n.d.

Fraser, Alexander. *Is There but One Return of Christ?* Pittsburgh, Pa.: Evangelical Fellowship, 1947.

Frost, Henry W. *The Second Coming of Christ*. Grand Rapids, Mich.: Wm. B. Eerdmans Publishing Co., 1934.

Fruchtenbaum, Arnold. "Problems with the Pre-Wrath Rapture." Tape on file at Post-Trib Research Center.

Gaebelein, Arno. *The Revelation*. Neptune, N. J.: Loizeaux Bro., 1961.

Grayzel, Solomon. *A History of the Jews*. Philadelphia: Jewish Publication Society of America, 1947.

Green, Thomas. *A Greek-English Lexicon to the New Testament*. New York: Harper and Bro., n.d.

Gundry, Robert. *The Church and The Tribulation*. Grand Rapids, Mich.: Zondervan Publishing House, 1973.

Hastings, James. *A Dictionary of the Bible, Volume 1*. Edinburgh:
    T & T Clark, 1898.

Huddliston, John Homer. *Essentials of New Testament Greek*. New
    York: MacMillian Co., 1949.

Ironside, H.A. *Lectures on the Book of Revelation*. New York:
    Loizeaux Bro., 1920.

Isidore, Epstein. *The Babylonian Talmud*. London: Soncino Press,
    1935-1960.

Johnson, Ken. "The Imminent Pre-Trib Coming of Christ." *Plains
    Baptist Challenger*, March 1995, pp. 5, 6.

Keach, Benjamin. *Exposition of the Parables*. Grand Rapids,
    Mich.: Kregel Publications, 1974.

Keith, George. "How Firm a Foundation." *Soul Stirring Songs and
    Hymns: Revised*. Murfreesburo, Tenn.: Sword of the
    Lord, 1986, p. 153.

The King James Version Bible.

Ladd, George. *The Blessed Hope*. Grand Rapids, Mich.: Wm. B.
    Eerdmans Publishing Co., 1956.

Lange, John Peter. *Lange's Commentary on the Holy Scriptures,
    Volume 7*. Grand Rapids, Mich.: Zondervan
    Publishing House, 1960.

Larkin, Clarence. *The Book of Daniel*. Philadelphia, Pa.: Erwin
    W. Mover Co., Printers, 1929.

Learsi, Rufus [Israel Goldberg]. *A History of the Jewish People*.
    Cleveland, Ohio: World Publishing Co., 1949.

The Liberty Annotated Study Bible. Lynchburg: Liberty
    University, 1988.

Lindsell, Harold and Woodbridge, Charles. *A Handbook of Christian Truth*. Westwood, N.J.: Fleming H. Revell Co., 1935.

Lindsey, Hal. *The Late Great Planet Earth*. Grand Rapids, Mich.: Zondervan Publishing House, 1970.

_____. *There's a New World Coming*. Santa Ana, Calif.: Vision House Publishers, 1973.

Lord, Walter. *The Day of Infamy*. New York: Holt, Rinehart & Winston, 1963.

Lumpkin, William L. *Baptist Confessions of Faith: Revised*. Valley Forge, Pa.: Judson Press, 1969.

MacPherson, Dave. *The Incredible Cover-Up*. Medford, Wa.: Omega Publications, 1975.

_____. *The Rapture Plot*. Simpsonville, S.C.: Millennium III Publishers, 1994.

_____. "A Long List of Post-Tribs." *P.O.S.T. Incorporated*. Box 49, Monticello, Utah 84535 USA.

Marrs, Texe. "Beast-like '666' Laws Forced on American Citizens." *Flashpoint*, March 1995, pp. 1, 2.

McClain, Alva J. *Daniel's Prophecy of the 70 Weeks*. Grand Rapids, Mich.: Zondervan Publishing House, 1940.

McManus, John F. "Top-Down Treason." *The New American*, Volume 11, 3 April 1995, p. 11.

Missler, Chuck, and Stewart, Don. *The Coming Temple*. Orange, Calif.: Dart Press, 1991.

Samuel Baxter, ed. *The Analytical Greek Lexicon*. Grand Rapids, Mich.: Zondervan Publishing House, 1970.

The New Scofield Reference Bible.

Pentecost, J. Dwight. *Things to Come.* Findlay, Ohio: Dunham Publishing Co., 1962.

Pink, Arthur W. *The Antichrist.* Grand Rapids, Mich.: Kregel Publications, 1988.

Reese, Alexander. *The Approaching Advent of Christ.* London: Marshall, Morgan and Scott Co., n.d.

Rice, John R. "No Signs of Christ's Coming." *The Sword of the Lord.* Volume 55, 29 September 1989, Number 20, p. 21.

Robertson, A.T. *A Grammar of the Greek New Testament in Light of Historical Research.* Nashville: Broadman Press, 1934.

_____. *A New Short Grammar of the Greek New Testament.* New York: Harper and Bro. Publishers, 1931.

_____. *Word Pictures in the New Testament.* Nashville: Broadman Press, 1931.

Rosenthal, Marvin. "Why Do We Celebrate Christmas on December 25th?" *Israel My Glory*, December/ January 1986-87, p. 3.

_____. "The Beginning of the End." *Zion's Fire*, January 1991, p. 20.

Ruckman, Peter. *The Books of Galatians, Ephesians, Philippians, Colossians.* Pensacola, Fla.: Bible Believers Press, 1973.

Scofield, C.I. *Will the Church Pass Through the Tribulation?* Philadelphia, Pa.: Philadelphia School of the Bible, 1917.

Scott, Walter. *Exposition of the Revelation of Jesus Christ.* Westwood, N.J.: Fleming H. Revell Co., n.d.

Springmeier, Fritz. *A Newsletter from a Follower of Christ.*" Volume 4, June-July-August 1995, pp. 5, 80.

Spurgeon, Charles H. *12 Sermons on the Second Coming.* Grand Rapids, Mich.: Baker Book House, 1976.

Stanton, Gerald. *Kept from the Hour.* Grand Rapids, Mich.: Zondervan Publishing House, 1956.

Steer, Roger. *George Müller Delighted in God!* Wheaton: Harold Shaw Publishers, 1981.

Thayer, Joseph Henry. *A Greek-English Lexicon of the New Testament.* New York: American Book Co., 1886.

Thiessen, Henry C. *Introduction to the New Testament.* Grand Rapids, Mich.: Wm. B. Eerdmans Publishing Co., 1943.

_____. *Will the Church Pass Through the Tribulation?* New York: Loizeaux Bro., 1941.

Walvoord, John. *The Rapture Question: Revised.* Grand Rapids: Zondervan Publishing House, 1979.

_____. *The Thessalonian Epistles.* Findlay, Ohio: Dunham Publishing Co., 1955.

_____, ed. "A Survey of the Eschatology of the Olivet Discourse." Bibliotheca Sacra, Volume 113, 1956, p. 200.

Webster, Noah. *American Dictionary of the English Language, 1828 Edition.* San Francisco: Foundation for American Christian Education, 1967.

Weiss, Philip. "Outcasts Digging in for the Apocalypse." *Time*, Volume 145, 1 May 1995.

INDEX

Have your friends been *WARNED* about The Pre-Trib Rapture Hoax?

For additional copies of

THE POST-TRIB, PRE-WRATH RAPTURE

WRITE TO:

The Post-Trib Research Center
7644 FARRALONE AVENUE, CANOGA PARK, CA 91304
(818) 340-6131

---

lease send me _____ copies of THE POST-TRIB, PRE-WRATH
APTURE for a gift of $12.00 each + shipping ($3.00 USA)

ake check or money order payable to: **Faith Baptist Church**

nd to: _____

_____

_____

Do you want to go to Heaven?

The Bible, God's Word, shows us the way to Heaven. There are certain things you must know and believe in order to go to Heaven.

1. Sin is the transgression (violation) of the law.

God's moral law is given in the Ten Commandments:

1. Thou shalt have no other gods before me.

2. Thou shalt not make unto thee any graven image, or any likeness of any thing that is in heaven above, or that is in the earth beneath, or that is in the water under the earth: Thou shalt not bow down thyself to them, nor serve them...

3. Thou shalt not take the name of the LORD thy God in vain...

4. Remember the sabbath day, to keep it holy. Six days shalt thou labour, and do all thy work...

5. Honour thy father and thy mother...

6. Thou shalt not kill.

7. Thou shalt not commit adultery.

8. Thou shalt not steal.

9. Thou shalt not bear false witness against thy neighbor.

10. Thou shalt not covet [desire that which is unlawful to obtain or possess; desire what belongs to another]...

2. We must know that we are sinners.

Romans 3:9 says, "...we have before proved both Jews and Gentiles, that they are all under sin."

Romans 3:10 says, "As it is written, There is none righteous, no not one."

Romans 3:23 says, " For all have sinned, and come short of the glory of God."

James 2:10 says, "For whosoever shall keep the whole law, and yet offend in one point, he is guilty of all."

3. We have all earned death and Hell.

Romans 6:23 says, "For the wages of sin is death..."

Revelation 21:8 says, "But the fearful, and unbelieving, and the abominable, and murderers, and whoremongers, and sorcerers, and idolaters, and all liars, shall have their part in the lake which burneth with fire and brimstone: which is the second death."

4. Jesus Christ paid the penalty for our sins.

Romans 5:8 says, " But God commendeth his love toward us, in that, while we were yet sinners, Christ [God manifest in the flesh] died for us".

I Peter 3:18 says, "For Christ also hath once suffered for sins, the just for the unjust, that he might bring us to God, being put to death in the flesh, but quickened [made alive] by the Spirit."

5. Jesus Christ is a living Saviour.

John 20:27 gives the words of the resurrected Christ to doubting Thomas: "Then saith he to Thomas, Reach hither thy finger, and behold my hands; and reach hither thy hand, and thrust it into my side: and be not faithless, but believing."

Hebrews 7:25 says, "Wherefore he is able also to save them to the uttermost that come unto God by him, seeing he ever liveth to make intercession for them."

6. **In order to be saved (delivered or set free from sin), you must REPENT (that voluntary change in the mind of the sinner in which he turns from sin), and you must BELIEVE (trust) in your heart in the risen Christ as your personal Lord and Saviour.**

Luke 13:3 says, "...except ye repent, ye shall all likewise perish."

Acts 3:19 says, "Repent ye therefore, and be converted, that your sins may be blotted out..."

Romans 10:9, 10 says, "That if thou shalt confess with thy mouth the Lord Jesus, and shalt believe in thine heart that God hath raised him from the dead, thou shalt be saved. For with the heart man believeth unto righteousnous...."

Romans 10:13 says, "For whosoever shall call upon the name of the Lord shall be saved."

If you believe these truths from the Bible, and if you want to be saved (delivered or set free from sin), call upon the Lord Jesus Christ right now, and ask Him to save you.